THIS LONG THREAD

Women of Color on Craft, Community, and Connection

JEN HEWETT

Roost Books

Roost Books
An imprint of Shambhala Publications, Inc.
2129 13th Street
Boulder, Colorado 80302
roostbooks.com

Cover art and design: Meenal Patel
Interior design: Kate E. White

9 8 7 6 5 4 3 2 1

First Edition
Printed in the United States of America

⊗This edition is printed on acid-free paper that meets the
American National Standards Institute z39.48 Standard.
♻Shambhala Publications makes every effort to print on recycled
paper. For more information, please visit www.shambhala.com.
Roost Books is distributed worldwide by Penguin Random House, Inc.,
and its subsidiaries.

LIBRARY OF CONGRESS CATALOGING-IN-PUBLICATION DATA
Names: Hewett, Jen, author.
Title: This long thread: women of color on
community, craft, and connection / Jen Hewett.
Description: First edition. | Boulder, Colorado: Roost Books, [2021]
Identifiers: LCCN 2021001397 | ISBN 9781611808247 (trade paperback)
Subjects: LCSH: Minority women—Social conditions—North America. |
Textile Crafts—Social aspects—North America.
Classification: LCC HQ1161 .H49 2021 | DDC 305.48/8097—dc23
LC record available at https://lccn.loc.gov/2021001397

This Long Thread

THIS LONG THREAD

Jen Hewett

JEN HEWETT

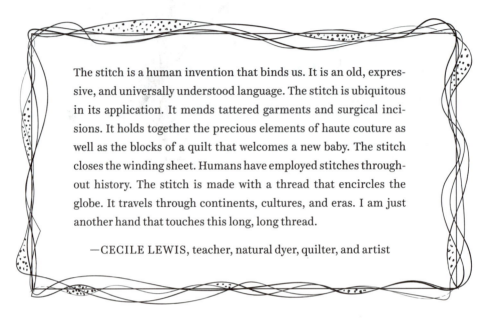

The stitch is a human invention that binds us. It is an old, expressive, and universally understood language. The stitch is ubiquitous in its application. It mends tattered garments and surgical incisions. It holds together the precious elements of haute couture as well as the blocks of a quilt that welcomes a new baby. The stitch closes the winding sheet. Humans have employed stitches throughout history. The stitch is made with a thread that encircles the globe. It travels through continents, cultures, and eras. I am just another hand that touches this long, long thread.

—CECILE LEWIS, teacher, natural dyer, quilter, and artist

In honor of my grandmothers:
Florence, Maria Fe, and Evelyn

CONTENTS

This Long Thread

INTRODUCTION

In January 2019, a blog post written by the founder of a knitting company, a white woman, went viral because of the post's neocolonialist undertones. Many rightly criticized the post, while well-intentioned, as racist. An Internet pile-on, the likes of which I'd never seen in craft social media, ensued. I was tangentially involved in the blog post (disclosure: the author is a friend of mine, her business was my very first licensee, and the trip she had written about was a trip I was leading to India later that year), so I read through many of the responses. I noticed that while many of the initial commenters who had taken the time to write thoughtful critiques of the blog post were people of color, a lot of the vitriol was coming from white women. The vitriol continued, even after the writer made a series of sincere apologies. I remarked to friends that it seemed the pile-on had become the "woke Olympics," with white women attempting to outdo each other in their vocal social media crusade against racism in the knitting world by attacking white individuals and white-owned businesses deemed racist online.

But, I knew from experience that the problem goes way beyond one person or one company. It is a systemic issue, not an individual one, and it extends beyond knitting to the larger fiber arts and crafts world. Professionally, I'm a textile artist and designer: I print my own fabric, teach classes on my process, and also design fabric for retailers and fabric companies. Outside my paid work, my hobbies include sewing and embroidery, I have a high profile as one of very few women of color in my industry. I have taught at craft retreats where I've been the sole Black teacher, was one of two teachers of color, or could count out of hundreds of attendees the number of attendees of color on one hand. I am one of maybe five independent Black fabric designers in the quilting industry, despite the long history of quilting among Black women in the United States. When I first started sewing clothing, I found very few indie-pattern designers of color. Yet, I knew that we existed in the craft world. We're here—we're just not represented.

I wrote about my experiences on social media and asked my white followers to examine their own craft communities. Who were they following the interviewee to tell her story as she wanted to. I edited the interviews, then sent them back to each subject to give her a chance to review and make further edits. I am not a journalist, and I suspect that this is not standard procedure. However, I wanted to make sure that the subjects were comfortable with what they had said and comfortable with the edits I had made.

I also commissioned essays from a handful of people. Jenna Wolf had responded to my social media post about my own experiences in the craft world and told me that, as a Native American woman, she feels completely unrepresented in the larger community. I asked her if she'd be interested in writing about that; she said yes. Shanel Wu had asked me if, as a nonbinary person, they could complete the survey. I encouraged them to. When they challenged my use of the word "woman," I asked them if they would like to write about that in an essay. They, too, were interested. Over lunch, Adrienne Rodriguez and I talked about how crochet is such an underdog in the fiber craft community, and she mentioned that she was researching the history of crochet through the lens of her own family. I asked her to write a bit about her findings. I commissioned five essays total; if I'd had a bigger budget and a larger word count, I would've commissioned even more.

Finally, the survey responses: I read through all of them multiple times. They are the thread woven throughout this book, the words that bind the interviews, essays, and my own story together. They allowed me to include far more voices than I could have if I had restricted the book to just interviews and essays. While I've incorporated many of the responses in essays and chapters, I have included complete survey responses from nine respondents who had written especially thoughtful responses. These nine respondents were also given a chance to review and edit their responses before I included them in my manuscript. I am grateful to all 269 contributors (listed on pages 363–66) for sharing their thoughts, opinions, and experiences with me.

It took me eighteen months to write this book. I finished the manuscript in fall 2020, a couple months before the US presidential election, at the tail end of a summer of protests against police brutality toward Black Americans, and in support of the Black Lives Matter movement. Like many Americans, I had been sheltering in place for six months due to the persistent threat of the coronavirus. The eighteen months between the initial pitch and the final manuscript were tumultuous on both a micro and a macro level. Once again, businesses were called out for their racist (and, more specifically, anti-

Black) behaviors. White people were encouraged to "melanate their feeds" by following more Black artists and creators on social media. In one week, I received over two thousand new followers. Once again, I took to social media to write about my discomfort with the colonialist language of "discovery" and this sudden burst of attention. People of color have been artists, makers, and craftspeople for millennia. We and our work often are largely unseen by the dominant culture until a cataclysmic event forces that dominant culture to notice the homogeneity of their communities.

As I was finishing the manuscript, Ebony Haight (whose essay is on page 294) asked me who the audience for this book is. It's a question that any writer has to address at the outset of the writing process, and my answer hasn't wavered in the eighteen months since I submitted the proposal. My primary audience is the diverse swath of crafters and artists featured in this book—people of color who are doing this work. They are people who have been practicing their crafts since childhood, as well as those who just learned six months ago. They are people who are doing this work professionally, and those for whom it is a hobby. They are women, and they are nonbinary. They are eighteen years old, and forty-five years old, and seventy-two years old. They are students, and they are retired. They are affluent, and they have to make do with limited means and resources. They are Indigenous, Black, Latinx, Asian, African, Caribbean, Middle Eastern, Canadian, American (and any combination of all of those). They are immigrants, they are descended from enslaved people, and their ancestors have been inhabiting this land for millennia. They are the people who are not often a part of the craft narrative, but they are here. We are here. This book is for us.

But, this book is also for anyone who wants to learn more about this rich, diverse community. As white folks grappled on social media with racism post–George Floyd, I saw many of them repeat the phrase "I'm here, I'm listening, I'm learning." The phrase has been repeated so often on social media that it's almost become a cliché. But, if the sentiment is true, then this book offers them a chance to spend time with our words, to listen, and to learn.

What I hope readers, regardless of race, take away from this book is that there is an unquestionable value in our stories and our work. I want to show that the fiber arts and crafts community is that much richer when there is space for our voices, not as window dressing but as an important and integral part of this community.

DEMOGRAPHICS

LOCATION

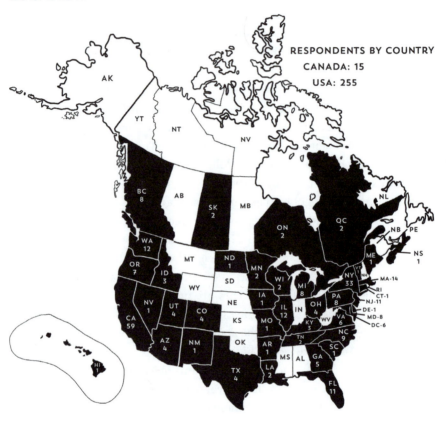

RESPONDENTS BY COUNTRY
CANADA: 15
USA: 255

AK

YT

NT

NV

BC
8

AB

SK
2

MB

ON
2

QC
2

NL

NB   PE

NS
1

ME
1

WA
12

OR
7

ID
3

MT

ND
1

MN
2

WI
2

MI
8

VT
NH
NY
33

MA-14

RI
CT-1
NJ-11

WY

SD

IA
1

IL
12

IN

OH
4

PA
8

DE-1
MD-8
DC-6

NV
1

UT
4

CO
4

NE

KS

MO
1

KY
3

WV

VA
6

NC
9

CA
59

AZ
4

NM
1

OK

AR
1

TN
2

SC
1

MS   AL

GA
5

HI
1

TX
4

LA
2

FL
11

AGE

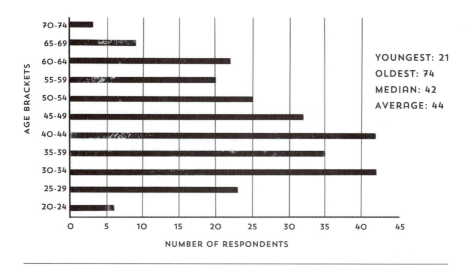

YOUNGEST: 21
OLDEST: 74
MEDIAN: 42
AVERAGE: 44

My grandmother taught me when I was young. When I studied knitwear design in college, I rediscovered my love for texture, color, and the ability to create your own fabric in knitting. I went on to design for industrial knitting machines but created hand-knit patterns on my personal time.—TINA TSE

The first thing I remember making was a stuffed dinosaur for my little brother when I was nine, with my mother's help. By the time I was fourteen, I made a skirt on my own that I wore to my first high school homecoming dance.—SALINA BURNS

My abuelita was a seamstress. It was really cool to tell her that the craft she used to support her family was something that I used to get a masters of fine arts.—LUCIA CALDERON-ARRIETA

HOW DO YOU DESCRIBE YOUR RACE AND/OR ETHNICITY?

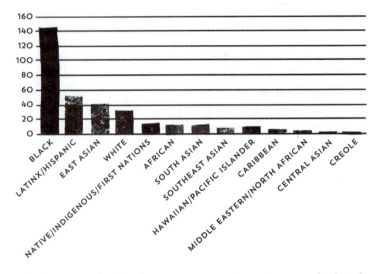

Respondents were asked to choose as many categories as applied to them and to add categories that they felt more accurately described them.

"African" and "Black" were separate choices to differentiate between people born in African countries and those of African ancestry who were born elsewhere and are part of the Black diaspora. While many respondents wrote "African American" in the "Other" section, African American wasn't a separate choice. "African American" excludes Canadians and people whose heritage hails from Mexico, Latin America, and the Caribbean who may not consider themselves American.

White was included as a choice because many people of color are of mixed-race heritage. Responses from anyone who claimed only "white" in their response to this question were not included.

Many Native/Indigenous/First Nations respondents also frequently selected Latinx/Hispanic.

WHAT TYPES OF FIBER CRAFTS DO YOU ENGAGE IN?

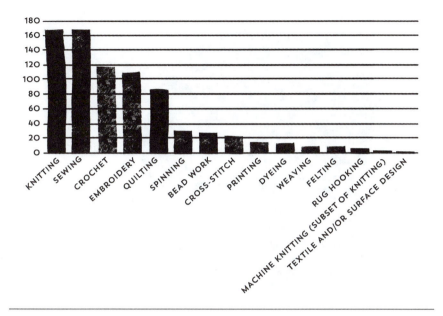

I predominantly knit at this point (learned as a child, became my main hobby in 2013), but I have at different moments spent time spinning (because of time we spent in South America), embroidering/cross-stitch (child into my teens), and weaving (in my teens and now a fascination for me).—CHRISTINA TORRES-ROUFF

I am a sewist/sewer of garments primarily, but I have quilted and knit before. I made my first and most difficult knitted object when I was eleven: baby booties for a neighbor. I had no idea that wasn't an appropriate beginner project! My main love, though, is garment sewing. I've been sewing now for over thirty-eight years! I started making doll clothes, and by high school I was experimenting with clothes for myself. Since college, I've been stitching a large percentage of my wardrobe, and I now average about ten to twelve garments per year.—LISA WILLIAMS

DO YOU ENGAGE IN THESE CRAFTS FOR INCOME OR AS A HOBBY?

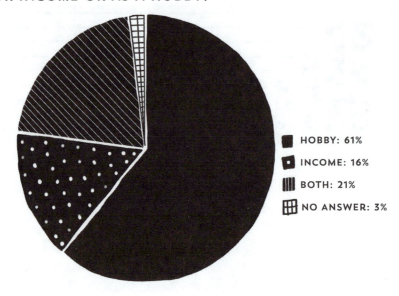

HOBBY: 61%

INCOME: 16%

BOTH: 21%

NO ANSWER: 3%

Entirely hobby. I purposefully have turned down several opportunities to make money via my crafts because I want to be able to unwind with them.—KRISTINA KOO

Trying to do this for income. I'm so done with the other types of jobs I've had—all in some kind of office, working on a computer. Handmaking really appeals to me now.—AVA CHAN

For art, for comfort, as spiritual practice, and for income.—JACQUI HOLMES CALHOUN

IF THIS IS A HOBBY, HOW MUCH OF YOUR TIME AND MONEY DO YOU ESTIMATE YOU SPEND PER YEAR ON IT?

Money/Year
Range: $100–$10,000
Time/Year
Range: 18–1,600 hours

Not a hobby but an obsession. Most of my waking hours and every cent I can lay my hands on.—CECILE LEWIS

Maybe 250 hours? 200? That doesn't include the time that I spend commuting to work with my eyes closed, constructing and deconstructing my latest piece, sketching pieces while I'm at a show or event, or reading a book, or volunteering at a clinic to help people immigrate, plus the way my other creative endeavors like performing directly impact my quilting.—SHUBHA BALA

Wait, what? I ain't tellin'! Too much! I am now in a space that folks send me yarn, so it's getting better.—GAYE GLASSPIE

DOES ANYONE IN YOUR FAMILY PRACTICE THIS CRAFT, TOO?

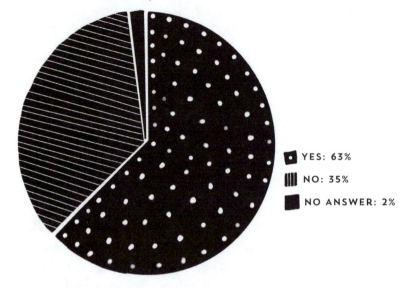

YES: 63%

NO: 35%

NO ANSWER: 2%

Yes. My 101-year-old mom still knits; she used to needlepoint and sew, too.—ANGIE FRANKLIN LORD

Not really. I'm from a family of immigrants. Crafting is a luxury to them, something they don't have time for when they were just trying to survive. I'm fortunate they did the hard work to allow me to explore art.—SARAH VANPHRAVONG

My dad used to hook rugs, my mom knitted, my paternal grandmother crocheted and embroidered prolifically.—ERIN EMIKO KAWAMATA

THE SURVEY QUESTIONS

Name

Age

What third-person pronouns would you like me to use when writing about you?

City, State or Province, Country

Citizen of

Website (if applicable)

Instagram (if applicable)

How do you describe your ethnicity? (Please check as many as apply and/or answer in your own words.)

What types of fiber crafts do you engage in?

How do you self-describe/identify yourself?

What's the first thing you remember making?

What are you making now?

How and why did you learn your craft(s) and/or your creative skills?

Does anyone in your family practice this craft, too? Are your pieces similar or different aesthetically?

Tell me about your creative community. You can define "community" as broadly or as specifically as you'd like.

When have you felt like an "other" within the context of your craft?

When do you feel recognized in your craft? Who recognizes you and how does that feel for you?

Are there aspects of your work that you feel are misunderstood?

Do you engage in these crafts for money or as a hobby?

If this is a hobby, how much of your time and money do you estimate you spend per year on it?

If you sell your pieces, who are your customers? How long have you been selling your work? What challenges have you faced in building your creative business?

What's your favorite thing you've made?

Do you have an artist statement or any principles that guide your work?

What adjectives do you use to describe your work?

Were you exposed to other people who looked like you who were engaged in this craft when you were younger?

Where did you get inspiration growing up? Who were your idols?

Who do you look to for inspiration today?

What colors are you drawn to and why?

Where do you get your materials?

How do you choose your materials?

Is there anything else you'd like to add?

TERMINOLOGY

PERSON OF COLOR (POC): A person who is not completely of European ancestry. I am using this term to refer to broad groups of nonwhite people of different races and ethnicities. When writing about and speaking with individuals, I prefer to use their specific self-identified race or ethnicity.

BLACK, INDIGENOUS, OR PERSON OF COLOR (BIPOC): An expansion of the term "People of Color." BIPOC attempts to emphasize that the oppression of Black and Indigenous people has been integral in the formation of the United States and Canada.

Why We Craft

OUR CRAFT ORIGINS

Survey Question:
How and/or Why Did You Learn Your Craft(s)?

I learned to knit about thirteen years ago. I took up knitting because I thought it would improve my hand-eye coordination and help me be a better surgeon. As an added bonus, it opened me up to a great community of other fiber artists and helped me realize how very much I love to make things.—TULLIKA GARG

All the women in my family worked in fiber, out of necessity. My grandmother was a dressmaker and so was my mom, who also taught clothing and textiles. My aunts all sewed. That was how they contributed to supporting their families. It wasn't until I came along that fiber art became something they could teach me to do for fun.—LOI LAING

I had been working in show business for a number of years. On a trip to Japan in the eighties, I became enthralled with the uniquely Japanese fashion of the day. I especially loved the knits by Kansai and the textiles that Issey Miyake was using. I decided I wanted to become a sweater designer when my showbiz career was over.—OLGALYN JOLLY

I learned to knit on December 13, 2002, on a bus back to Providence from Woonsocket, Rhode Island. I was in an AmeriCorps program called City Year and the Corps member I supervised knitted all the time. She taught me how to knit on the bus back to Providence. She had long, metal Sally Bates needles and a vibrant royal-blue ball of acrylic yarn. I know this date because it's my birthday, and she taught me how to knit as a present. Thank you, Bryn—you changed my life trajectory!—DIANE IVEY

I was hospitalized due to an illness that made it very difficult for me to walk and take care of myself. I couldn't work and was so stressed because a diagnosis couldn't be found, and my life was changing very drastically. Having been a super independent and active person, I wasn't sure how to create structure and joy in my life from my bed. My roommate at the time was a very accomplished knitter and offered to teach me. It was the best thing ever.—DINA ALI

I learned sewing in college because, at the time, I wanted to pursue graduate study in electronic textiles with my undergraduate degree in electrical engineering. There was a professor that had studied apparel design and had her PhD in computer science, so I felt she had the best balance of engineering and design. She recommended I take courses in textiles, garment sewing, and pattern design. I ended up taking two of three courses, but I really excelled. Learning how to sew brought me a new love.—ADRIANA BLANCO

My mother taught me. We traveled from Detroit to New Mexico in the car and I talked a lot! To crochet, I needed to count and pay attention. She got some silence.—IZOLA GARY

I wanted to learn a new skill. I also wanted to be an interesting older person with a passion.—GAIL PETTIFORD WILLETT

JEN HEWETT: I first learned to sew when I was in fifth grade, at a summer day camp for girls. Much of what feels so instinctive to me now—winding a bobbin, sewing with the right sides together, backstitching to begin and end a line of stitches—are steps that I learned from my kind, gentle sewing instructor over thirty years ago. I spent every bit of free time I had that summer sewing on the camp's machines. But then, I stopped sewing when camp ended because I didn't have a sewing machine at home.

I didn't start sewing in earnest again until two decades later. By then, the DIY movement was in full swing and crafts like sewing, knitting, and woodworking were becoming popular again. The DIY movement overlapped with the emergence of blogs. In addition to sharing their DIY projects on their blogs, people were often also sharing their processes. This made craft more accessible. There are gatekeepers and barriers to entry, and getting past them can sometimes require a guide. Bloggers often served as those guides. When I needed someone to guide me through the completely unintuitive process of working with a Big Four dress pattern whose instructions were written for someone who already knows what they are doing, I turned to a blog sew-along. When I needed help figuring out which fabrics to choose and where to buy them, I turned to a blog post that listed exactly what fabric the blogger used and included links to online shops. These resources were invaluable.

While a handful of people surveyed for this book initially learned their crafts from books and blogs, most, like me, first learned in person. Many reported that their family members were their earliest teachers. Bhavana Dhaman, a sewist from California whose relatives were rangoli artists, knitters, crocheters, and sewists, responded, "Making is almost hereditary." Similarly, Maybelle Taylor Bennett, a weaver and knitter from Washington, DC, wrote, "My grandmother had fourteen children. . . . Everyone learned handcrafts, so my grandmothers, aunties, and mom taught me how to crochet and knit." Cynthia Martinez, a knitter and crocheter from Washington, responded, "I come from a long line of seamstresses, so it was inevitable that I would learn to sew." Roxanne Masters, a knitter from Oregon, says she learned to sew because she had no choice. "I was my mother's helper. I cut out patterns, pinned cloth, and threaded needles very early on."

Others learned from friends. Aria Velasquez, a knitter from Washington, DC, learned to knit from a group of girls in her sixth-grade class. "It became a micro-fad that they picked up in 4-H, and then it spread." Jocelyn Murray, also a knitter from Washington, DC, "first learned to knit from a friend behind the bar in college," and Christine Tawatao, a quilter and sewist from Washington, learned to quilt from her college roommate. While Charnita Belcher, a knitter from California, learned how to knit from her grandmother, she didn't make anything more complicated than scarves and blankets for years. Decades later, a coworker challenged her to try knitting something more complicated during their daily "stitch and bitch" lunches in the company cafeteria. Through these lunches, she built up the skills and courage to knit her first sweater.

Some learned, as I did, in more formal settings. Rosie Chapman, an art quilter from Michigan, learned to sew in seventh grade in her Detroit public school, while Kaiya Herman Hilker, a multidisciplinary crafter in Michigan, attended a Waldorf school, "where handwork is a necessity." Bonnie Hsueh, a self-described aspiring textile artist from British Columbia, has been taking classes and workshops over the last ten years, "slowly acquiring some skills."

While many of the respondents who learned their crafts as children did so out of necessity, almost everyone who either continued with or learned their crafts in adulthood did so as a hobby. Though I initially learned to sew because it was a summer camp elective, I picked it up again in my thirties out of choice. I was working a corporate job at the time, and I wanted a creative outlet. Sewing (and screenprinting, another craft I learned at the same time) fit that bill. Sewing my own clothing eventually became a way for me to express my style, to create a uniform of my favorite silhouettes and prints, free of the ever-changing dictates of fashion and retail.

Ava Chan, a felt maker and seamstress from Massachusetts, echoes this. "I've returned to garment sewing because the usual department store offerings are hideous. If you go the small-sewing route, there are so many

---

Clothing communicated for me, and sewing allowed me to create my visual lexicon.

---

fashion styles, types of fabrics, and practical details (pockets!) that one can have." Likewise, Julie Robinson, a fashion designer from New York, says she would see clothes in magazines that she wanted, but couldn't afford or find in stores, or would want if they were slightly altered. She writes, "I learned to make things so I could have exactly what I pictured in my head." Atiya Jones, a multidisciplinary crafter from Pennsylvania, says that, as a teenager, "Clothing communicated for me, and sewing allowed me to create my visual lexicon."

Jones also writes that learning to sew in sixth-grade home ec allowed her to alter her clothing to fit her tall, thin frame. Other respondents also learned to sew so they could create clothing that fit their body types. Aria Velasquez writes that following sewists on Instagram motivated her to learn how to sew. "I was always really impressed with their talent and how they could make things that didn't look like anything available in mainstream stores or online, and that made them look so happy and comfortable in their bodies." Grizel Esquivel in Oregon writes that she sews her own clothes because they make her feel "cute and confident," adding, "As an overweight woman, plus-size clothing that's made for the mass market is shapeless, boring, and made using only the saddest, darkest prints."

Many also reported learning—and practicing—their crafts as a way to be connected to others. Kristine Caswelch, a knitter from Ohio, learned to knit while she was her grandmother's caregiver and struggling with feelings of isolation. She calls knitting her "saving grace." She participated in her friend's knitting class, becoming friends with "an amazing group of women" who became her support system during this time. Lisa McClendon, a knitter, sewist, and crocheter from Los Angeles, originally learned to crochet because crocheted clothing was in fashion at the time. But later, she writes, "It would be the craft I did while my mom knitted and had chemo treatments. When she passed, I inherited all her knitting items, and one day, I just said, 'Maybe I'll knit.' I love knitting and it makes me feel like my mom is always with me."

Others wrote about practicing their crafts as a way to be connected to themselves, to build identity and self-esteem. Lisa Merriweather, a knitter from California, calls knitting "my meditation, and something that helps me cope with the challenges I've faced. Knitting has been a big part of me rebuilding my identity as a person." Carmen Ali, in Ontario, started sewing in high school, but stopped because she let perfection get in her way. She started sewing again a year ago and writes, "It has transformed my confidence. It has helped me to let go of my perfectionist ways, to be creative, and to commit to self-care."

So many of the responses I received are about the ways that craft is intricately linked to connection. People often learned their crafts as a way of connecting with their family and friends, even if craft was an economic necessity. They continue to practice their craft to connect not only with others but also with themselves, with their desires, needs, and creativity. As Maria Parker, a multidisciplinary crafter from Virginia, writes, "There is no reason why, other than that I love it. I can't imagine not being able to create. It is who I am." Our crafts often become a part of who we are. Regardless of how or why we learned our craft, we continue to make because our craft continues to give us the creative outlet, the community, and the connections we want and need.

INTERNATIONAL STYLE ICON

Interview with Sonya Philip

JEN HEWETT: I was just learning to sew clothing when I took your sewing class for your Dress No.1 pattern. But, at what point did you start sewing?

SONYA PHILIP: I took a needlework class in sixth or seventh grade. I know I sewed before then because my mother had a sewing machine. But, that needlework class was my first memory of actually having to sit down and do a project with the expectation of doing things from start to finish. One of my school assignments was to make a pillow. I wanted to make a pillow that was shaped like a pencil. I was trying to use fusible interfacing, and there was going to be a stripe on it. I didn't turn the edges under. It looked hideous.

Then my mother helped me, and when I say "helped" me, I mean she ended up doing most of it for me. It looked wonderful, but it was just this clear distinction of what I did didn't work, and then the project got taken over by my mother and done to make it look right. I remember the feeling of, "Well, I'm glad it looks this way, but do I really have ownership of this? Did I make it myself"? No, I didn't. It was finessed. That experience also helped inform my own teaching style. I'm not going to do things for people. I will show them how to do things. I can sew a seam or I can sew bias tape, but I can do that because I've done it over and over and over again.

There's no shortcut. They're going to have to put in the time to gain the manual dexterity and the hand-eye coordination. That was probably the inflection point where sewing and myself started bridging apart. I liked fashion just as any teenager trying to figure out who they were liked fashion. But I think I had this feeling that I was not capable of executing the ideas that I had, making them look like the pictures in my head.

That continued throughout my twenties. My mom gave me her sewing machine. I still have it. I carried it with me in moves. It would sit in the closet for most of the time, and then I would take it out. I would do things like make a Halloween costume. Or, just little things here and there.

I lived in these small places where I never had a space dedicated to sewing. Even if you have a sewing machine set up, if you don't have a cutting table, that's going to make sewing difficult. It might not take a lot of time compared to, say, knitting or weaving. Yes, you can put together something really quickly, but it does use a lot of space. And, the time you do need to invest in it needs to be focused and uninterrupted.

Then I discovered knitting in the early 2000s when Debbie Stoller came out with her *Stitch 'n Bitch* book. There was this big resurgence in knitting. I also had a child in a Waldorf school and everything coalesced—handcrafts from the Waldorf school, the existence of knitting groups, and more yarn stores. I also found knitting communities online through Flickr and blogs.

JH: Flickr was so great for community.

SP: It really was. I know people who I've kept in contact with to this day who were old Flickr and blog friends. I started knitting and took to that. Everyone got hats one year for Christmas or scarves another year. I had a knitting blog. I thought that I was going to be a knitter or I was going to be a pattern designer. But that did not happen.

Through Flickr, I got to know people who were knitters, but also other people, too, like ceramicists, printmakers, or people who sewed clothes. I would leave comments like, "Oh, I love what you made. I wish I could sew." I'd convinced myself I couldn't sew. I could knit, but I couldn't sew.

JH: Why had you convinced yourself that you couldn't sew?

SP: I think because I had had enough disasters. We got an old sofa and I decided to sew a slipcover. That was an ambitious thing, and I made it. But, I didn't finish any of the inside edges, so the first time it got washed, all the threads on the inside unraveled. And, we knew a woman who was an incredible seamstress and she would sew her daughter's birthday dresses. I had a daughter. I thought, "I'm going to sew her birthday dresses." I sewed her a dress, and I was able to get it on her head, but I wasn't able to get it off again. I had to cut her out of it.

There were all these moments when I proved to myself I couldn't sew. First was the pencil pillow, then the birthday dress. I made peace with the fact that I was lacking something, maybe the patience, to sew. I think also I'm convinced to this day that my mother's sewing machine was cursed somehow. It was this finicky thing because I would always have tension issues.

JH: I'm convinced, though, that inanimate objects absorb stuff from us. I don't know where that comes from, but I do think that there's something to be said for a thing that is unlucky. I too have a sewing machine that I got when I was thirteen, and it was a workhorse. It's the machine I learned how to sew on. And it just decided to die. I tried to revive it a few times. I was convinced that the machine was telling me, "I've taken you as far as I can, and it's time to upgrade."

SP: Yeah, time to pass the baton. I found a sewing machine on the side of the road. I was out driving and thought, "That looks like a sewing machine case." And I stopped the car. That sewing machine only went at half speed, but that was perfect. Probably 50 percent of the dresses for my project, *100 Acts of Sewing*, were sewn on that machine. I think that the change of machine made a big difference.

   I also took a sewing class with Cal Patch. Just her style of teaching and the way she explained things made it clear to me that I knew a lot more about sewing than I thought I did. I'd thought that I couldn't sew and I that didn't know how to. She demystified it, putting the pieces together, drafting patterns, and constructing garments.

JH: But, there's a bigger story behind taking Cal's class, right?

SP: Yes, there is. I was frustrated with finding clothes to wear. I had had two—or was it three?—kids by then. I think in between the second and third, having young children, I didn't care what I was wearing, didn't really pay attention to how I looked. It's like, "Eh, this is comfortable. A kid is going to spit up on it. I don't care." This is where Flickr comes into it, too. I joined a group called Wardrobe Remix.

JH: I remember Wardrobe Remix. I wasn't a part of it, but I remember looking at the photos.

SP: Wardrobe Remix was started by a woman named Tricia Royal who I just thought was the coolest person ever. She always just had amazing hair, and she sewed, she designed, she knit. You know that if you were in the same high school with her, she would be in some arty band or something. Wardrobe Remix was a Flickr group where people would share photos of themselves. It was what would now be considered "#outfitoftheday."

But, it was not done widely then. It was more like street style—all sorts of people, young people, old people, wearing clothes they'd made, clothes they'd bought or thrifted. Someone could be wearing high-concept looks. Someone else would be wearing all these layers and look like they stepped out of a Russian storybook. It was people from all over the world, all walks of life. It was super inspiring. I decided to start taking pictures. Prior to this, I really hadn't liked having my photo taken. I think this was like 2007, 2008. Having kids had changed my body. I thought, "Oh, I don't like the way I look. I look fat." Having a photo taken, I would have to confront the fact that I looked fat.

I decided that instead of hiding from the idea of looking fat, I would embrace it and then try to minimize it by wearing clothing that I thought would make me look less fat. Plus-size clothing back then was not what it is now. The clothes were all-black, they were stretchy, maybe they had bell sleeves. Or, everything was wrap dresses, which I could never wear. I like natural fibers, and they didn't make plus-size clothing in natural fibers.

JH: So much polyester.

SP: Yeah, so much polyester. And I couldn't find natural fibers in my price range. There were more expensive brands like FLAX, CP Shades, and some European brands. All I wanted was to get a pair of black linen pants. I thought, "Oh, if I just had linen pants, then everything would be terrific."

I got more interested in what I was wearing. For my first Wardrobe-Remix photo post, I stood outside my front door. I was dressed in blues and yellows, and I decided I wasn't going to hide my body anymore. I like color, and I'm going to celebrate it and wear what feels good. That was very clearly a turning point for me, getting that support on Flickr where I met people who would leave lovely comments like, "Love what you're wearing." Then I would comment on theirs. It was a very nurturing community.

There was this financial gap between what I wanted to wear and what was available to me. If money was no object, yeah, I could dress myself. But, the reality was we had one income, three kids, and were living in an expensive city. There wasn't a lot of disposable income to put toward clothes, so I would go to the thrift stores and look at eBay. I found this one secondhand linen dress from FLAX. It was this dusty pink color I never would have chosen for myself, but I loved the way the dress looked. I thought, "Okay, if I could pair this dress with some linen pants and a hand-knit sweater, I would wear this every day." I then started coming with ideas; how could I replicate this?

I remember at the time, my friend Kristine Vejar, who owns the yarn and fabric store A Verb for Keeping Warm, said, "You should just sew something yourself." I was like, "No, no, no. No. I can't do that. No."

JH: As you know, I sew a lot of my own clothes. For a long time, I refused to learn how to put in an invisible zipper because I was terrified of it. So, I'd do all these workarounds to avoid the invisible zipper. When I finally jumped in and did it, it was so easy, and it completely changed how and what I could sew.

SP: I think we convince ourselves that we can't do something, and we butt up against it. Even though doing it will open up these avenues or expand things. We close ourselves off to it because it intimidates us. I took Cal's class. It was a basic pattern drafting class, and I think we learned how to draft a skirt and a dress. The class was on a Saturday. Monday, I dutifully went out and bought the materials that I had learned that I needed in this class, and I drafted a pattern and made a dress. It was too big at first, so I redid it and got my muslin to where it was like, "Whoa, okay, this looks good."

Then, I cut into this fabric that I had previously deemed too special to cut into. It was this black and white fabric that I thought that if I touched it, I'd mess it up. But I was like, "Oh, I can do this now." I was encouraged by this class. I made the dress.

There was this funny moment when the logical steps became clear and I saw sewing as this interlocking puzzle. I think that that partly came from Cal's explanations and realizing sewing's not this mysterious thing. It's logical.

I made that dress. I had a studio outside the home at the time, and one of my studio mates had a mirror, so I went over into her space and I looked at myself. It's cheesy—I describe that moment as the clouds parting and this ray of light shining and the music swelling: I had made this simple dress. It was this eureka moment of "I made this, I would wear it, and all my hopes and dreams and wishes have been realized." That was on a Monday. By the end of the week, I had made four dresses.

I've always loved fabric, and I could use fabric to make clothes that fit me and express myself. I could wear things in ways that were not available to me until then. It was practical and creative and expressive. I was in my room, I had hung the dresses up, and I was looking at them like, "Oh my gosh, look at these." I was so pleased with myself.

JH: I still do that with every single garment I sew. I hang it on the back of my closet so that when I wake up in the morning, the first thing I see is what I've sewn.

SP: There's something about that combination of being functional and decorative. It's very special.

JH: Let's talk about that, though. You had said in another interview that clothing as a form of creative expression is something that . . .

SP: Has been diluted.

JH: You talked about Wardrobe Remix and that it was never about brands or status, right?

SP: No.

JH: It was actually about a form of expression that was kind of divorced in a way from consumption.

SP: Yeah, because it was based on this street style and the differentiation between street style versus a runway style.

So, instead of what you're seeing in the fashion houses and magazines, it's what people are doing with those pieces of clothing. These were people who were making do with what they had and what they could get their hands on. That might be thrift stores or borrowing or trading because they did not have all the money and could not get the latest trends.

Certain brands now have this status where people are waiting in line—be it a physical or digital line—to get things. There are clothing brands where there are whole communities set up for trading and swapping. There's the aesthetic, but also all the things that come with it that transcend the aesthetic. Like, "When I am wearing Brand X or when I have Brand X hanging in my closet, then I am leading Brand X lifestyle. These brands are markers of success. This will indicate that I earn this amount of money, I think this about the planet, I send my children to this kind of school, and this is the car I drive or don't drive."

That is where I see ready-to-wear clothing being. That it's more a marker of "This is where I am in society." That's how it's always been. But I think that social media exacerbates that. Also, thanks to the Internet, we can almost get anything. So many of us don't have a connection to the clothes because they are just these external markers of our wealth. . . . Not even just wealth. I think it's also so aspirational. It's like if I wear these clothes, then I might not be this, but I want to look like this.

JH: Right. It's how we want the world to perceive us.

SP: Yes. You might not be able to afford a closet full of these really expensive clothes, but you don't even have to buy them now. You can rent them.

JH: I had a really interesting conversation with a friend of mine who has a very corporate job and she has a lot of money, and she was making fun of one of her coworkers who rents her expensive things. She doesn't own them. My friend said, "Am I mean for looking down on her for this?" I said, "Actually, yeah." One, it's none of your business. But, two, clearly these things are important to you, and therefore they're important to all the people in your social circle. The coworker feels that she has to have them to fit into this job, this circle. And if she can't afford to buy them, if she still needs to have them, she's going to get them. It's not just her doing something that you think is shady or somehow déclassé. It's also that you're attaching value to these things makes them valuable for her.

SP: I think that's exactly right. Ascribing the value, ascribing the status to those things. Looking at renting luxury items as déclassé is the fact that it's opened them up to people who couldn't otherwise afford them. It astonishes me how so many things in this gig economy—rental, even ride-sharing, grocery delivery—all of these are things that previously were only available to people who were very wealthy. But now, you can do it in this kind of piecemeal fashion. You might not need to buy the luxury purse, but you can rent it and sort of occupy that lifestyle for a time.

JH: There's this whole general idea of democratization of luxury that it's no longer luxury and it's no longer special, and so we're constantly seeking out the new and the different on such a regular basis to signify . . .

SP: Yes, wealth. And, I think, to signify and differentiate your position in the hierarchy and that position, because you always want to be above someone else. To me, shopping for clothes was never a rewarding experience. I remember very clearly at one point, my daughter had a weekly acupuncture appointment downtown. There's an Anthropologie right there. Sometimes, we'd go into Anthropologie. Everything's beautiful, everything's lovely, they're "borrowing" from artisans—and also employing artisans too. It was, again, part and parcel of that whole aspirational aesthetic that you, too, could look like you live in the French countryside.

JH: Or, you've traveled the world and you've brought back all this stuff from your travels. I hate the word "curation," but I think it's apt here. Somebody has curated the experience, so it's not just the clothes, it's also the layout, and the music, and the lighting.

SP: Everything is curated. That will be the word for this period in time: curation.

JH: Right. Because if you have access to the world, if you have access to everything, then you're relying on someone usually outside of yourself to curate what you see.

SP: I would go in and I remember everything was tiny and couldn't fit. It was like, "Oh, there's this sweater." I tried it on, and oh, it fit. I wouldn't ordinarily buy things new in stores, but this thing fit, so I bought it. I brought it home and thought, "I like the way this sweater looks, and there was another color. So next week, I'm going to get it." Was it there the next week? No, it was gone. That was my experience of fast fashion. Anthropologie isn't H&M,

it's not ZARA, but it still has that high turnover. It's gone, and never to be seen again.

It reminds me of a scene in *The Wiz* where Dorothy makes it to Oz and they're in the Emerald City. Everyone's wearing red because red is the color, and they're dancing and they're saying, "Red, red." Then there's this fanfare and they're like, "Red is no longer the color. Now we're going to wear blue." The lights change and then everyone's wearing blue. They're like, "I wouldn't be caught dead in red." Now, they're singing about blue. Yes, it's exaggerated there. But they're talking about, "Oh, the fashion's changing." That thing that just a few minutes ago was to die for is now passé, and now we're going to see this. It's lampooned there in a very fantastic-seventies style.

Fashion changes, and we don't have any control of it. We have a total lack of agency. And, it doesn't matter what you're comfortable in. It doesn't matter what you're comfortable exposing or not exposing or what colors you like or don't like. Of course, there will always be trends, but they happen so quickly now. I felt like I was insulated from the trends just by dint of not being able to fit into standard clothing sizes.

JH: You started your *100 Acts of Sewing* project in 2012. What was that project?

SP: I made the first four dresses. At this time, I was used to working in a series. I studied creative writing in school, and a lot of my poems were in series. I was also doing fiber art, and I had a couple of series there as well, so I was very comfortable in that sort of method of working. So, perhaps with that mindset and also with this flush of enthusiasm of making these dresses, the number 100 popped into my head. The words "I am going to make 100 dresses" came out of my mouth. I couldn't stop making dresses, so I had to justify the fact that I was making them. I created the project to enable myself, and also maybe justify the mania. I put together the scaffolding of this project and I documented every dress, started posting them first to a Tumblr and then to a website. Then I was going along and just doing that.

In a way that is not like me, I started planning. I started a spreadsheet and I started tracking how many dresses I had made. I started numbering them. The first several were all the same kind. I was making lots of sleeveless dresses, A-line shifts. I began asking myself, "Well, how many dresses do I need?"

So, I started making dresses for people because I didn't need them all, but I also had this sort of caveat of, "I want to make you a dress." I crafted an email where I'd say, "I want to make you a dress. Give me your measurements. Tell me what you like. You can have this dress, but I may also need it in the future at some point if I want to ever display these all together."

JH: Were you using your own patterns or were you using commercial patterns?

SP: A mixture of both. At first, I used just my own and then I branched into making some garments using commercial patterns. It turned out to be a wonderful education. It's one thing to make garments for just one size. It's another thing to make them for different sizes and different bodies. I wasn't able to find what I wanted among commercial patterns, which was a simple pattern in a large range of sizes. I wanted a simple dress pattern that was more of a canvas, because I love fabric. I wanted a pattern where the fabric could do a majority of the talking and the garment would be about this fantastic fabric. The design elements would take a back seat completely.

It was creative, yet having that one-year time constraint, it was also just like "Don't think, just make. Just get it done." I needed to photograph and post each dress, too. When you have a time constraint and you just have to get something done, it's not so much saying, "This is good enough," but more, "This works. I've got it to the point where I want, and now I'm going to move on to the next one." No one thing becomes overly precious. I was just in the trenches, doing the same thing day after day and building my skills.

I wasn't finding what I wanted pattern-wise, so I thought I'd just make my own. The hubris of the unschooled. But also, I think that my approach to making things work and making patterns that work for me has a lot to do with both being a larger size and being mixed-race. I have gone through the world not fitting in. The idea of not having a place and having to straddle two worlds means I just figure things out for myself.

I worked with a pattern maker and a grader to get the first dress out, Dress Number One. I also had some different styles I wanted. I taught myself how to digitize, how to grade, how to apply pattern drafting principles. What if you took a garment to not its simplest form but to a simple form? Could you use just one piece and then just cut two of the same piece and adjust? That is not how it's done, but the result is something that looks like a dress, feels like a dress, and holds together. Maybe it's not everyone's bar for success, but if it holds together through the wash and doesn't fall apart when you're wearing it, that's successful.

It's interesting to me that with sewing, the mark of a fine garment or a good garment is one where the indicators of the garment being handmade

---

The clothes that you make do not need to look like what is hanging in the stores because those are designed to be made in an assembly line. They are designed to be made and possibly also designed to be cut in the most economical way. What works for a ready-to-wear garment does not necessarily work for a home sewer, so why are you, as a home sewer, trying to achieve that?

---

are minimized or erased. So, you hide things. You hide the hem by doing a blind hem. It's unusual to me that the goal is to eliminate the evidence of the maker's hand. Where, to me, the hand is interesting.

The clothes that you make do not need to look like what is hanging in the stores because those are designed to be made in an assembly line. They are designed to be made and possibly also designed to be cut in the most economical way. What works for a ready-to-wear garment does not necessarily work for a home sewer, so why are you, as a home sewer, trying to achieve that?

JH: I also think that it's in many ways undervaluing the labor that goes into those ready-to-wear clothes that are in the stores. That you, as a novice, can come in and do the work that someone who has been doing this for forty-plus hours a week for ten years can do.

SP: I have taught classes where people are so adept at sewing. They know their way around the sewing machine because maybe they're quilters. Quilting, it's precision work. When learning to sew garments, quilters are making that leap from a two-dimensional object to a three-dimensional one. Again, the idea of pushing yourself to another level can be scary. They can't. They don't want to.

JH: Do you think there's also this fear of going from making this two-dimensional object that lies flat on your bed to making something that you wear, and all the stuff tied into body image and style and taste?

SP: Definitely. I have a whole other theory. With quilt-making, you have the idea that it's in service.

JH: It has a bigger function, which is to keep you warm?

SP: Yeah, but not necessarily you personally. When you make something that is just for you, then you have the concept of things being selfish. But I think that it's not selfish. If it's just serving you, then that is important. Why can't we, meaning the collective "we," condone gaining pleasure? Like you have to put this moniker of it being selfish and selfish is a bad thing. And even if it's said with kind of a cheeky wink, and like, "This is my selfish thing," no, you're still perpetuating the idea that you shouldn't be doing this, that somehow this is wrong.

JH: It's so interesting too because it's such a big difference between art and craft. For the most part, when an artist is creating "art," they're doing it for themselves first and foremost. You're doing something that's coming out of your vision that you need to execute. No one ever calls that selfish, right?

SP: And it doesn't have a purpose. It's on the wall, but you don't question its purpose.

JH: Yet, when we talk about craft, especially when we talk about sewing, it has to have a purpose. But with sewing, too, this idea that it's inherently selfish because you're doing it for yourself seems so regressive to me.

SP: Absolutely regressive. Especially when I think of how much sewing has contributed to my life and how much joy and healing it's given to me, given to other people. So much of why I want to teach sewing and sell patterns is because I'm proselytizing. I want to spread this because I can say that I am completely different in so many ways than I was before I started this. The way I think of dressing myself. That I don't have that fear or discomfort of thinking about how I look. That I've made clothes that I want to wear, and so when I wear them, I don't have to think, "Oh, what? Does this look good?" I wear things, I post things online, and people compliment me. I have developed a style where people want to dress like me.

In some ways, it's like, "This shouldn't be." I am overweight. I am short. I am in my midforties. What is going on here? I joked when I posted one of my

---

So much of why I want to teach sewing and sell patterns is because I'm proselytizing. I want to spread this because I can say that I am completely different in so many ways than I was before I started this.

---

first handmade outfit photos on Instagram. I was joking with someone that it's like, "Yeah, international style icon."

JH: That might be your subtitle on this.

SP: We're force-fed this idea that you have to look a certain way to be a taste-maker or influencer. I don't know if it's just being a certain age, but I don't aspire to look or to dress a certain way. Something that I also chafe against is when women talk about being invisible when they get to a certain age. I've never understood that and perhaps I never understood it because, well, when you mean "invisible" do you mean "sexually viable"? Do you mean attractive and that you're gaining certain looks, and then at some point, you're not getting them anymore? Well, as someone who is overweight, who is ethnically ambiguous, I've felt largely invisible my whole life. Welcome to the club. We're happy to be here, invisible.

JH: I think it's been a nice shift for me because of how badly I used to get harassed just existing in my twenties and early thirties. There were certain bus lines at certain times that I would avoid because the harassment could be relentless. If I'm suddenly invisible, it actually isn't a bad thing. I haven't missed it. For a lot of women, I think particularly middle-class white women, it sneaks up on them because they've always been given lots of attention. They're lauded for their appearance.

SP: Ta-Nehisi Coates had a great talk about the idea that when you go through the world being able to go anywhere and all the doors are open to you, and then all of a sudden, when you can't have this one thing or say this, or something is closed to you, then it's like, "But what are you talking about?"

JH: Making your own clothes instead of buying your clothes is deeply subversive because when you're buying your clothes, you're trying to fit into whatever is out there. When you're making your clothes, you're actually making the clothes for who you are and what you have. You're making your clothes for the body you have.

SP: Someone left a comment on one of my Instagram posts saying she had used one of my patterns and made something badly, but has still worn it a lot. This was one of the first things she made and she went on to then change it up, but she wore and still wears the first one. She later went and tailored subsequent versions to better suit her idea of what she wanted to wear. You can make something that might not be the realization of everything that you've ever wanted, but it still serves its purpose, it's still functional, and you made it, and that's fantastic. And maybe the next one will be closer to what your ideal is. It's, yeah, absolutely a never-ending process of building upon things and working not toward perfection but toward just what you want.

UN MANTELITO BLANCO

Essay by Adrienne Rodriguez

IN THE CORNER of my living room, a white crocheted doily lays quietly on a side table. It's prominently displayed with a few plants, and we try to keep it uncovered by the various piles of books and knitting projects that seem to accumulate in every corner of the house. The doily is in the shape of a flower head with multiple points radiating from the center. It is not only one of the only pieces of crochet I own but also the only object I have from my maternal grandmother, Nana Sara. She passed away in 1983 when I was four years old. My memories of her are very vague: She was in a wheelchair and only spoke Spanish. Her eyesight was poor and she had stopped crafting when her health declined.

My mother decorates my childhood home with numerous doilies crocheted by Nana Sara. One doily greets you as you enter the living room and is used as a placemat for the crystal candy dish on the coffee table. In the guest bedroom, they soften the dresser's surface. The doilies serve as a constant and silent reminder of my Nana Sara's handwork. My mom shared with me that she never learned to crochet, but she noted my grandmother was a prolific crafter. She had a Singer sewing machine with a treadle she used to make clothing. During the 1940s, she also supplemented the family's income by working from home as a seamstress. I find it ironic that I co-own a yarn and fabric store, but did not grow up crocheting or knitting. I did not learn to knit until I was twenty-four years old and was finally proficient enough at age twenty-six to knit a hat for myself. I could blame the ADHD for not getting the skill right away. It took at least five times to catch on and stick. The entire culture was also very foreign, a different language, and not a part of my history. Knitting felt awkward, and growing up in the desert of Southern California, I never even saw anyone knitting or crocheting! Knitting for me is a seasonal craft done in the winter, usually surrounded by friends who are also knitting. My partner, Kristine, learned to knit at a very early age from her maternal grandmother in Illinois. It made such an impact on her that we now co-own a store called A Verb for Keeping Warm, specializing in textiles and natural dyes. She knits and sews year-round and our home is filled with soft wools ready for their destiny. However, I still do not know how to crochet! No one in my family knows how, either. I know how to chain stitch, but beyond that, it's a mystery. So, as a child, as I do now, I look in wonder at the doily; it's history, how and why it was made.

> Originally a convent art, crochet was the technique that nuns taught to impoverished women during the Irish Famine of 1846, giving the women a sellable product that might keep them and their families from starving. Small crocheted textiles could be made relatively quickly, and the resulting openwork pieces, often worked in cotton, were touted as a kind of inexpensive lace."[*]

Sara Castillo Acosta was fifteen when she became an orphan in Chihuahua, Mexico, in the early 1900s. She was sent to a Catholic orphanage for the rest of her schooling and attended a Catholic high school in Chihuahua. After high school, she moved to Southern California and married my grandfather, a childhood acquaintance, in 1920. My mom tells me that as a child, she remembers my grandmother visiting with friends, either knitting or crocheting as they chatted. My Nana Sara would make clothing for her children and small decorations for the humble casita. My grandmother had eleven children, but somehow found time to relax with her friends while crafting, not only a functional duty but also a moment for herself. Creating an object where she was in complete control. Possibly a doily that illustrated her creativity and individuality. My family is unsure how my grandmother learned to crochet, but knowing it was taught in Catholic convents around the world, we could assume she learned in school. While researching the history of crochet in Mexico, I found a lot of conflicting information on the origins. Mostly because other techniques preceded contemporary crochet, but are not exactly the same. For example:

> Mexico has a pre-Hispanic craft called *randa* that is very similar to crochet. Originally, thread from the maguey cactus plant was used in this technique to produce detail almost identical to that of crochet.

* Beverly Gordon, "The Push-Pull of the Doily: Revered, Reviled, and Reconceived," *Piece-Work*, November/December 2017.

The tradition continues in some areas of Mexico such as Tlacolula, Oaxaca, where very fine thread is used to produce extremely delicate pieces that look almost like lace.[*]

Regardless of how it came to be the craft we know today as crochet, I consider it a link to my personal history. A link that I enthusiastically share as a contemporary fiber artist. Whether I know how to crochet is irrelevant. No matter how or why a crocheted piece was made, the most important thing for me is who made it. It is an intergenerational link that I can cherish every day. A way to have my grandmother part of my daily life. I'm not sure she ever had that in mind when she made these doilies, but nonetheless, the doilies are reminders that the creative spirit lives on and inspires. So much so that in reflection of her work by researching and writing this essay, I have promised myself to learn to crochet so that the legacy of the craft in our family will continue.

[*] Susannah Rigg, *Interweave Crochet*, Summer 2017.

SURVEY PROFILE

Claudia Carpenter

Age: 46
Location: Escondido, California
Profession: Artist/Vlogger

What types of fiber crafts do you engage in, and how many years have you been engaged in each?
I've been crocheting for about five years.

How do you self-describe/identify yourself?
I am an artist.

What's the first thing you remember making?
I crocheted a small scarf for my daughter, who at the time was five years old.

What are you making now?
I am working on a beautiful shawl made of merino wool and mohair.

What's your favorite thing you've made?
My favorite make is a shawl design that pushed me to learn a new crochet technique (interlocking crochet). It mimics a knit brioche look and it is stunning. The design is called Rapture by Rosina Northcott.

How and why did you learn your crafts?
Growing up in El Salvador, I lived in a multigenerational home with my great-grandmother, grandmother, and father. I shared a room with Great-Grandmother Maria, who crocheted. My home had various pieces of crochet. The idea of wanting to crochet is something that was always with me. Even remembering as far back as when I was around nine or ten years old, I remember having a hook and yarn in my hand and making a chain of crochet stitches. It is all I knew to do. Many years later, in my early twenties, I had

a friend who was involved with crochet. An elderly neighbor had taught her basic stitches. When that neighbor passed away, she inherited many beautiful pieces, two of which she gifted me. Again, I was in awe of the craft and wanted desperately to learn, but I felt too shy to ask my friend to teach me. Moving on to my thirties, I was determined that this time I would learn. I bought a book that was supposed to help a beginner learn to crochet. I tried and tried and could not make sense of the instructions and illustrations. Wedding planning and a new life took precedence over learning to crochet, and I moved on.

In my late thirties, my daughter was five years old and I wanted to crochet her something. I found that old book I had purchased many, many years before and looked up the terms and techniques on YouTube. Hallelujah! I was finally able to make sense of the book. I bought other books and more yarn, more hooks, and finally, I was able to enter this creative space. The world of fiber with all its magic became a real thing for me.

Does anyone in your family practice this craft, too? Are your pieces similar or different aesthetically?
No one in my immediate family crocheted until I started to spread the crochet love. Now, I have a sister-in-law and a cousin who actively crochet.

Tell me about your creative community. You can define "community" as broadly or as specifically as you'd like.
My creative community has its foundation on Instagram and YouTube. This is where I have made most of the friendships and relationships that have enriched my creative journey. They are truly international and multicultural. My creative community has expanded my creativity in so many ways. It gives me insights into the fiber community that I would have never been exposed to if not for their Instagram profiles or YouTube videos. Last year, I made a trip to Skipton, England, for the fiber festival Yarndale. There, I met in person many of my online friends and had the most amazing time. It was wonderful to interact with these women who I considered friends and who were exactly how they came across on social media. They were genuine, creative beings that are an important part of my life.

When have you felt like an "other" within the context of your craft?
The times I have felt the most uncomfortable have been when I have visited yarn shops or attended yarn crawls. The uncomfortable feeling starts at the

parking lot. *How will they treat me? Will I be made to feel like I don't belong?* Frankly, going into an all-white space makes me uncomfortable, and yarn shops tend to be predominantly white spaces.

For me, there are two things at play when I visit a yarn shop, yarn crawl, or fiber festival: First, am I feeling uncomfortable because I am a POC in a white space, or because as a crocheter, I am entering a knitting space? My running joke is, "Are they being rude because I'm brown or because I crochet?" My craft is always underrepresented in yarn shops, except for one in the area where I live. There are ten yarn shops in San Diego (where I live). There is only one that represents crochet with the same respect demonstrated to knitting—*one!* It is the one farthest from where I live, and it is the one I like to visit the most.

I wish my local yarn store and shops all over could wrap their minds about how intentional and how difficult it is to walk into a yarn shop as a POC. The mental preparation it often takes to go in and to be prepared for it to go bad real quick or to take that breath of relief and know that it will be okay . . . this time.

When do you feel recognized in your craft? Who recognizes you and how does that feel for you?
I don't crochet, design pins, or maintain a YouTube channel for recognition. I crochet because I love my craft, and I want the whole world to crochet and to see how beautiful my craft can be. It feels great to get positive feedback in my

---

> I think crochet is misunderstood by yarn companies, yarn shops, and indie dyers.

Etsy shop for the designs I create for my pin-back buttons. I am happy that people appreciate my crochet vlogcast on YouTube, but I don't do any of it for recognition. I want everyone who crochets to feel proud of what they create. I am happy that people recognize me, but I am happiest when people reach out and tell me they are trying a new technique or pattern because of something I have shared on social media or the vlogcast.

Are there aspects of your work that you feel are misunderstood?
I think crochet is misunderstood by yarn companies, yarn shops, and indie dyers. This idea that crocheters only work with acrylic or worsted-weight

yarns is utter rubbish. I don't see anything wrong with either of those things. Both are a part of our crochet community, but it is a stereotype that has to stop. I work with both acrylics and natural fibers. My enormous stash can attest to it. Crocheters are a part of the fiber community; we spend our hard-earned money making purchases of fiber of all types. It's time that those in the business of selling yarn wake up to this fact.

Do you engage in these crafts for income or as a hobby?
I engage in the crafting/fiber community as a maker and as a business. I derive income from the sale of pins I design for my Etsy shop. These pin-back and enamel pins are about crochet and fiber love. I want to promote crochet, and I design pins that promote crochet in the best possible way. My YouTube channel is monetized so I do receive some small revenue for the videos people watch, but it is not much. I don't sell crocheted items, but will take the odd commission here and there. I love to crochet, so I crochet patterns that capture my interest and use the pretty yarn because it makes me happy.

DESIGN WITH INTENTION

Interview with Seema Krish

JEN HEWETT: Tell me about young Seema. Where did you live? What were you interested in?

SEEMA KRISH: I grew up in Bombay in an apartment with my parents and my brother, and I didn't have a family connection to textiles, design, or art. My father worked a corporate job for a big company. He was a managing director. My mother did not work, but she raised my brother and me and she was interested in—is still interested in—yoga, and she teaches yoga. She's been doing that since I was a little girl and tried to get all of us to do yoga, but none of us expressed an interest because it was her "thing." It's funny coming to the United States and that's when I'm like, "Oh, I need to do yoga now." It's always when it's given to you free, it's not interesting, right? Especially when it's your mother telling you to do it. I try to remember that as I raise my daughter. I don't always succeed, but definitely try.

So, that was my growing up. The consistent theme was that I was very interested in art and design all along and was always painting and drawing. Instead of doing homework, I was always doodling. It was always the battle in the house: to focus and do my homework and not constantly be drawing. I did take art classes with a close friend of my parents—an artist, who became a mentor to me when I was in sixth or seventh grade. She gave informal art classes to a bunch of kids at her home. She would teach us to paint and draw using pencils, charcoal, and oil paints. I enjoyed that.

When it came time to pick colleges and to start thinking about what I wanted to do, I really wanted to formally pursue art, and my mother was pretty open to it. My father was, well, "I don't want you to be a starving artist. I want you to make a living." It was a big shift in his mind to support that. But, he would take me to a bookstore on the weekends and I would always pick books on art, so he realized that art was a calling that I couldn't contain.

When I had to start picking colleges and my career path, I wanted to study art. It was a little bit of a battle because my parents are super supportive of everything I want to do, and always have been, but they are also practical and entrenched in reality. There was that sense of "What are you going to do with your life if you study art?" It required being open-minded on their end, and in the late eighties, it was a time in India when everybody was focused on becoming a lawyer, doctor, or engineer. That thinking has shifted now with there being a lot more opportunities for youngsters today, but that's the India I grew up in. I decided I really, really wanted to study art. I was able to convince my dad. He compromised, saying, "Well, I want you to pick a path that will have earning potential." We discussed advertising as one avenue, and I enrolled in a local art school in Bombay, which offered a Foundation Art program, with the intention of eventually picking advertising. But during that Foundation year, I realized how much I loved textiles. There was just no going back from there. My dad also agreed with textiles being a viable career option, one we had not thought of previously.

JH: It's interesting that he thought it was viable.

SK: Well, I guess because of the strong garment production industry in India, right? That's very prevalent and viable. I think he could envision that, whereas it wasn't something we discussed when we were discussing options. Advertising was in his realm as it related to his business. Once the decision for pursuing a textiles path was made, my parents fully supported me. After completing the Foundation program in Bombay, I decided to go to New York and study at FIT (Fashion Institute of Technology). I applied to different schools, was accepted at RISD (Rhode Island School of Design) and FIT, and then picked FIT because of its location—New York City.

That was my plan. I loved the program at RISD maybe a little bit more, but that is in Providence . . .

JH: Can you imagine those winters after living in Bombay your entire life?

SK: Exactly. New York felt very much like Bombay. City-wise, it felt like a big city: a lot of noise, a lot of people, a lot of activity. So, that's where I ended up going to college. It was an amazing experience. I got a lot more out of it because I really connected with my weaving professor. I had a deep interest in weaving at the time, and she was a weaver. She would register me for a print class and we would end up doing one-on-one weaving projects instead. It was a tailor-made program.

It was incredible to have that rapport and relationship, and she's a woman who's still very much in my life. We still visit each other. She even came to our wedding in India. It is one of those unusual relationship things. I feel lucky that throughout my career in textiles, I have had amazing mentors. I don't go looking for them, but they just show up when I need them.

Early on, being exposed to the fashion industry at FIT, I decided I didn't want to work in the fashion industry. I did one summer internship with a mill that wove fabrics for fashion. I was a hand weaver in their office, basically weaving and creating the sample swatches for fabrics that went on jackets and women's clothing. The swatch was designed and woven in the studio, and then after approval, it was produced in mills overseas. I was the hand weaver creating these swatches. It was super fun for me, but I got the experience of being in a fashion environment. This was one of the good things about FIT. They have deep connections with the industry, making these kinds of opportunities available. Personally, after this internship experience, I quickly realized that I didn't enjoy the pace of the fashion industry. I felt that wasn't suited to me.

I learned more about the interior design industry. That seemed to be more of a fit for me. I liked that, within the interior design industry, there's a lot of development time for a product because it stays around for so much longer. Fashion is so much quicker. You're just developing it and then you're on to the next season. Textiles for interiors have longevity, so we end up putting more thought into the making of the products.

I was lucky that while in school, I decided I wanted to work in the interior design industry. The school had set me up for an internship with a textile mill that wove fabrics for interiors, specifically contract interiors, which means office and commercial spaces. The internship was a major part of my last term. Once again, I learned a lot about weaving and the requirements for interior design, but I didn't like the product. When I graduated, they offered me a job at their design studio. The mill was in Pennsylvania; the studio was in Manhattan.

At the time, I was a foreign student. If I accepted the job, eventually they would need to do my visa paperwork, so I would have been committed to them for several years. I was not inclined toward doing that. I felt I would be better off going back to India and working with Indian textiles, which would be a lot more exciting. I turned down that job. My family definitely thought I was crazy.

While I was figuring it out, I learned about the D & D building (Decoration and Design). I thought that I would've loved to work with a company that was represented in that environment as their textiles are gorgeous, decorative, and used for high-end residences. I noticed a job at my school's job office for cutting swatches part-time in one of the companies in the D & D building. I didn't know the company name, but it was basically cutting and making samples.

I thought to myself that at least I'd be around the right products while I was figuring things out, and I'd see where it led. The job was part-time, so I could still interview, research, and explore other things. When I walked into the interview, the company was Nuno. I was not familiar with the name Nuno, but I had seen their textiles displayed at the Cooper Hewitt Museum a couple of weeks prior! At the museum, the textiles had the name of Junichi Arai, one of the founders of Nuno Corporation. I was excited as I actually got to touch the fabrics that I wasn't allowed to go near at the museum. I got the job of cutting swatches and being a helper for the Nuno showroom. Nuno is based in Japan, so they have someone who owned that showroom in New York, which distributed their product.

I did that for about two, three months while I was exploring other things, but nothing else was panning out. During that time, the one full-time employee left because the distributor was a little bit difficult and a bit quirky. The distributor asked me, "Well, do you want to work here full-time?" The job involved a lot of sales, going to architecture firms, showing the collection, and selling the line. The product was so beautiful, it sold itself most of the time. The company was pretty high profile; they were shown at the Museum of Modern Art, so there was a lot of museum interaction, press interaction, plus interacting with design firms.

I told him, "I can do the job. I'm confident of that. But I'm a designer. I don't really want to be selling. If I commit to doing this, I don't want to just be selling. I want to at some point do design." He said, "We can definitely discuss that. If you can help me out right now, then we can figure out how to make it work down the road." I was open to that and I took the job. It just became incredible from there. A couple of months later, some of the Japanese team came over for an exhibition and they asked, "Oh, but you design?" One thing led to another and I got to jump into the design part and go to Japan, work with them on projects there.

JH: What luck, though.

SK: Real luck because I think so many textile designers try to work for that company, but it's such a small company and it's really hard to get in. I feel I just got in through the back door almost. I got really lucky. It was a dream to have this as a first place to work.

After Nuno, I decided to go back to India because I wanted to engage with Indian textiles. I hadn't had any experience with them before, and by the time I went back, my parents had moved from Bombay to Bangalore. That worked in my favor because there was so much more textile production there. When I talked of leaving and moving back, Nuno said, "Whatever you do, we'd like to stay engaged. We'll be your first client with whatever you make." That was really encouraging.

I set up a little weaving studio. I didn't know what I was going to be doing, but just was interested to weave because I was so inspired by everything I had learned and absorbed through my experience at Nuno. I wanted to do my own interpretation, so that's why I started. I made some things for Nuno like *bojagis* and wove some fabrics with silk for Nuno that I would have produced in an open market.

I also made a little collection of accessories—scarves and sellable things—that I sold in India through high-end design stores and through a few stores that I'd interacted with through my time at Nuno. My products were sold in stores in the United Kingdom and New York, so I was able to connect to some of those people. I think the tremendous calling card was being able to say, "Hey, I previously worked at Nuno," and people would be interested in seeing what I did.

I also got engaged with the Indian government because they have weaver centers in different cities. They were working on revival projects for certain crafts because people were wearing fewer saris. In certain villages, weavers were becoming redundant, so the government had initiatives to bring in designers to help revive some of those paths and find new avenues.

It was awesome. I got involved with a lot of that, worked with little villages, did work with weavers. I enjoyed that aspect of it. I think, again, having worked at Nuno and seeing how they worked with Japanese craft and found new directions for it, I was primed well to do that in India as well. The third thing I did with that weaving studio is I wove different experimental swatches. Because of having had that selling experience at Nuno, I would come back to the United States every few months and show my swatches to companies like Donghia and Jack Larsen. They would buy the samples and often ask me to connect them with mills that could produce them. I didn't want to take on making production for them—I was just selling them the design idea.

JH: You also had the technical ability so that you could.

SK: I could help them make the prototype. I could connect them with mills. It was a really interesting time, doing a lot of different things. It was very fun and engaging. Then I met my husband, which was a good thing, but he lived in Boston at the time, so we had this long-distance thing going for a while. We realized one of us was going to move, so I went and checked out Boston to see because I didn't know anything outside of New York City that much.

The only company I knew in the area at the time was Robert Allen. I think I got lucky again because they had a job opening. I was in the right place at the right time, and it was probably harder for them to find talent in that area. So, I decided I would take the job. I went back to India, wrapped everything up. Robert Allen even moved me back to the United States. They moved my loom as well. I started working with them as a director of design.

It was interesting for me because I'd been in the world of art textiles prior to that. This was really industry; they bought from a lot of mills around the world. It was very numbers-based, very budget-driven, very much of all that had not been on my radar at all. It was a good learning experience. It was like business school, almost. There was also a lot of travel because they bought from a lot of mills around the world. I learned a lot about textile production in different countries, the nuances of which country produced what, and what they were known for.

It was an amazing experience from that point of view. I did that for about five years, and then I felt like I needed to get back to doing something that I really, really loved. I had started thinking, *Well, do I really want to do all that?* I'd just had my daughter, and I took some time off. When I started thinking about what I wanted to do, my first thought was *There's just too much product, and do we need more product?* I'll come back to you and tell you what I'm thinking now about all that, but at that point, I struggled with that thought. I'd be putting more stuff out there, and I'd seen so much overconsumption and overproduction and warehouses filled with fabric. And you feel at some point, *Where is it ending up, right?*

It's something you just feel bad about. So, that was my initial reaction, but then we're artists and we need our expression, too, so I felt maybe if I can find a context for everything. For me, that meant going back to India and working with craft. So, those were my two commitments: I would work with India and work with craft. I think India was also good from the perspective of staying connected with the country myself. That tied all that together for me. I felt if I could just bring a new context to the craft, which again, I was sort of primed to do after having worked at Nuno and then having done that revival work with the government projects.

I decided to work with Indian craft and do it in a modern way, bring my own viewpoint to it. I decided to do pillows, thinking it would be easier and I wouldn't have to stock fabric or deal with high volumes. I did one season and the collection sold successfully, but I realized that, again, every season you're switching it up. It's not fair to the craftspeople, not fair to the process; again, going back to that fashion environment of fast product.

I said, *Maybe I'm better suited to fabric by the yard.* I jumped back into that. With fabric by the yard, there's a lot more quality that goes into it because of repeatability and making sure you can deliver according to the sample and what the client needs. Whereas, with pillows, it's a one-off.

Before I jumped in wholeheartedly, I moved to India for a year, in 2012. My daughter did kindergarten there. We stayed with my parents and my husband traveled back and forth. That's when I worked with the craftspeople, the group that I still work with, and spent the time training them. I was confident that I could deliver the quality that I wanted, and then came back and found the first showroom.

JH: Do you work mainly through the showrooms or do you have clients that come to you individually too?

SK: We primarily work through the showrooms, but we will definitely work with people if they come to us independently. Our primary clients are interior designers and architects, traded through the showroom. I think those lines have been getting blurred more with things being online, so we'll have clients who will reach out and say, "Can we buy a product?" We're not going to turn them away. But that's a very small number because I think most people feel a bit daunted as well when it's a to-the-trade business. How do you approach it? How do you buy it?

JH: You've always worked in kind of a rarefied world.

SK: Yeah. I think that's one thing that I do struggle with because I wish there was a way to make it more accessible. It's not the life I live. If I had to buy my textiles, not being in this world, I wouldn't be buying them. That's the reality. I think that's a big struggle for me.

That's my biggest struggle. I think the values of the consumer and of the product are different. Having said that, yesterday, we had a wonderful experience where an interior designer brought her client, who is a millionaire and was really interested in knowing where his product came from. He actually came in, met us, and spent the time to hear our story. But that's one in a thousand, one in, I don't know how many. We've never had that experience before. He cares about how the product is made. It was nice to see that someone who is doing their home at that level who doesn't have to care wanted to work with local people and wanted to hear the stories. That gives me hope that there are some people out there that care, but . . .

JH: Hopefully, that will trickle down a lot more.

SK: Yeah, I hope so.

JH: We talk about it in fashion a lot now, but we don't talk about it so much in interiors. I think it's that feeling, too, that these are expensive items already for a lot of people. A $2,000 couch is expensive for most people, but in the grand scheme of the lifetime of that product, it's not bad.

SK: Yeah, and I think again, it's the mentality of buying it cheap at retail and then switching it out constantly versus getting something that you live with for a very long time. I think part of it is in this whole interior design world, none of that is accessible either. The reupholstery is so expensive.

JH: It's the same as the cost of the item.

SK: Sometimes, more than the cost of the item. I think we don't have that infrastructure in place. Which, for example, growing up in India, it was so easy to do. We had tailors, we have all those things, and I grew up living like that. If I wanted a new shirt, I would go to the tailor and buy the fabric and he would make it. We didn't even have that many stores growing up. Literally, I would make my clothes with the tailor.

JH: When I was in India, the owners of the hotel where I stayed were renovating their family fort. One of them said, "You know, the thing about India is if you need to have a 400-year-old fort restored, you can just walk out to the village and there are people who know how to do this."

SK: Yes, exactly.

JH: I have two more questions for you. The first: Do you have an artist's statement or a business mission?

SK: Specifically, it's about bringing new context to traditional craft, being committed to craft, working in sustainable environments, and bringing a modern vocabulary to traditional craft.

JH: Well, then that segues nicely into my last question: How is the work that you are doing different from traditional craft?

SK: I think it begins with the designs themselves. They're bolder and more modern and not as traditional in design. I think the second part of what we do different is the way we combine things.

The layering, adding the embroidery to it . . . unexpected layering, I would say. I think that's how I do things differently. For example, in this pattern, the one with the big ogee motif, you'd typically not see a block like this.

It would be much finer and more carved. When I started this pattern, the printers would print it and you would see the variation on it. They were really unhappy with that. They would try to go back with a brush and even it out. I was like, "No, that's what I want. I want more of that, that *wabi-sabi* kind of imperfect." I think that's what makes it different: making the imperfections visible, glorifying the imperfections.

WHAT ARE YOU MAKING NOW?

A cardigan out of my hand-spun wool.—VERONICA SEW

I have a number of works in progress at the moment. Two partially made quilt tops. One quilt that I'm about to start cutting the fabric for. An indie pattern for a top that I bought/washed/dried the fabric for and I'm waiting to cut into it after I maybe finish a couple of the quilts on my list first. Reusable gift bags in lieu of using paper wrapping paper. Reusable mesh produce bags.—SHIRLEY KARNOS

Recently, I've been trying to incorporate other fibers and objects onto my embroidery pieces. I'm really hoping to build more texture onto my fabric. For example, yarn, thicker cotton string, and shells. I want to eventually merge into making woven wall hangings. I'm really inspired by the organic texture, style, and design of Asmaa Aman-Tran's work.—DETIARE LEIFI

Learning Our Craft

< Naiomi Glasses's blankets, rugs, and bags

BEYOND BARBIE CLOTHES: CREATING FOR WHO WE ARE

Survey Question:
What's the First Thing You Remember Making?

I sewed a cloth drawstring bag for my sponge hair curlers. I made the draw-string with a single crochet chain yarn. When my family and I were camping, our dog Nipsey chewed up all the curlers, but the bag remained intact. It was a sign, I was not sure of what, but definitely a sign.—CHARLENE JACKSON

The first thing was a small knitted purse with a big button closure. My mother always said that I learned to knit by watching her when I was five. I think she actually taught me, and that was a lovely fabricated memory!—AMY CREWS

I would have to say [my first creation was] doll clothes, with my mother's help. We made clothes for my Barbies. But, before I could make things, I would design the things I wanted me or my Barbies to wear, and my family members would make them.—JOCELYN MURRAY

My first project was a striped scarf that was meant as a gift for my friend. My mom was so excited to teach me how to knit that she gave me the yarn and needles to be able to make it. The width of the scarf changed as I kept adding or losing stitches, and the stripes were varying lengths. My friend still loved it and was amazed that I had made it. This was enough magic for me to fall in love with the fiber arts.—NORIKO HO

Satin heart pillows for Valentine's Day; I used to sell those to my classmates. —EBONY LOVE

[The first thing I made was] Barbie clothes out of those stretchy Styrofoam things that come on Asian pears. It was what I had easily available to me, and

I vividly remember making a "dress" out of one of them and tying a string "belt" around it.—KRISTL YUEN

I first sewed when I was twelve years old. I loved Barbies at that time and used pretty scraps from tailoring shops to hand-sew clothes for my Barbies. I loved it! I must have made at least thirty-five outfits for my dolls!—SOUMYA MUPALLA

A cotton smock top to wear over a steel back brace I had to wear every evening after I came from school! My aunt sat me down to a mint green Singer sewing machine and my love of crafting began.—REGINA C. GEE

I made a leopard button-up shirt with matching pants for a 4-H competition. —EMILY CLARK

JEN HEWETT: The first thing I remember sewing is a striped purse with a long shoulder strap and an oversized plastic button. I made it in the sewing class I took at summer camp. I was incredibly proud of that purse and proceeded to make replicas for my sewing teacher and my friends.

Because so many of the respondents learned their crafts as children, it isn't surprising that the first items many of them remember making are stuffed animals and clothing for their stuffed animals and dolls. Bretony McGee remembers how she "somehow managed to (horribly) sew a small teddy bear and stuff it with cotton balls" and even had "an ambitious idea of starting a teddy bear company." At eight years old, Shannita Williams "crocheted a stuffed dinosaur for [her] grandmother . . . made of peach-colored, scratchy, cheap acrylic yarn, and she loved it." But, what surprised me was the number of respondents—twenty-two, or 8 percent—who specifically remembered making clothing for their Barbie dolls. Deborah Henry, a multidisciplinary crafter from Oregon, responded that the first thing she remembered making was a dress she hand-sewed for her Barbie when she was six years old. Christine Tawatao, a sewist from Washington State, recalls, "My very first makes were clothes for my Barbie dolls when I was little. That was when I first learned how to sew. We used to make them from scrap rags, like old underwear and T-shirts."

I, however, didn't have a Barbie doll when I was little. She was contraband in my house. I don't remember what reasons my parents gave for this ban at the time. I just remember that when an aunt gave me a Barbie for Christmas, the doll disappeared before I had a chance to play with it.

Before writing this chapter, I asked my dad why he hadn't allowed me to have a Barbie doll. "They always seemed kind of sexist," he said, "and they had blonde hair and blue eyes and unnatural proportions. They didn't seem right for a kid like you. I figured you could decide for yourself when you were a bit older, like eleven or twelve." To be fair, my parents had also banned G.I. Joe figurines because my dad, a Vietnam veteran, didn't want my brother to play with toys that glorified war.

But my dad's reason behind the Barbie ban surprised me. My parents aren't very feminist. They each have fairly traditional gender roles in their marriage and raised my brother and me within those norms. Nor did my parents talk to us about race much. It was the eighties, and they both believed in the American dream of a true meritocracy. My mom, who is from the Philippines, long believed that all you had to do to succeed in the United States was work hard, save your money, and stay out of trouble. My dad, who is Black, hoped that raising my brother and me in a middle-class home and giving us the opportunities that he hadn't had would shield us from much of the racism he had encountered.

Though I had lots of dolls and stuffed animals, I desperately wanted a Barbie as much as my brother wanted a GI Joe. We finally got what we wanted when my uncle took us and our cousins on a shopping spree at Toys R Us. But, I quickly figured out that Barbie was only interesting to me as long as she was contraband. She didn't look like me, and preteen me found her proportions embarrassing. Once I finally had a Barbie, I was ready to go back to playing with Legos, stuffed teddy bears, and my collection of Strawberry Shortcake dolls.

Studies have shown that playing with dolls teaches children empathy and helps them work through emotions and make sense of the world. I don't disagree with other people's childhood love for their Barbie dolls. I, too, wanted a Barbie doll so badly as a child. And, the messages about normative beauty standards that my parents worried that Barbie channeled bombarded me daily anyway, thanks to mainstream media. Survey respondents playing with dolls that look nothing like them is probably no more harmful than growing up in a world where you rarely see yourself or your family positively presented in media. Barbie, it turns out, is a symptom of the problem rather than the problem itself.

For survey respondents, sewing clothes for their Barbies appears to have been a passing, childhood hobby—no one responded that they're currently working on clothes for Barbie dolls. And while some, such as Raquel Busa (profiled on page 136) and Katia Ferris, create dolls in their adulthood, they make them in the likeness of the recipient. But, many more respondents report that they're currently making clothing for their loved ones and themselves. Likewise, when I started sewing again in my thirties, I learned to sew garments that fit me and my tastes. I took classes and read books about pattern drafting so I could make exactly what I want. There's a certain amount of liberation in being able to create something that is exactly what you want. As I mentioned to Sonya Philip in our interview on page 23, making your own clothes instead of buying them is a deeply subversive act. Rather than trying to fit into whatever fashion designers and retailers have deemed a trend or what a standard body type or size is, you're making the clothes for who you are and the body you have. In essence, making is an act of creating and asserting your identity.

SEVENTH-GENERATION WEAVER

Interview with Naiomi Glasses

Yá'át'ééh! Shí éí Naiomi Glasses yinishyé. Hashk'ąą hadzohi nishłį. Tł'áásh-
chí'í bashishchiin. Áshįįhi dashicheíí. Tó'aheedlíinii dashinalí. Tsé Nitsaa
Deez'áhí déé naashá. Ahéhee!

Hello! My name is Naiomi Glasses. I am of the Yucca Fruit-strung-out-in-a-
line Clan. I am born of the Red Bottom people Clan. My maternal grandfather
is Salt Clan. My paternal grandfather is of the Water Flows Together Clan. I
am from Rock Point. Thank you!

JEN HEWETT: Why don't we start by you telling me about anything you
want us to know about who you are, where you live, what you do . . .

NAIOMI GLASSES: I am from a small town called Rock Point. I live in a
weird area that is closer to another town, but I technically live in Rock Point.
It's in between two towns. I live in the complete middle of nowhere. It's pretty
nice out here because it's so quiet that it allows you to have a clear head, free
from distractions. For an artist, that is such a blessing.

    I am twenty-two now, and I've been weaving rugs on my own since I was
eighteen. So, that's four years. I grew up in the valley of Phoenix, Arizona. I
lived in a suburb for the first twelve years of my life. I'm coming up on almost
ten years of living on the reservation. It's a completely different life out here.
It's crazy. I have to go back to the city quite often for appointments, and it's so
different from when I was younger. When I was younger, when we were living
on it, I didn't mind it. Out here, you get used to the silence of everything and
the carefree movement of life. It's just so much calmer and more slow-paced.
But, whenever we go out to the city, there are honks and police sirens, and it's
a lot, I feel like. It's so different, but I really love it out here. My parents were
both extremely surprised by how well my brother and I adapted out here so
quickly. We're like, "Okay, so we live here now. We're going to start adapting.

We're going to make the best of it." So, that's kind of how I see it out here, now. I'm just making the best out of the life we have out here.

When I was younger, I always wanted to learn how to weave Navajo rugs because my paternal grandmother weaves rugs. We would come up for the summer and I would see her weaving. I would always ask her, "Grandma, I want to learn. Teach me." She'd just tell me, "Just watch." Because that's how they teach up here. You watch someone and you learn from that.

It wasn't until I was about fifteen or sixteen, somewhere around there, that I started weaving. My brother, Tyler, had also started weaving. He started weaving before me. I learned from him because he was like, "Oh, just help me close up the rug." Then I started helping him close up rugs. Those were baby steps into learning how to use my hands with the warp and the weft, everything.

Then, I started helping my grandma close up her rugs. Finally, I think my brother and my grandma were like, "Okay, it's your turn now." So, they got a loom and threw me onto it and I just started weaving. That first rug was a saddle blanket and it had a bunch of squares in the corner, like steps. They were different colored steps. I believe I did it in natural hand-spun colors because, at that time, my grandma would just shear her sheep and then she would put aside wool. She would not really use it. At that time, she told us that a lot of the traders didn't like the thick, chunky hand-spun wool, so she would use the store-bought wool. So, my brother and I were like, "Well, there's all this hand-spun wool laying around here. Why don't we just start using it?"

I think that's kind of what set us apart because a lot of traders said they weren't seeing much of the thick, hand-spun stuff. They're like, "Oh, wow. You guys are doing it old-school with the hand-spun wool."

JH: Do you dye your wool, too? Or, are you using just the natural color of the sheep's wool?

NG: We usually use wool in the natural color of the sheep. So, we use natural white and natural brown, natural black. The browns and the black colors are really hard to find. We had little black lambs, and when they started growing up, they started losing their black colors. They're getting sun-bleached. I don't know how other people get such a rich black color from their sheep. I don't know. But sometimes, we have to go out and find people who have black sheep and ask, "Hey, can we get some of your wool?" We'll buy some from them.

There are feed stores that buy the wool from these Navajo grandmas who would raise their sheep, and then they'll shear yearly or twice a year, but our grandma does it once a year. The feed stores don't buy a lot of colors, though. If the wool is black or brown, the price goes down on it. So, I think that's why.

JH: I would think that it would be the other way around, since it's so rare.

NG: That's what you would think. But, I think they're thinking more that white can be dyed and more stuff can be done with white. It's more versatile. Whereas, if you get black, you've got to hope that you get another black color that matches closer. Maybe it's a little more difficult, but if you're a weaver, it's great.

JH: So, unlike most people who are weavers, you're actually kind of doing everything, right? So, you're raising the sheep and shearing the sheep. Do you card the wool, too?

NG: Yeah. We card the wool. We'll do the yearly shearing and then we pick out the best fleece that we know can be carded and spun into something. The rest, we'll send to a border town like Gallup, New Mexico. My grandma will take it over there. She'll sell it.

The good wool, we'll keep that here at home. Our process is to get it really clean with the carding because I feel like a lot of debris comes out from carding. I know some people wash it before they card it, but my brother and I have tried that, and it kind of seemed a little more difficult doing it that way. I don't know. It works in different ways for different people.

So, we'll card it and then we'll spin it and then we wash it. Then, we hang it up to dry and let it set. We wash it several times, though, to make sure it's pretty clean. But, we try to keep that sheep smell there. When I first started weaving, I sold mostly to traders and that was something they really liked because it brought back that old memory of back in the day when Navajo weavers would come in and they'd have these rugs that were hand-spun, everything handmade.

A lot of them would pick up our rugs and they'd be like, "Oh, it smells so good. You can smell that sheep." Which is silly to my brother and me because we're around sheep all the time, and we're like, "Oh, my gosh, that sheep smell. What are you even talking about?"

JH: What is it about weaving that you like? Because you could have done many other things. Why did you choose to become a weaver?

NG: I have no clue. Something about weaving just drew me to it, really. I always saw it as a kid, growing up, whenever we would come and visit. It was just so magical to me at that time. "Wow, Grandma does this?" It starts with just what looks like just strings, and then all of a sudden, she has a blanket at the end, which is amazing because I never saw her map out her designs or use patterns.

I remember at one time when I was a kid, I really wanted to get into knitting. Or, it was either knitting or crocheting. My maternal grandmother does a lot of knitting. I remember going out and buying the little templates and everything. I was begging my parents, "Oh, my gosh, can I get this? I want to try it. I want to do something with my hands, make something."

I tried learning how to do it from my maternal grandmother, and she was just like, "Oh, well, you just do it like this." She made it look easy, but I was—seven or eight? And I was like, "Oh, that is definitely not easy."

So, I guess I've just always been drawn to doing stuff with my hands. I was also really into drawing as a kid. I guess it's like a form of artistic expression. I've just always been into doing stuff with my hands. I don't know how to even explain this because it was something I always wanted to do and did; I've never been asked this question.

JH: I mean, I totally get it. I have friends who have very normal office jobs. They're accountants and they're lawyers and they followed a path and they knew this was what they wanted to do. So, they followed the path and that's how they got there.

But, I'm an artist, and I feel like I tried to do everything else, but art just kept coming back to me and saying, "No, this is what you're going to do." I can't talk logically about why I like doing it. It just is something that I think happened to me. I tried to resist it and then I realized that it was silly to resist it.

NG: Exactly. I have friends that also went on that same path. A lot of my friends right now are graduating from college and everything, but I started weaving as soon as I got out of high school. I was thinking, "Okay, I'm just going to do this for the summer and I'm going to go to college." Once it came around, I hadn't enrolled, but I realized, "Oh, my gosh. I can make a career out of this." So, then I was like, "Okay." It's something I love, so I decided to just go with it, and I really like where it's gotten me right now.

I'm just working on trying to do better than I did on the last rug. Because I feel like in Navajo weaving, there's no such thing as perfection. I'll see rugs and I'll think, "Oh, my gosh. This is perfect." But, at the same time, the weaver will be like, "Oh, well, I made this mistake here." I guess we artists are our own biggest critics. I guess my big thing is just trying to be better at the next rug than I am at the last rug. I'm just trying to better myself.

JH: I love your patterns. I love that they've got this real geometry to them, yet still a lot of movement and vibrancy. Are you working with traditional patterns? Or, are these ones that you've made up? Or, is it a combination?

NG: Because there are standard patterns that came with the trading post, there was a demand of "Oh, this is what we want. This is what we can sell." The trading post patterns are beautiful. They're extremely detailed. They're nice, but I feel like it kind of fits you into a mold, like you do one pattern, and that's the only pattern. There's not much innovation within that same pattern.

We like to take older styles and add a twist. We'll take little elements, like the crosses we do. That's an old design motif that you would see in older rugs. We use that a lot.

And then, stripes. A lot of blankets back then were more utilitarian, so they were banded. Not really fancy. I don't know. There's something about stripes, too. I love stripes. Stripes are so beautiful, and a lot of people overlook them because they think, "Oh, you're just going back and forth, back and forth." But I get to this point where I want to make [the stripes] as straight as I can make them, and that takes a lot of back-filling and standing back to see if they are even. They're a lot harder than I feel like a lot of people give them credit for. Especially if your warp is uneven, which thankfully I've kind of gotten better at making my warp a little more even so when I weave, it doesn't bunch up in one area as badly as it did when I first started weaving.

Also, we haven't done this design motif in a while, but when we first started, we were obsessed with whirling logs, which people outside of the Navajo land would see as swastikas. But back then, they used to mean good luck, fortune, just prosperity. Good things in life. But then, Hitler came in, took it, and turned it into . . . what he turned it into. I see a lot of young artists, even older artists now, trying to reclaim that design motif, as if to say, "This is what it means and this is what it stands for, and even though someone tried taking it and making it bad, we're here to let you know that it's still a good design and this is the original meaning behind it." I really like that one.

JH: I think that you have one of the most beautiful Instagram feeds that I've seen. It's just visually so stunning. Well, and I think there's always a trend that goes on, and right now, the trend is all these white backgrounds and kind of subtle colors. Yours is so different because there's just so much color, and then there's the richness of the landscape. Then you pop up and you're modeling every few photos—I just love it. And, I love that you're using technology in this way that supports a tradition. I just find it fascinating.

Are you selling your work mainly through the Internet and social media? Or, are you still having to go through trading posts?

NG: That's something I love about technology. It has opened a lot of doors for me. I feel like right now, we're talking because you found me through Instagram. This opportunity wouldn't have happened if I hadn't been on Instagram. I've gotten a lot of customers through Instagram—especially with the purses. Those are popular among a lot of people. A lot of people really like the purses. Also, it's something that you can take with you anywhere. I think that's why it does better. Because with a rug, it'll be in the house. You can show it off at your home, but a purse, it'll be with you all the time.

Sometimes, I'll go to a trader because sometimes I have horses that need to be fed, dogs that need to be fed, and sheep that need to be fed. But when I first started out, I didn't get the prices I wanted. At that time, I was still a young weaver, and they'd say, "We'll see if it sells. If it does, we'll give you a better price." Thankfully, my rugs were popular enough that at the trading posts, they were able to sell.

I understand that I sell it to them at a wholesale price and they mark it up. That's also because of their overhead costs. They have a storefront and they have to keep operations running. So, I'm completely fine with that.

The first one I sold in Gallup, New Mexico, and the second one I sold in Cortez, Colorado. I just saw the receipt for that one the other day and I think I only got $175 for that at that time.

It was a lot of work. I remember being discouraged, but then the [trader] told me how he works with his stuff. Some stores will double the [wholesale] price [for retail]. Some triple or quadruple it. But, he told me that he'll give me more than half the price that he'll sell it for because he sells it to other people and other traders back East. I have no clue where that rug is now!

A part of what taught me to try and perfect my craft was talking with these traders and trying to better each rug so it would sell for a higher price. I mean, it's kind of sad when you think of it like that, but I think it also made me into a pretty confident and tougher person in a way.

Because before, I remember the first time someone told me . . . It was my first rug and I sold it at Perry Null's in Gallup, New Mexico. The guy said, "I'll give you this much for it." I felt like, "What? I put all this work into it!" I remember so badly wanting to cry right then and there, but I thought, "Okay, that's a good price. I still need to feed my dogs. Okay, I'll do this." I sold it to him.

But over time, I have definitely gotten better speaking skills with these traders. It's okay if I sell to a trader because I get a better price now. I go to only a few of the trading posts. Well, they're not even trading posts. They're more like galleries.

They sell Native jewelry and rugs, but they don't do trading anymore as they did back in the day. But, I like them because they treat me well and I've gotten to know quite a few of them really well.

I do have customers from Instagram, so that does work, also.

JH: Twenty-two years ago, you couldn't have done this. You would have relied only on the traders and the galleries, which is kind of a crazy thought.

NG: That is crazy. Or, unless you didn't do markets. Like, there's Heard Indian Market in March and Santa Fe Indian Market in August, which are the two biggest ones for a lot of weavers in our area. But I don't know about other areas. I know from a lot of my weaver friends, they say that those two are the ones that treat them the best. They get the best sales at those markets. See, that's what's great about those shows. I haven't entered one yet. I always miss the deadline. So, this year, I'm definitely putting it on my calendar, setting like a million alarms, like, "Get your application in so I'm on time."*

---

* After this interview, Naiomi entered a purse into the Gallup Inter-Tribal Ceremonial and received first place in her division. She also submitted an application to the 2020 Santa Fe Indian Market and was accepted.

JH: Will you have to spend every waking hour to have enough to sell at the markets?

NG: Oh, yeah. I mean, that's not much different from what we do already. We're always weaving something or we're always dealing with our wool, either spinning or just preparing the wool. Even the warp. We buy it in skeins, and so then we have to ball it up. I think a whole skein of warp takes two hours to ball. It's a lot of preparation. I feel like weaving the actual rug is the easiest part, compared to everything else that goes into it.

JH: How long does it usually take you to weave a rug?

NG: I measured my most recent rug earlier. 29 inches by 24 inches. It wasn't that big, but it took us a month. But it was a fun project, so we had fun with it.

JH: How much time do you spend per day weaving?

NG: A lot of people ask me how many hours it takes, and that's the thing. I feel like when you are your own self-employed person, you kind of just work. "Oh, I'll work now. I have this time. I'll work." So, I don't know. Weaving, we try to spend eight hours a day on it, but I'll sometimes be at it for twelve hours. Sometimes, I just drink a bunch of coffee and I'm up all night, weaving. Sometimes it happens that way. Sometimes, I tell myself, "Okay, well, we've got to go do this."

Today, right now, since I'm looking for goats, I'm not weaving.* So, sometimes that takes away time from the loom. And then, because we live out so far, you have to plan to go to town. If we're going to get groceries, like a good amount of groceries, if we go to a bigger town like Gallup, it would take us two hours to go over there and then two hours back.

So, that's four hours. But see, that's the thing. When you live out here, two hours doesn't seem like a lot of time. It just seems like, "Oh, okay. Gallup. It's right there. It's like a small drive away." Yeah. Time adds up. Like, when you're out in town, going to go get groceries in Gallup is a whole day thing

---

* Naiomi's family's goats had escaped from their pen shortly before I interviewed her, and she and her brother, Tyler, were driving around the reservation looking for them.

because then you realize, "Oh, yeah. We have to get this while we're out there. We need to get the truck serviced. This thing is wearing down at the house, so we have to get a new thing for that."

So, sometimes when we go to a bigger town, it's a whole day thing, which means a whole day of not weaving. It's kind of difficult living out here, not having the convenience, because I grew up having a store less than a mile away. I think that was one of the biggest shocks coming out here. Because I mean, I had experienced it in the summer, but it was a small dose. There are smaller towns that have one grocery store, but even the selection at that grocery store is kind of limited. So, even if we go to one of the smaller towns here, that's still about forty-five minutes away. And the nearest gas station is, like, twenty-five minutes away. So, to get gas, you have to have gas.

JH: I heard you say in your radio interview yesterday that you are from seven generations of weavers? Is that right?

NG: Oh, my gosh. What would it be? When they came back from the Long Walk* . . . okay, let's count it out. There's my grandma. There's her mom. And then her grandma. And then her great-grandma. Her great-great-grandma. And then . . . Yeah, so it's about four greats. My great-great-great-great-grandmother learned how to weave when we were in Bosque Redondo, which is where they held the Navajo people when they tried to move us off our land. And so, out of that, my great-great-great-great-grandmother learned how to weave. At least, that's as far back as my grandmother could trace it when we talked to her. From there, she taught her daughter and then her daughter taught her daughter, and it came down. Now, here I am, weaving.

It's something I want to keep alive—the tradition. When I eventually have kids, I want to teach them how to weave. I want to teach my nephews

---

* The Long Walk is the forced removal by the United States government of the Navajo (Diné) people from their native land in modern-day Arizona to the Fort Sumner Bosque Redondo internment camp in eastern New Mexico. Between 1863 and 1866, the US military marched more than ten thousand Navajo men, women, and children to Bosque Redondo, where they were interned until the 1868 Bosque Redondo treaty. Over two thousand Diné internees died in Bosque Redondo. ("The Long Walk," Smithsonian National Museum of the American Indian, accessed March 9, 2021, https://americanindian.si.edu/nk360/navajo /long-walk/long-walk.cshtml.)

and my nieces. They'll watch me weave and they'll ask, "Oh, can I try that?" I'll say, "Yeah, sure. This is how you do it." Then I'll show them. It's just great seeing something that has lasted in our family for this long still going on. I feel like it's just something you rarely see.

JH: That amazes me that you can count back all the generations, all the women in your family who have woven and that that line is essentially unbroken. That it's just been passed from person to person. That touches me in just this huge way. I feel like you're very, very lucky to have had that.

NG: I have to sit back and realize that sometimes, too. It's crazy because when you're weaving and in the moment, you're not really thinking of it. But then sometimes, I'll be using a weaving tool. For example, I have my great-grandmother's batten and I use that sometimes for rugs. It's crazy to think that the same weaving tool she used, I'm using it at that moment. It has all the little grooves from being used so much. It's crazy to think that I have something that old and I'm still using it.

My paternal grandmother taught all of her kids. It didn't matter to her if you were her son or her daughter. I know there are some people who try to put weaving into a gender role, saying, "Oh, you're a boy. You can't weave," because it's typically a woman-dominated craft. But I notice now, the younger weavers my age who are weaving and are out there doing everything, they're mostly male weavers, like my brother, Tyler. They're doing really well and trying different things. They're also about revival weavings. We hadn't seen a lot of these designs in a long time. They're like, "Well, let's bring them back. Show that our ancestors were innovative with their designs." Just focus on the old, but make it new.

It's crazy seeing where weaving is going, and I love it. It's great seeing that there are still young people taking it up.

JH: And you're one of them!

NG: Yeah! I'm also a part of the young people taking it up. Sometimes, I start talking and I feel like I'm so much older, and then I'm like, "Wait, I'm twenty-two!"

HANDMADE INHERITANCE

Essay by Mia Nakaji Monnier

I LEARNED HOW to craft from my mom. She was always making things: clothes for my brothers and me, scarves for my dad, cross-stitched wall hangings, holiday cards, bread, a tube of fabric to block the draft that came in under the front door. Her mom, my *obaachan*, worked as a tailor in Japan, leaving her small hometown in coastal Wakayama to go to a high school that specialized in sewing. My mom still has some of the clothes my obaachan made her—a brown velvet jumper dress, a pink tweed skirt, and a matching jacket—that she's packed and unpacked more than ten times over more than forty years.

My family moved often while I was growing up, seven times back and forth across the country before I finished high school, and in each new town or city, there was always a period of time when we had only each other. For fun, we went to bookstores together, and my mom kept us stocked with arts and crafts supplies. Early on, she taught me how to string beads onto elastic cord, make origami animals, and sew with felt and embroidery floss. Mostly, though, I wrote to keep myself company, filling notebooks with single-minded focus and bad poetry.

Each move we made jostled us a little more than the last. We were often looking back: me to old friends, my parents to theirs, plus a home owned and not rented, a kinder school for my brother, Japanese American relatives now half the country away. My mom, in particular, often seemed haunted by the memory of her parents in Japan and all the time she spent away from them. She talked of how she abandoned them, how she abandoned her younger brother to take care of them as they aged and eventually died. From our years of moving, I understood loneliness and nostalgia, but I had no idea how my mom must have felt about her parents until I became an adult.

I began knitting seriously around the time I developed anxiety and depression, in the years after I finished college and moved back to Los Angeles from Vermont. I lived in an apartment only an hour from my parents, but I found myself worrying about them all the time. To spend more time together, my mom and I signed up for a shawl-knitting class at a yarn shop in Hermosa Beach. Before then, I'd knitted mostly scarves. My mom taught me to knit for the first time when I was eight, with a scratchy wool yarn that didn't speak to me. In middle school, I tried again with candy-colored Lion Brand acrylic, in high school with ribbon and confetti yarns, and in college with a variegated Manos del Uruguay worsted-weight single-ply wool from the yarn shop in town.

In our knitting class, most of our classmates were women my mom's age or older, who told us they thought it was nice that we knitted together, mother and daughter. "You never know where she'll live in the future, so we might as well do something together for now," my mom always replied. I'd just accepted a spot in a writing program at the University of Southern California, a guaranteed two more years in LA, and already my mom sounded afraid to lose me. In college, when I studied abroad for a year in Kyoto, she had told me, "Don't fall in love with a Japanese person and stay there forever. Though if you do, I guess it serves me right because that's what I did to my parents."

As I made my shawl, a crescent-shaped design with several different lace sections and a picot edge, I began to see the possibility of knitting beyond scarves. In the seven years since, I've learned how to sew, embroider, cross-stitch, weave, needle felt, make animal-shaped pom-poms, and crochet. Still,

---

I feel most like her when I'm knitting, not casually or while holding a conversation but totally immersed, hours into a project and accompanying Netflix binge, hunched in my office chair, my responsibilities just over my shoulder.

I'm best and most obsessive at knitting. After making that first shawl with my mom, I made a second one in another color, then a gold-colored cowl with teardrop-shaped lace formed by drop-stitches, a simple sweater with Noro yarn, fingerless mitts, and socks. Like those first shawls hold the memories of the class I took with my mom, the others hold memories of sitting outside in the grass with my childhood dog in his last days, or helping my youngest brother move into his first dorm room, or starting grad school with the vaguest hope. Mostly they remind me of my mom.

Of course, crafting is just one of the things I've inherited from her. Now that I'm in my thirties, I recognize more of her in myself than ever: her body type, her sweet tooth, her obsessive tendencies (to not just knit a project but knit practically nonstop until it's done), her overeating, her cheerful defensiveness in the face of loved ones' intervention, and her complex feelings for her mom, interwoven with guilt and shame. I feel most like her when I'm knitting, not casually or while holding a conversation but totally immersed, hours into a project and accompanying Netflix binge, hunched in my office chair, my responsibilities just over my shoulder.

The way I used to lose myself as a kid, in notebooks, writing for hours, has become more fraught now that I'm a professional writer. It's harder now to remember writing as an intimate, ultimately solitary craft, without imagining all the possible ways a piece will be received after I finish it. To reach that trancelike state of flow, I first have to force myself to sit with my internal chaos and begin writing, loosening my mind and rearranging words until finally, I can give myself over to the process, and it's all so frustratingly intangible.

With crafting (also because I don't craft or design patterns for a living), there's nothing but a tangible process. I unwind a skein of yarn, stretch it across my yarn swift, and crank the winder to turn it into a ball. I cut embroidery floss to size, loop it onto a thread minder, pluck a strand at a time as

---

The way I feel while I'm making an object doesn't affect the way it looks, and I like that about crafting, the way it takes my intense feelings and turns them into something pretty and soft.

I need it, and peel off two plies. All this feels good not because it's easy but because it's physically cumbersome and often difficult. I like the resistance of denim against a sashiko needle, and the way crocheting fast requires tension. I like the clear beginning and end of each step, how easily a project can be broken down into smaller pieces, how reliably I can expand my skills by choosing the right projects and moving step by step. The way I feel while I'm making an object doesn't affect the way it looks, and I like that about crafting, the way it takes my intense feelings and turns them into something pretty and soft. But, that also masks the point where crafting turns from enrichment to numbing mechanism. Everyone in my family has one of these, whether a substance addiction or something easier to downplay. How much is too much of a good, harmless thing?

Most times, when I walk through my parents' front door, I see my mom lounging in her chair across from the computer where she streams Korean dramas, knitting or crocheting beside piles and piles of yarn and craft books. She can spend whole days like this, often staying up late and waking up early, falling asleep in her chair in a position that makes me worry about her neck. I struggle to let go of anything I inherit from my mom. The way she keeps her mom's hand-sewn clothes, I keep the handknits she made me while I was in college. When I have given one of her handmade objects away, I've felt sad and ashamed, like I'm abandoning a piece of her. When I look at my body in the mirror and want to lose weight, I also think this body looks like my mom's, and how mean am I to want to change it?

From watching my mom mourn my obaachan, I've learned that this complexity of inheritance will only get harder when my mom is gone (many years from now, knock on wood). What I want is not to shed her influence, anyway, or to stop crafting. What I want, I think, is to face myself without running away, to tolerate loneliness without fear of abandoning or being abandoned, to sit in the silence with a blank page and all my tangled thoughts, with the faith that a thread, patiently unwound, will be worth the discomfort.

It's no coincidence that I almost always craft in front of a TV show, which allows me to binge while having a finished object to show for it, but also to stitch without having to hear my thoughts. Last night and this morning, though, I mended a pair of jeans. The process required a tabletop and lots of potential to stab myself with a needle and pins, so I did it without Netflix, making rows of horizontal running stitches, then whipstitching around the torn hole, then going over the running stitches with vertical ones to make tiny, irregular square crosses. My mom used to mend my brothers' jeans similarly when we were kids; I didn't let her do it to mine because I found it ugly. As I worked, the fabric began to change texture, the raised cotton stitches and the gentle warping they caused gave it a quilted feeling, elementally comforting. In the silence, I noticed it with my full attention, and then I found the words.

MAKING, LEARNING, AND ENCOURAGING

Interview with Latifah Saafir

JEN HEWETT: Tell me about your childhood. Were you always a maker?

LATIFAH SAAFIR: I was born in my mom's hometown, which is Cincinnati. We moved to California when I was under a year old. We lived in LA for the first, I don't know, ten or twelve years of my life. It's interesting 'cause we lived in South Central LA. That environment was very formative.

We didn't have a lot of money, so we were relegated to living in poor neighborhoods. But, my parents tried to protect us as much as they could in those environments. They put a lot of focus on education. We were super serious, quirky kids. We were raised without a TV, and when my mom wanted to finally get one, we fought her about it because we were like, "Well, it's going to take away our free time." And, we were raised with a lot of social consciousness. It's funny now, like especially being in this community where all these—um . . . what's the best word for it?—women who are not of color have suddenly become socially conscious now.

You are already raised with social consciousness being Black, period. But our parents put a really strong focus on it. I was raised Muslim. I don't necessarily align myself with that right now. But, that's still the closest faith that I've aligned myself with because that's how I was raised. It was just all about community-building and being Black.

When I was ten or eleven, my sister and I started our first business. The story is kind of funny and I don't tell it often because a lot of people can't relate to it. We started this business so that we could fund this organization that we wanted to start. We were raised in South Central Los Angeles. In our little apartment complex, there was the prostitute, the drug dealer, and we knew all of this was going on around us. Our organization was called Adolescent Jihad. "Jihad" is the Arabic word meaning "struggle." So, it's the struggle of the youth, and we needed money to run this organization. We made greeting cards. Felt and lace and paper, all of that. My dad got us crafting when we were young. I think it's because I'm the second oldest of seven and he needed something to keep us busy.

He got us making greeting cards when we were around six, seven years old. We were young and my mom taught us to sew around the same time as well. So, that's kind of my foray into, you know, crafting and creating and making, and I've been making ever since.

At twelve, we moved after a bullet came through my parents' window and the boy down the street was killed. My parents were like, "Okay, we're leaving," so they moved us to rural Texas. We lived outside of Weatherford, Texas, in the middle of nowhere in a small Muslim community. I have these two opposite ends of the spectrum as far as how we were raised—the freedom of the country and being in that environment, and being in Texas with all the race relations you have to deal with there. And that versus being raised in South Central Los Angeles. Some things are very similar, but some things are totally opposite as well. I went to high school and college (Prairie View A & M) in Texas, and then I moved back to California after college. I've been back in LA ever since.

JH: Both my dad's parents are from Houston. My grandparents moved out to South LA. My dad would go back to Texas in the summers. My dad was recently talking to one of his aunts, who's in her nineties now, and telling a story about going from living in an all-Black area in South LA to Texas and having to learn how to call everybody "ma'am" and "sir," and who you could look in the eye and who you couldn't look in the eye. And, as a ten-year-old, never having been exposed to this, having to learn it real fast.

LS: We moved to Texas when I was twelve. We got in trouble for not calling adults "ma'am" and "sir." We were very respectful kids, but as a child raised in LA, saying yes and not yeah was respectful. Going from LA to rural Texas, we knew what stores we weren't welcome in. It wasn't Jim Crow days, but I was up at midnight doing homework in high school and we would hear a truck slowly going around the corner by our house and someone would scream out "n****r" in the middle of the night.

The flip side of it is, in some ways, I'd rather deal with racism in your face versus racism behind closed doors, which is what you have in California, you know? I lived in Ontario, just outside of LA. There was an LAPD officer who lived in our community, and when he raised his garage door, he had a Confederate flag hanging. I'd rather know. But, it was a really interesting experience growing up and having that urban experience be so strong and then move to a completely different environment.

JH: So, then you go off and you get a degree in mechanical engineering, and you're a mechanical engineer.

LS: My parents made a lot of sacrifices for our education when we were growing up. We were homeschooled just about all the way through. And, we were raised with one major expectation: we were going to go to college. But, they couldn't afford to pay for it, so we had to get the grades and keep our grades up enough to where we could get scholarships. I think six out of the seven kids went to college on a full scholarship.

I think a lot of quilters, at least quilt designers, are very left-brain/right-brain balanced—we have a technical background and still are very artistic. If I take those left-brain/right-brain tests, I'm right down the middle, 50/50 every single time. It's kind of a blessing and a curse. I embrace it more as a blessing now, but so often we're slotted into a certain type of career path, and you have to pick one or the other. Quilting embraces both, which is pretty amazing. I wanted to do a pure math degree, but I didn't want to be a teacher. In the end, I decided on engineering, and it was strictly an economic decision. I could do anything with that degree and I could get a great job out of college with that degree. I don't regret it at all, but if I had to do it over, I may have made a different decision.

My forty-three-year-old self, looking back on it, thinks maybe that wasn't the best basis for making a decision. But when you aren't raised with a lot, you make decisions based on that. The degree served me well, and at the end of the day, it's a degree, and people respect it as well. It was an easy degree for me, using the [analytical] part of my brain. I do that part easily, but it doesn't always bring me joy. I need the art element, the other side of my brain, to work along with it to bring me joy. In engineering school, I did do a minor in merchandising and design, which at the small school that I went to was kind of the closest thing that fit what I thought I wanted to do.

JH: What did you do out of college then? Were you working in engineering?

LS: No, because I remember interviewing with ExxonMobil, going to the plants out in the middle of nowhere in Texas and Louisiana. I just remember thinking, "I'm going to be so depressed working in this environment." I thought of the challenge of working in this very male-dominated field, and remember—not only was I African American and a woman, but even through college, I also wrapped my hair, too.

So, I had these three minority strikes against me going into this field. So I thought, "Okay, let me pick something where I'll deal with different sides of my brain." I went into a technical leadership program with General Electric. It was a technical sales program, and I was in that for about a year and a half. I quit that because I had gotten pretty sick. I had gone through depression after college. I probably dealt with it most of my teen years and finally got it treated after college. Then I met Thomas Meeks, this amazing, self-taught, Black engineer—an inventor—and I went to work for him. I worked for him for six or seven years. He owned his own business; he had patents and developed technology. I got to do a little bit of the engineering stuff and I helped him to run his office. It was pretty amazing. I learned a lot about intellectual property. And I learned a lot about what to do and what not to do in a family business. He passed, and his business closed as a result.

Then I worked for Salesforce.com in their Santa Monica office for about six years. I got laid off from that job, and that's when I decided maybe I could do something that I enjoy and love. I started to make my way through the quilting world and tried to figure out how I could build a business in that. I took a job as an educator for Janome. On the side, I was slowly building my product base and teaching and doing. I do this full-time now.

JH: I read that you started the Modern Quilt Guild after only having made one quilt.

LS: Yes. But, you have to realize I had been sewing my whole life. I didn't have to learn how to sew to quilt. I had to learn a few quilt-specific things, but I wasn't afraid to explore at a machine. I had sewn everything from my business suits when I interviewed for my engineering jobs when I graduated from college to my mom's dress that she wore in her renewal vows. I can sew just about anything. I'd made maybe two small quilts before 'cause I'm a serial crafter. I had to prove to myself that [quilting] was something I was gonna stick with and finish. But, it was my first quilt that I designed that I finished to bring to the Guild meeting, which is probably my third quilt.

JH: Why did you start the LA Modern Quilt Guild?

LS: I always say it's a very selfish thing—and not in a negative way. There was a very active online community at that time. I had gone to the Quilts Inc. Quilt Festival in Long Beach. But at that time, modern quilting lived almost exclusively online. You wouldn't see modern quilts at quilt shows. You saw very few modern fabric stores that were dedicated to only modern fabric. When I came back from that show, I felt kind of disappointed. I see all these people online—where are they in real life? Alissa, who's the lady that I cofounded the Guild with, posted on her blog that she had the same experience. My response in the comments was, "We should start our own guild." The show was in July. We had that conversation in August 2009.

By October, we had our first meeting. That's literally how it started. The timing was a big part of it. We had the idea, we jumped on it, I threw up a website, and at our first meeting, we had around twenty members or so. It was a pretty interesting, crazy experience.

JH: You seem to have this tendency to just decide what you want to do and do it, where a lot of people would overthink it and never launch anything or over-engineer it. What is it about you or about your personality or experience that you think makes you be the person who just gets stuff done?

LS: Hmm, that's an interesting question. I don't know. I'm the sort of person who dives into things sort of headfirst for better or worse. That's not always a good thing. I have a tendency to hyper-focus on things. If I get excited about something, I go all in. I've never really analyzed that part of myself, so that's why it's hard for me to come up with the answer to that.

JH: Fair enough. One of the things that I've noticed recently has been that people who are the most successful as artists or crafters, and who are doing this professionally, are ones who had a regular job before or during the time that they jumped into this. There seems to be a certain amount of discipline and planning that you learn or start to execute on to the point where you don't even think about it anymore. You decide you want to start a guild. You already have the technical skills. You can put up a website. You know how to organize people. Maybe I'm putting words in your mouth . . .

LS: I think you do have a point there. It's interesting because, in our world, there are a lot of people who have never been in the business world and have never had jobs outside of the home. And they do operate very differently.

JH: Often because they have a spouse or partner who is footing all the bills.

LS: It's a reality. It's a struggle for me. They can run what I call hobby businesses. They don't have to necessarily have an income at the end of the day. They run them because it's fun to do, it's something to do.

JH: Then they lower the teaching price expectations for the rest of us, which is a constant battle that I have, especially with quilt guilds, of how much I need to get paid to make teaching worth it.

LS: I've dealt with people who do work for me, whether it's a longarm quilter or whatever, and I say, "I'm paying you this because this is what your prices should be and I encourage you to raise your prices." What you do does impact everyone else, you know? I've had one of them who didn't take it so kindly. I did it with the best of intentions, and I've had others that have come back to me and thanked me. It's also amazing that some of the larger companies in our industry are also not run very professionally.

It's really strange trying to run a business in this industry. This is all I do. I haven't figured out how to branch outside of quilts. I'm not an illustrator. My business is strictly patterns and designing quilt tools. So, within the quilting industry, it's kind of a struggle to figure out how to put all the pieces together to make a solid business that I'm thriving on, and not struggle from day to day.

JH: I totally get it. The designers Molly Hatch and Justina Blakeney both shared how much they make in a year. When they said that, I thought, "Oh good. I feel like I'm doing okay because that's what these women are making.

I'm completely in line with that." Then I mentioned it to my friend who works at Google and she said, "Holy shit—that's it?" I said, "Yeah, that is it." That's not to say that it's not possible to make more because it definitely is. Also, I run a lot of expenses through my business. Plus, I'm not going out to eat because I'm not miserable at work. I don't commute. So, I have a lot more take-home pay than most people would think.

LS: I didn't hate my job. Salesforce is actually a great company, and I worked with a great team. The benefits were unsurpassed. But, I dreaded going to work every single day. I think I was raised with this entrepreneur mindset. I said I started my first business when I was eleven or twelve. My dad never really ran his own successful business. He always worked for someone else, but he always wanted to. So, we were raised in this kind of environment of do-for-self. So, every day, I went to work at my Salesforce job, I felt like I was making a whole lot more money for the company than for myself.

I had no motivation at work and I'm the worst corporate employee because of that. I have no desire to climb corporate ladders. I'm fully capable and able, but I didn't have it in me. But now I work on my business 24/7, which is probably not healthy, but I love it.

I'm always like, "Ooh, what else can I do? How can I do this? And can I do that?" I'm starting to develop safer boundaries for myself, as far as what I do to put into it. And, I try to make time for other things that are important outside of it. But, I never dread doing the work. Whenever I get to thinking that it would be so much easier from a financial standpoint to have a job, I think about how I felt every morning when I worked for someone else.

JH: Walk me through all the different things that you do for all the different aspects of your business.

LS: I'm at the point where I need an assistant, so I'm going to have to start to make room for an assistant to get to the next level. We all as creative entrepreneurs get to that point, and it's a very scary step to take. I've been thinking about it for like a year and a half, so I know I need to do it. But it does feel very overwhelming. I do everything with my patterns. I do farm out technical editing, but outside of that, I write all my patterns and make all my samples. I farm out my longarm quilting sometimes. I do all my illustrations. I learned the Adobe Suite so I could do it. I taught myself Illustrator and InDesign. I do all my photography. I do all my page layouts. I handle all my shipping. I mean, you know how it is. You have to do it, all of them, from the beginning to the end. And the big picture piece that I know I'm missing now because I get so bogged down in the details. Sometimes, I do big picture rather well. But sometimes, when I'm trying to get a project out, I'm so hyper-focused on it that I don't step back and think, "Oh, I really need to market these things now that they're out in the world."

This year, I have a couple of pretty big projects that I'm finalizing. One is launching my line of patterns that teach kids how to sew. I'm relaunching Quilt Cadets with new patterns and a new website. Once I get that out into the market, the whole rest of the year is just going to be focused on marketing because that's the big area where I know that I haven't put as much of a focus. I tell people I spend very little time on my sewing machine. I sew maybe a month out of the year, the month before Quilt Market. The rest of the time, I'm in front of my computer.

JH: You have patterns that you sell. You have templates . . . Do you have a book?

LS: I've never done a book because when I looked at the bottom line of what it would make it, I would rather put the time and energy toward patterns. And, I've been able to get far enough in my career where I have name recognition, so I didn't need that expensive business card necessarily. I would like to do one book, but I want it to be my *one* book. You know what I mean? I want it to be something that reflects who I am. And I also didn't want to just put any kind of book out through the craft publishing companies that I wouldn't have 100 percent creative control over, because I need it to be my book.

I need it to look like me and people to pick it up and say, "Oh, this is Latifah's" without even seeing the byline, you know? So, that's why I haven't done books. I've designed fabric. I rely heavily on the design team at Hoffman Fabrics.

I listened to an audiobook for marketing. It talked about how you're distinguished in the industry. I think that one of the things that distinguishes me is my technical side. If you've ever seen Clammy, one of my templates, it's a pretty unique and original tool. I think that's the kind of thing that really differentiates me. The book was like, "Focus on that, and create your own subcategory in the market." Anyway, I was thinking about it this morning.

Because quilting is a really busy marketplace. Everyone thinks they're a pattern designer now, so it takes a lot to distinguish yourself from the crowd. I try to look at what is successful for other people and pattern myself off that. But, that's a lot of work either way.

JH: Explain what Clammy is.

LS: Clammy is a clamshell-shaped cutting template. It's nice because not only can you cut the clamshell but you can also cut all different types of curved shapes, so it's a multifunction template. From a business perspective, a single-use template is not the best use of my time or my customers' money.

I thought only if I made a multiuse template would I put it out. I was able to design it. It's ingenious. It's a template set and it comes in four different sizes. I have seven patterns now that are based off the template, and literally, I could build a whole business off it if I'm disciplined enough to do so. I have another tool that I developed two years ago that I want to get out in the market, but I can't do it yet until I market Clammy fully, so I can build off it. I can build a whole business off this template set, but my artistic brain is all over the place, so that makes it hard. I have to be disciplined enough to keep focusing on that and not be everywhere else.

JH: Are you completely self-funded? You're just plowing all your profits back into the business?

LS: A lot of them, yes. And sometimes, that's what paces delivery. I initially launched using Kickstarter and all those funds went straight into products. Since then, I dump most profits right back into growing the business. I have three existing patterns for my Quilt Cadets product range that I never really promoted. I partnered with Annabel Wrigley from Little Pincushion Studio to design four additional projects. So now, I have a total of seven. We're doing new covers on the old ones, but to print four additional patterns, it costs four or five grand. So, how do you fund that? How do you get it out? It's been interesting figuring out how to juggle everything and make it all work and still pay my health insurance.

JH: So, what's next? What are you working on or excited about?

LS: I'm at a weird stage right now where I'm trying to figure out how I can hone what I'm doing and figure out what's next. I have a lot of products that I need to push and get out into the market. I have patterns. I have some strategies for how I can take existing products and refresh them. I'm hacking my own patterns, taking an existing pattern, and then saying, "Okay, you can do this with it and you can do that." I have a whole series of blog posts planned around doing that—using existing content and repurposing it. I'm at the stage now where I feel like I've had my head in the dirt, just constantly working, working, working, working.

I need to learn how to work smarter instead of working harder—because I've been working really, really hard. I'm at that stage where I'm taking a slight step back and just looking at what all is going on—what should I focus on, what's been most profitable, and what's not working? Sometimes, you have to know when to just stop something. I get my stubbornness, honest, from all sides of my family. And persistence is really great. Stubbornness isn't always. Persistence means you have a drive to be successful, but sometimes you have to know when to say, "Okay, that's done, let's learn from it, and move on to the next one." It's not a failure, it's just a part of running a business and growing and learning.

I feel firmly in that stage of taking a step back and saying, "Okay, what's next?" I have lots more ideas. I think it's because such a large part of my brain deals with the technical stuff. I don't consider myself an artist. In some ways, I do. I've always been a maker, but when I started quilting, that was the first time I've ever felt like I was an artist. But by the same token, I'm so controlled by both sides of my brain that I feel like that's one area that's lacking. I would love to take classes in drawing and flex those muscles a lot more. Because I've had no formal training at all in that.

So, I'm in it and I'm gonna stay in it. Even if I had to go back to work, which I'm not too proud to do, I think I'll always do this because it brings me so much joy and personal fulfillment.

JH: Do you have a coach or anybody who advises you?

LS: I have a lot of peer support, but we're kind of wading through this together. I'd like a coach—someone who's either done it before or has experience. I don't have that, but I want it.

JH: Same. I have a licensing coach, and she's trying to get me to talk about my brand and where I want to go. Because I'm in it all the time. If it were up to me, I would just draw and print all day. But, it's not up to me in many ways because I have bills to pay.

Who are your peers?

LS: Who do I rely on? I try to find people who are more successful than I am, even though I still feel like we're peers, but I rely heavily on or talk to people. I'm in constant contact with a lot of the Black girls in the industry.

And then I have people who are not in the quilt world who I can ask, "Am I crazy for thinking this?" Like putting things in perspective—that is helpful too. Because sometimes our world feels a little bit inbred. Everyone knows everyone. So sometimes, it is good for me to talk to someone who has never sat at a sewing machine in their life, but they give good, practical advice.

My belief is that the world is big enough for all of us to be successful. So, if I can help you out, if you come to me and say, "Latifah, you've done this before. What is your advice?" I'm going to give you everything that I can give

---

So, it's no sweat off my back to help you out, to help boost you, because I think the more successful you are, the more successful it makes our whole community and our whole industry, and the more successful I have room to be as well.

---

you because a lot of work goes into it. What I give you is going to help you, but you still have to put blood, sweat, and tears into it to make it happen. So, it's no sweat off my back to help you out, to help boost you, because I think the more successful you are, the more successful it makes our whole community and our whole industry, and the more successful I have room to be as well.

I've learned that other people don't believe that, though. People know who I am, and people probably consider me one of the cool kids now. But, I don't care about having a name and having people look up to me and all of that. It's more important to me that you're a great human.

At this point, I'm surrounding myself with people who are like-minded, who are not with all the bullshit, who are just about, "Let's create something beautiful." That's what we're trying to do through our businesses. We're trying to create a life for ourselves. But, we're trying to make beautiful things

---

We're trying to create a life for ourselves.
But, we're trying to make beautiful things and
encourage other people to do the same thing.

---

and encourage other people to do the same thing. If it's not done in a spirit of love and togetherness, then . . . you know what? Just focus on the people who are doing it.

WHAT ARE YOU MAKING NOW?

Currently cutting and sewing a summer cardigan. It's a sewing pattern of my design and sewn with fabric I developed. The pattern was digitized and trued by someone else, and so this will give me the chance to test the digitized version. It's also the first time that this shorter version of this design will have been sewn. I designed the longer version in one of my heavier fabrics that appeared in *Threads Magazine* #200 (December 2018/January 2019).—OLGALYN JOLLY

I'm designing a new collection of fabric.—WHITNEY MANNEY

Embroidered fiber art pieces that incorporate painting, as well as abstract punch needle pieces.—LOI LAING

I am currently working on a birthday dress for my six-year-old daughter and some summer clothes for my nine-month-old. I am also working on building the inventory for my Etsy shop.—SOUMYA MUPALLA

Craft as Business

< Jen Hewett's screenprinting tools

THE BUSINESS OF CRAFT

Survey Question: Do You Engage in These Crafts for Income or as a Hobby?

I wish there was more income, but it's really a hobby since the income is very minimal. I wanted this to turn into something that would provide an income while I also take care of my kids. I gave up being an art director when I moved abroad and miss having an income.—ELAINE TOM

No income, just hobby. I don't take commissions because once someone else's money is introduced into the equation, it stops being about fun. If I were to start selling things I've knitted or sewn, I would have to consider how much time I put into something or how much yarn costs and how much I would have to charge to break even on my time and my materials. Sometimes, I just don't feel like knitting for weeks or months at a time and I don't want to introduce some kind of financial penalty in my life for what is essentially the basic ebb and flow of a hobby.—ARIA VELASQUEZ

This craft is my full-time job. I make, teach, and sell *bojagi*, and I lead textile tours.—YOUNGMIN LEE

This is my full-time work (although my husband is currently the majority income earner). Business has been picking up steadily ever since I decided to be full-time.—YETUNDE RODRIGUEZ

Trying to do this for income. I'm so done with the other types of jobs I've had—all in some kind of office, working on a computer. Handmaking really appeals to me now.—AVA CHAN

Both! I am a knit and crochet designer, but I also love fiber crafts and will unplug by working on other projects (not my designs) for hobby!
—NORIKO HO

For me, crafting is a hobby with a small income. It also helps to augment my portfolio, which in turn helps me book more clients for the jobs that actually pay my bills.—JULIE ROBINSON

In a sense, it is both. I have a full-time job for income, but designing hand knits is more than a hobby for me. I've been designing my whole career, in and outside the hand-knitting community. But, I do knit patterns from other designers as a hobby.—TINA TSE

HANDMADE BEGINNINGS: MY BUSINESS STORY

JEN HEWETT: I started screenprinting in January 2008, in the early days of Etsy. Etsy was founded in 2005 as an online marketplace for hand-made goods and everything listed on the site had to be made by the sellers themselves. Handmade was making a comeback at that time. "Artisan" had become a buzzword, a slow-movement, handcrafted alternative to the con-sumer excesses of the booming early 2000s. We were in the Great Recession and shoppers wanted more of a connection to the things they were buying. Storytelling was essential to the marketing of handmade goods, and I leaned heavily into my own story.

My story begins with that first screenprinting class in 2008. I signed up for the class thinking that screenprinting would be a creative respite from my corporate job, but I knew the moment I pulled my first print that I wanted to become a professional printmaker. When I was laid off from my corporate job a week before Christmas 2008, and no jobs doing the kind of work I'd previously done were available, I decided to plunge fully into printmaking. I lived on my small savings and went to the shared printmaking studio as often as I could.

I didn't print on fabric for the first few months. I was on a budget, and fabric was far more expensive than the paper I was printing on. I told myself that my skills weren't yet good enough to justify the cost of making mistakes on fabric. It wasn't until my first craft fair, when multiple customers asked me if my work was available on fabric goods, that something clicked. A print on paper requires work on the customer's end. They have to figure out where to display a print, then buy a frame and a mat for it. I learned that the pros-pect of having to do that work prevented customers from buying my prints on paper. I suspected that if I made products that were utilitarian—a dishtowel or a zippered bag, for example—I'd have an easier time selling my work.

So, I went to a drop-in class at the print studio and asked the instructor on duty to show me how to print on fabric. Within a couple weeks, I had (decently) printed fabric, (poorly) sewn it into little zippered bags, and added them to my Etsy shop. Those bags went as viral as something could in 2009 and were reposted on so many Tumblr sites that I stopped counting. The success of that bag—plus my love of fabric and sewing—convinced me to keep working with fabric.

But, that success also showed me just how difficult it is to make a living selling my own handmade work. Each bag required multiple steps: cutting the fabric, preparing my screens, printing, heat setting, sewing, pressing, and tagging. At a certain point, I was able to outsource much of the cutting and sewing. However, I never found a local screenprinting shop that could do my complex, multicolored prints on unfinished fabric. Doing all the printing myself left me with little time to work on new designs. I did time studies and discovered it took me eight days to design, print, and pack just one hundred tea towels. At one point, my back went out from the demands of so much physical labor. Yet, I couldn't charge enough money for my products to fairly compensate me for my time. To make my handmade work profitable, I'd need to move my operations out of my tiny print studio at home and into a more industrial, streamlined setup. I would also need to hire and train a team to do the production work so I could focus on the creative and business aspects of the work. I had neither the start-up capital nor (more importantly) the inclination to move into the larger-scale production that would make the work that I was doing myself financially sustainable. It was clear to me that if I wanted to have a long career in fabric, I either needed to minimize the amount of time I spent doing production work or dramatically increase my prices.

I wasn't the only artist/designer/maker facing these issues. In a 2009 *New York Times* article,[*] the writer Alex Williams interviewed Yokoo Gibraan, who had earned six figures in a year by making her hand-knit scarves and accessories and selling them on Etsy. However, that success came at a price. She knit thirteen hours a day to keep up with the pace of sales. Brandi Harper, who is

---

[*] Alex Williams, "That Hobby Looks Like a Lot of Work," *New York Times*, December 17, 2009, https://www.nytimes.com/2009/12/17/fashion/17etsy.html.

profiled on page 324, talks about charging $120 for a scarf that took her ten hours to knit. Lisa Hsia, an embroiderer, sewist, and visual artist from Oakland, California, writes, "I used to sell my fiber crafts, but now it's a hobby. I've thought about re-monetizing what I make, but I have hand/wrist problems, back strain, etc. I don't think I would feel charging what it's worth to me, to spend my life energy doing this kind of intensive hand work."

As Etsy sellers became more successful, keeping up with the demands for their handmade work could be both overwhelming and physically debilitating. Etsy did gradually allow its sellers to work with manufacturing partners, as long as the sellers still had a hand in their products' design process. Etsy, which became a publicly traded company in 2015, has since moved away from its original mission as "Your place to buy and sell all things handmade" to one whose motto is "Keep commerce human." Its focus is now on independent sellers who may or may not make the products they sell themselves rather than on artists who make all their merchandise by hand.

Faced with the realities of running a completely handmade business, I decided to gradually move away from that business model to a model that has multiple revenue streams. I still occasionally print my own work, but that's not the core of what I do now. I license my designs to manufacturers who essentially rent my work from me for a specific period of time and a specific use and pay me a royalty based on their sales. The bulk of my surface design income comes from licensing my designs for fabric sold by the yard and fabric for home goods. I occasionally outsource small projects to manufacturers and sell those products in my online shop. I've taken on increasingly larger illustration jobs. And, realizing that there's a large market of people who want to learn my crafts, I began to teach screenprinting and block printing, both online and in person. In my classes, students learn not only how to create their own work but also how much work goes into handmade objects. I hope that this knowledge informs how they view and value handmade products.

I'm now more than a decade into my career as a printmaker and surface designer. While I still do a small amount of production work, I have the luxury of only taking on those projects when I want to. The bulk of my income now comes from licensing my work, selling my products directly to consumers, and doing illustration work for clients. And, I continue to print as part of my design process. I still carve blocks and print them, then scan in those prints and digitally manipulate them. I refer to my old screen-printed fabric for inspiration. A good portion of my current licensing portfolio consists of work I made in the early 2010s, when I painstakingly did everything by hand for little money, working other jobs to financially support myself. While producing handmade work myself may no longer be the core part of my business, it remains at the heart of my design process.

My story is, of course, only my story. I'm sure that there are thousands of makers in the United States and Canada who have successfully managed to sustain themselves on their completely handmade, utilitarian products. And many, like Sonya Philip (profiled on page 23), Brandi Harper (profiled on page 324), and Latifah Saafir (profiled on page 74) earn a living from selling sewing, knitting, and quilt patterns to hobbyists. Some, like Candice English (profiled on page 285) and Adrienne Rodriguez (who wrote an essay on page 37), run thriving businesses that hand-dye yarn and sell it to knitters, crocheters, and weavers. But, I know from personal experience that handmade is a tough business. Craft that has a utilitarian rather than a fine art purpose often isn't valued enough to command the prices that would make it sustainable to its makers as a business in the long-term.

I'm happy with my hybrid business model. It allows me to earn a living without having to be the sole means of production. And, maybe more importantly, it allows me to practice the craft that got me to this place—printmaking—on my own terms. My business may no longer be a strictly handmade one, but my hand is in all aspects of it.

THE ARTIST KNOWN
AS TWINKIE CHAN

Interview with Stephanie Lee

JEN HEWETT: How would you describe your work and what you do?

STEPHANIE LEE: I first hit the crochet scene creating food-themed scarves. It's very specific, very niche. I was making them for myself. I had too many piling up in my closet, and I knew I wasn't going to wear them. This was in 2004, 2005, and people were just starting to make their own vanity websites for whatever silly reason. I figured I would join the trend and put up a website for fun. I threw up maybe a dozen scarves and they sold right away. I think the scarves are what put me on the map and what I became known for. But these days, my crochet also spans toward more the *amigurumi*, the little toys. I tend to stick with food themes. It wasn't an intentional branding—it's just stuff that I like. It makes me happy. So, that's usually what people associate me with.

JH: You have a very specific color sense that's really . . . well, how would you describe your color sense?

SL: I love saturated color. I don't think I have a particular color palette. I don't wear a lot of brown or gray, so I don't work with a lot of brown or gray, except I love bread. If I'm crocheting a bread loaf, I have to work in brown. But otherwise, I'm drawn to candy colors, cupcake frosting colors, and things like that.

JH: When did you start crocheting? Were you creative as a kid or was this something you picked up later?

SL: I currently live with my best friend, and our mothers were also best friends. When we were young, we would go shopping and would want something. They would always tell us to put it down, go home, and make it. We even

93

think about that now when we're out and about. "This is really neat!" "Yeah, you could totally go home and make that." I don't know if they were encouraging our creativity, or maybe they were just trying to make us not spend money. But, it encouraged us to think about things that we wanted and things that we needed, and if we could create them on our own.

It was my best friend's grandmother who taught us both how to crochet. We were staying with Grandma Wendleton in San Diego for a week or so, and she was very crafty. She was the classic grandma who crocheted afghans and toilet-paper covers with the Barbie doll on top and the dress to cover the toilet paper. She was also an amazing sewist, so it was like craft camp when we hung out with her.

JH: Where did you grow up?

SL: In the Bay Area, on the Peninsula. We lived in the Woodside, Redwood City area. I think I'm what you might think of as a stereotypical first-generation Asian child. I went to a private school; I played piano until I was eighteen. I had all these extracurricular activities. I was very much encouraged to think about going to law school or med school—that clichéd track of the tiger mom leaning over the piano going, "You must practice every day." That was the household that I grew up in.

But, my parents were also pretty liberal. I mean, they always had ideals for what they wanted us to be, but they always gave us the freedom to do what we wanted. Because my dad felt a lot of pressure from his parents to join the family business, and my grandfather always wanted a doctor in the family, I think my dad was really careful about not putting that on us, which was progressive and awesome. They're really supportive of what I do now. It's not what they thought would happen, but they're cool with it. We were highly encouraged to be successful in whatever it was that we chose. Just whatever you're doing, be the best at it.

JH: At some point, you started crocheting scarves. Why did you start crocheting food scarves, of all things?

SL: Well, the scarves were purely utilitarian. I moved to San Francisco in my early twenties. I know people who come from a cold climate think that

San Francisco is not cold, but when the fog rolls in and you're not used to fog, it's cold. It's relative. So, I started making scarves for myself because I wanted to wear something I couldn't find in the store. I wanted to have something unique.

At that point, Etsy wasn't really a thing. A lot of indie sellers were on eBay at that time. I was looking at what other people were making, and there was a lot of animal-themed stuff, like bunny scarves or kitty scarves. I was just trying to find that thing that didn't exist yet. And, I have always had a weird love for faux food.

I don't know if this is part of your childhood memory, but Fisher-Price sold these plastic fake food sets, and I wanted to collect all of them. That was all that I wanted to collect. And there was the little McDonald's-themed set. My mom kept it, and now my niece and nephew have it. They are these cool, plastic, weird toys that have kind of lasted the ages, but are so cool and so cute.

I think that it's nostalgia for me, too. There's something about the look and the color and the shapes of food that I just think is so fun. There's a joy and a nostalgia, and I think when people put on the scarves, they feel that, too. There was an older man in a business meeting I was in one time—I think he was an accountant—and he put on a bacon-and-egg scarf and said, "I feel young again." That's totally the point! I just think that food is cool. I don't think I'm a foodie, but I'm very into seeking out novelty desserts. I just think it's all very visually appealing.

JH: You then made the leap from selling products to designing patterns. How did that come about? Because those are actually two different skill sets.

SL: I had never intended to sell the patterns. That was never my plan. I wanted to be an accessories designer, a knitwear designer, and I was surprised that I started receiving so many requests for the patterns. I was really against it first because you're basically giving away your trade secrets.

At the time, around 2008 to 2009, I had a business partner, and he said, "You can never write a book. Don't give away the patterns." But, we came to the realization that those two markets are very different. Someone who wants to buy a scarf probably doesn't know how to crochet or knit, and the person who crochets or knits probably is not going to buy a complete scarf from me because they think they can make it.

So, those two different roles really do work together. Unfortunately, when you do share patterns, people are going to create products with them and sell them in their own stores. Even if you didn't share the pattern, they would try to reverse engineer it and figure it out. That's always going to happen when you share your work—that's something you just have to accept as a business-person. It's harder to protect things like crochet and knit designs than a visual graphic design. So, that's kind of part and parcel of the business.

But, I found that I liked designing and selling patterns, and I do actually enjoy when people start opening their own stores selling things they've made from my patterns. It's like I've helped someone else start their business. I've helped someone else start their creative journey. I was closed off to it in the beginning, but the teaching component is something I had never imagined. I think a lot of it was studying other people's patterns, figuring out what I liked and didn't like about other people's patterns, and then learning and teaching myself from there.

JH: Why crochet? And not knitting?

SL: It's just what I learned, what I learned first.

JH: A lot of what I'm reading in the survey responses for this book is that crochet is totally looked down upon by knitters. Do you have thoughts on that?

SL: Definitely, and I think some crocheters may dislike my thoughts on it—

JH: That's fine.

SL: I mean, I get it. I think the look you can get with knit apparel can be much more . . . I don't know what the right word is. When you crochet a garment, it doesn't have quite the same drape as a knit garment. The stitching can veer toward looking like a granny square, or a little old-fashioned, or very seventies. Specifically, for fashion. If I were to purchase a kit to make a sweater, I would probably personally lean toward knit. I just think it's visually more appealing to me personally. I get how crochet can still have this funky grandma aesthetic.

I think I've stated that on social media somewhere. Not in a mean way. Just in a personal opinion kind of way. And other crochet designers were like, "No no no no no. There's so much new in crochet now. Check out this person and this person and this person." But, I can still tell this is a crocheted garment—it's a different aesthetic. I don't know that it's my aesthetic. But, I do think there are vast differences in what you can do with knitting. I think it does veer toward more of a higher fashion aesthetic. The techniques produce different results and it's about the look you want to go for. But, crochet is definitely cool for more 3D objects. It can be more sculptural, so I think that's a big advantage of it.

JH: And, your work is super sculptural.

SL: It has leaned that way, but even with the flat things like scarves, it's much easier to navigate an odd shape, like the shape of a slice of toast. You can get more round corners with crochet.

JH: Your work has followed the rise of social media and what, back in the day, we called Web 2.0. Tell me about your start and how you've ridden the changes that have happened. Because you totally are one of the OG public crafters out there.

SL: To be honest, I'm always very slow to adopt. But I think I'm just aware enough to hit it. I know there are some crafters and bloggers who were on Instagram far before I was. I was like, "What is this thing? Do I need this?" Because I always feel like we have a certain amount of time, and a lot of it should be crafting and designing. The social part of it and the promotion part of it is important, but it's really easy for that to take up the majority of your time.

I think TikTok is starting to be the new thing. They asked me to create content to encourage people to see TikTok not just as a channel for little music videos or for sketch comedy but also to display your crafting or to do a quick tutorial. I think that they're trying to encourage different uses, but I'm still like, "Do I need another app on my phone?" I have a weird push-pull with it.

JH: How have you maintained your longevity? Fads come and go, and I know a lot of people who started when you did who are not doing this anymore.

SL: I think that comes from just what you genuinely enjoy. I think that affects your longevity. If you're on Instagram trying to figure out what content is popular and what people like, and you're altering maybe what you actually like posting, it's going to start feeling like a job. When the algorithm changes and you don't get the response that you're used to, you're going to get discouraged. You kind of have to let it go.

I know the numbers are important—I used to be the social media manager for another company, and analytics are important—but, if you're coming at it from your own business, I think you just have to remember what you love. If you love it, you're creating your own longevity. You're just doing it because you like it, and if you've created your own community around your work, other people are bolstering you too and encouraging you. And that's really cool. So, that's sort of an energizing source. You don't have to think of social media as a draining thing. It can be a very encouraging thing also.

JH: You have a craft that is physically demanding. It's a lot of hand work, a lot of really close-up eye strain. How do you manage that? Keep yourself healthy?

SL: I'm surprised that my hands still work right now. I'm just now starting to feel pain in my elbow.

I like creating the pattern, and I love the creation of that first sample. I do not like making copies of it. If I want twenty cactus scarves for my shop, I'm not making twenty of those. That's not my passion. I'm done after the first one. So, I hire out that help.

I'm very careful to put my energy into what I like. If I like something less, and it's physically demanding, I make a budget for that, and I hire out that help. I'm not 100 percent generating everything on my own. My time and attention can also be toward non-crocheting, less physically demanding things, like blogging. I'm not blogging that much anymore, but I was pretty hardcore blogging for a couple of years.

I was also licensing my work for a while. There were things that were taking up my time that weren't just sitting at home crocheting because that definitely would be physically draining.

I don't do special stretching or exercises for my fingers or anything like that. I think it was just a lot about taking breaks and making sure those breaks were productive also for the business.

JH: So, you have a business where you're doing one-offs. You're having other people crochet for you. You were doing some licensing. You publish patterns. And you've also written books. Again, I think you were one of the craft bloggers who made that transition to craft books pretty early.

SL: I used to work in book publishing. I'm very aware of the business, how it worked, and what I needed to do. So, it seemed to me like a very attainable thing. Publishing is changing, too. There's a lot of self-publishing now. But, I think ten years ago, publishing was still sort of this weird, mysterious leviathan, and people wondered how they could ever break into that business. But I didn't have that barrier. Once I was okay with sharing the patterns, it was easy. It was just kind of like an easy flow for me.

JH: Was your business ever your full-time gig or have you always had another job on the side?

SL: It was my full-time gig for a while. I just went back to the office about three years ago. I was on my own from 2010 to 2017.

JH: What were the jobs that you had before and after?

SL: I worked in publishing for over ten years after college. And then after that publishing job, that's when I started trying to do my crochet business full-time.

Just as a side note, I never thought that my Etsy shop was going to bring me a living wage. My whole strategy was to license and to get the product produced elsewhere, and to create a brand around it. That's what my hope was. That didn't quite pan out. I'm glad I tried it, but you know sometimes things don't always work out the way you hoped.

That's when I got a job in social media and digital marketing for a small clothing and gift company. Now, I work at Creativebug. It's just a part-time contract right now, but I work on the back end, organizing the classes and coaching artists through their shoots.

JH: On your blog, I noticed that you have a lot of patterns that are free. People don't have to go on Ravelry and pay for it, which is counterintuitive to a lot of messaging out there, which is "Give nothing away for free."

SL: Yes, I agree with that as well.

JH: So, why have you been publishing patterns for free on your site? Is there a larger thinking behind that?

SL: I'm doing it a lot less now that I'm working basically full-time. But back in the day, people did it because they were trying to earn ad revenue from the blog. They were trying to make revenue from the ads to offset the revenue that they're not making from selling the pattern. It seems exciting for the person who gets the free content, but nothing is really free, right? The blogger is still attempting to make revenue in some other form. At that time, there were different indie platforms for monetizing your blog.

In that way, you're like, "Okay, I can make x-amount of money a month from just blogging. So sure, free content." Frankly, on Facebook when you post, "This is a free pattern," it's shared more. Sure, you're losing revenue [by giving away a pattern for free], but there was also that feeling of, "Oh my gosh—25,000 people have seen this post."

What I did to differentiate my free content from my paid content was share a lot of the stuff I was making for fun for myself for free on my blog—it's not a Twinkie Chan–branded product. It might be like an animal toy or something that I normally wouldn't sell in my Etsy shop, so I felt okay making that a free pattern because it just wasn't really what I thought a Twinkie Chan pattern was. Or, they could be really short little projects that I didn't think that I wanted to make someone pay for. I don't normally put a full scarf pattern for free because that's my thing. If people want that, they need to pay for it.

JH: Okay, that makes sense. And I think the days of blogging to earn money are over.

SL: Because Instagram and Facebook are so hard to penetrate now, there's talk about blogs coming back. I don't think we're there yet, and I don't know if we will be. Because now search engine optimization is a huge nightmare also. But, I think there's an awareness that we can't always be dependent on other people's apps or other people's websites because we can't control that. There's the philosophy that we can control our own website. I don't know if that's 100 percent true, but I like the idea of it.

JH: Tell me about your brand's name. Was Twinkie a name you chose for yourself when you were older or is that your nickname?

SL: It was a name I chose solely for the business because, at the time, I was working in publishing and my real name is so common. I was worried my clients would Google me and see that I was doing this other thing and be like, "Why aren't you devoting more time to my work?" That probably never would have happened, but that was my thought behind it. Also, at that time, privacy was still a huge issue.

JH: Oh, I remember privacy.

SL: Remember not posting where you were at exactly in that moment so people could come and murder you? Back then, no one was showing their face. No one was using real names. Everyone had a fake name. No one was using their real name because that was crazy. Chan is my mother's maiden name, so that's a nod to her. Twinkie was just . . . I don't know. Sometimes, you just hit it randomly. I wanted something fun and food-related.

And, Twinkie, no one uses it anymore, but in the eighties, it was a reference to Asian kids who grew up in America.

JH: Yeah, like a banana or a coconut, yeah.

SL: Sometimes, when you share that, people say that it sounds offensive. But I'm talking about myself, and I'm not offended by it. Sometimes, I'm hesitant about mentioning it, but that was the genesis of it too.

JH: For people who are reading this who may not know what kind of slang or the derogatory meaning of "Twinkie" is, just explain it.

SL: Well, it's because the Twinkie is yellow on the outside and white on the inside. So, I get how that's super not cool now, but in a way, you're taking it back. It's just fun and it's light, and we're obviously not yellow on the outside.

JH: Or, white on the inside.

SL: I know, it's ridiculous. But it's sort of like a wink, you know, to that old-school thinking.

There's maybe one person in the history of my business who was like, "Does that mean what I think it means?" I was like, "Yeah, you know it, girl." One person. No one knows. These were not ever things that my peers and I called each other or other people called us, but it was in the cultural awareness that these terms existed. I don't have personal experience with them.

JH: Tell me about your influences. Who or what has influenced your work?

SL: In the very beginning, I think I was just influenced by my childhood love for faux-food toys. LiveJournal, speaking of Web 2.0, is where I think things really hit for me. I found myself in this community of like-minded people on LiveJournal who were very into Japanese street fashion, which I didn't know anything about. I was like, "What is this? This is amazing. It's colorful, it's fun, it does have that sort of childhood wink where there's a lot of ruffles and polka dots, and I am so into this." I sort of fell down the rabbit hole of that.

I felt like you could wear the scarves that I was making with a T-shirt and jeans—it would be totally cute. But, if you wanted to go full out with some Sweet Lolita or Harajuku theme, I kind of went into that whole "More is more" aesthetic. That became a really big inspiration for me.

As far as forming a community and being inspired by other people, a lot of people ask, "Who are other knitters or crocheters who inspire you?" That's actually not my community, which might be odd to some people. I'm more drawn to aesthetic more than skill set.

A lot of my friends and inspirations are painters, clothing designers, or jewelry makers. I'm looking just more at that colorful, fun, cute aesthetic than "You crochet, too, and that means we have all these things in common," which I don't think is true at all. There are so many different aesthetics within the crochet/knit world, and I fall into a very, very tiny corner of that. So, try to build out your own corner in your own way.

JH: That leads to my last question. You have such a distinctive personal look that works with your work. There's an ecology of what you do that seems to bleed out into everything else about you. Have you always been that way or is this something that you consciously curated and created?

SL: Have I always been that way? So, now I have to think about who I was when I was little. I mean, I think with any one style, it's a mixture of both. You kind of like what you like, but every day, you're sort of curating yourself, even if you don't think about it in a super intentional way. When I start walking around, people will say, "Oh, you must really like pink." And I look down, and there is a lot of pink happening here. But when I woke up today, I didn't think I was going to bring out my pink purse. And I know my hair is pink but then I have to match it with my pink shirt and my pink sweater. It's not that curated, but when you start gathering things that you like, it just starts happening on its own. So, to answer your question, it's a mixture of both: being influenced by things that I enjoy and then incorporating them into my life.

SURVEY PROFILE

Stephanie Brown

Age: 47
Location: Vallejo, California
Profession: Owner of a lifestyle boutique

What types of fiber crafts do you engage in and how many years have you been engaged in each?

I have been a passionate weaver for almost ten years now. I have been brimming with creative energy ever since I was a kid. I started taking photography classes when I was in elementary school and discovered that I had a keen eye for composition and a strong sense of color and proportion. I feel a relentless urge to create and have turned into a Jill-of-all-trades, and yes, master of none. I have dabbled in everything from knitting and sewing to furniture refinishing and woodworking, ceramics, leather working, you name it—but nothing ever gripped me like weaving. I feel a calm giddiness when I sit in front of a freshly warped loom and then somehow magic happens. I wish I could say I was the organized, streamlined type that sketches out ideas first and then sets off to work, but I just fling open my cabinet doors, touch and feel the yarns, and wait for inspiration to strike. I am forever excited at what keeps flowing out of me creatively, and while each piece is totally different— there definitely is no signature "Rebel Yarn style"—they are all entirely me.

How do you self-describe/identify yourself?

Mama. Free spirit. Fiber artist. Rebel. Roller skater. Shopkeeper. Ever-evolving.

What's the first thing you remember making?

An eight-inch knit teddy bear in elementary school, memorable only because it was the worst in the entire class. Thanks to my complete and utter lack of skill, my teddy was literally big (and hole-y) enough to be worn as a sweater. That failure lit a fire in me and sparked my obsession with fibers and textiles.

What are you making now?

I just pulled a new piece off the loom this afternoon: a tapestry woven in a very textural way with organic wool and an earthy-brown suede. My five-year-old son titled it "Land-Cloud," and it fits perfectly. It's a lovely experimentation in texture and materials that I am super excited about.

What's your favorite thing you've made?

My son Brixton was three when I was working on my first chunky roving piece, and when my husband came home, he said, "Look, Daddy! Mami's building a cloud!" That first "cloud" will forever be my favorite; I had a really hard time sending it off to its new home.

How and why did you learn your crafts?

I saw this beautiful woven textile in an Anthropologie catalog, looked at the $275 price tag, and arrogantly thought, "Surely *not*." I set off to the craft store to buy materials and whip this thing up real quick. I learned quickly that weaving is a very involved craft (in a sense of time and materials) and that the price tag was absolutely warranted. I also instantly found my passion! After watching several instruction videos online, I was hooked. I remain fascinated by the endless possibilities of the craft and feel most at home and at peace in front of a loom.

Tell me about your creative community. You can define "community" as broadly or as specifically as you'd like.

I live in Vallejo, California, which is literally the most diverse city in the United States, and I am blessed to be surrounded by an obscene amount of wildly talented people! I own a small lifestyle boutique with a focus on locally hand-crafted goods, so I get to collaborate with a lot of artisans and makers. I love the Vallejo spirit and sense of community; we all admire, inspire, and cheer each other on around here. I am excited to have the opportunity to provide fellow craftspeople and artists a space to show and sell their work—I know how hard and nerve-racking it is.

When have you felt like an "other" within the context of your craft?

I don't really spend a lot of time checking out fellow fiber artists' and weavers' work. I had an obsessive research phase when I first got on Instagram, but realized after a while that when my head is swimming with images, inspiration can't flow through. So, I stopped. Now and then, friends or clients will send me pictures for inspiration, but I focus on the pieces, the techniques, and designs rather than on the artists themselves. I have to admit that I am now curious, though, and will have to seek out other weavers of color.

When do you feel recognized in your craft? Who recognizes you and how does that feel for you?
I feel recognized and full of wonder and gratitude every time I sell a piece. I am especially humbled by custom orders and commissions. The fact that people trust me (and my point of view) to create a special piece for their homes lets me know I am on the right path. Being authentically yourself and receiving validation for your work is elating.

Are there aspects of your work that you feel are misunderstood?
Art is a subjective thing. My pieces are bound to mean different things to different people. They mean different things to me at times. I try to create and release!

If you sell your pieces, who are your customers?
I used to give my pieces away to friends, who kept urging me to participate in a craft fair or market. It took me a whole year to work up the nerve to do a pop-up at a West Elm store, and as nerve-wracking as putting myself out there was, it ended up being just the kick and confidence booster I needed to really spread my wings. I have been selling my pieces at events and pop-ups for about four years now and, most excitingly, in my very own brick-and-mortar store for the last two and a half years! I have taken on several commissions and have just recently started teaching classes as well.

What challenges have you faced in building your creative business?
The biggest challenge for me is finding a balance between running a business on my own and being creative. I am just now finding my stride and am fighting to make time to weave—it's the one thing that elevates and keeps me grounded.

Do you have an artist statement or any principles that guide your work?
In true free-spirit style, the answer about an artist statement is no, but my

life in general as well as my work are guided by the principle of going with the flow. It always takes me just where I am supposed to be.

When you were younger, were you exposed to other people who looked like you, or who were from similar backgrounds as you, and who engaged in this craft?
Absolutely not! I grew up in Germany and was mostly the only Black kid in school. Somehow, that was less of a problem than it would have been here in the States; no one ever emphasized my skin color so I was never acutely conscious of my "otherness."

Where did you get inspiration growing up?
I have always been inspired by nature—as a whole and in single magnified details. I remember spending hours roaming around city parks, cemeteries, and woods with my camera, documenting the beauty all around me. I was always and forever out and about, soaking up every sight, scent, sound, and sensation.

I looked up to the strong women in our family who worked with steely determination to make things happen and still knew how to live life to the fullest. I always carry their spirits in my heart.

Who do you look to for inspiration today?
I mostly seem to find inspiration within. Being a total introvert, too much external stimulation (especially in the form of social media) makes me shut down. Inspiration usually happens in my light-filled backyard studio that is full of vases filled with dried wildflowers, grasses, and feathers; baskets of driftwood and branches; and bowls of rocks and broken shells. We routinely bring home a hoard of found objects from our family adventures.

What colors are you drawn to and why?
Earth tones all the way! I have always preferred a more muted palette, and that bias just got intensified during my first visit to New Mexico. The high desert is a magical place to me. I will be forever haunted by the shapes and colors out there. The desert calls me whenever I need a spiritual reset. I suppose I am drawn to the calming sparseness, which puts my mind at ease and gives my spirit room to soar.

How do you choose your materials?
It's mostly a tactile thing for me. I love the feel of yarn running through my fingers. If I like the way a fiber feels or I come across an interesting texture, color, or dye process in a yarn, it's definitely coming home with me.

WHAT ARE YOU MAKING NOW?

I'm currently working on my very first knit sweater! I usually make skimpy stuff (because I can normally only afford one skein at a time), so this is a bit out of my safe zone.—BRETONY MCGEE

I'm spinning some local mohair/wool roving that was milled and dyed in LaFarge, carding some local Suffolk [wool], knitting some cabled socks, and knitting a prototype for a new design that will be published in a book!—LAUREN MCELROY

I'm working on a lace blouse, one of my own designs.—TRACEY RIVERS

CREATING WHAT I WANT TO SEE

Interview with Rashida Coleman-Hale

JEN HEWETT: I know you had a really interesting childhood. Tell me about it.

RASHIDA COLEMAN-HALE: I was born in Orlando, but we lived in Winter Haven. My grandparents raised me because my parents were traveling the world. My dad was BB King's drummer for years until he [BB King] passed away. My mom was in Japan, modeling. She moved there when I was three and then she sent for me a couple of years down the line, so I went to Japan and lived with her for a little bit. But I liked the States better, so I ended up coming back home.

It was strange being in Tokyo. It's so safe there. I was nine years old, roaming around Tokyo by myself because my mom was working all the time. I rode my bike to school or took the bus or the subway, and after school, I would go explore. It was a really cool experience. I really feel like that helped me to be so open-minded. I was able to experience all these adventures on my own. It made me super independent, too. I was an only child, so I had to entertain myself somehow. After I came back to the States, I spent my summers in Tokyo all the way through college. I went back in 2020, after not having been there since maybe 2004. It was amazing! Tokyo played such a huge part in my life.

JH: How did your mom end up modeling in Japan?

RCH: She was a flight attendant for Braniff, and Carlos Falchi discovered her. He was like, "You need to be in Japan, modeling." She had done a couple of local modeling gigs in Florida and DC, but then she thought about it and was like, "Well, why not? I'm super young. Let's go explore. I've never been overseas." My family's from St. Kitts, so besides being in the Caribbean, she hadn't been anywhere before. I think she had that sense of, "I can do whatever

I want. I've got opportunities." I think also being a flight attendant opened that door for her. So, she went and checked Tokyo out, found an agency, and ended up staying. They loved her in Japan, and the rest is history.

JH: Is she still there?

RCH: No, she's in Florida now. She moved around a lot, but right now she's in Florida. She doesn't know how to stay still. I know she's still got a few more adventures up her sleeve.

JH: Who were your creative influences as a kid?

RCH: I was an only child, so I kinda had to entertain myself. My grandmother was at an age where she had raised her children. By the time I came around, she was in her forties, and she wasn't the type to sit on the floor and play with Legos.

So, I basically had just me, myself, and I. I drew all the time, and I got in trouble in school because I was always doodling and not paying attention. I used to make little storybooks. I drew the pictures and made up the stories. I was always doing something, making something, or creating something. I used to take my toys apart all the time. My grandfather had to hide his tools from me because I wanted to see what was in the toys, crack them open. That's still one of my favorite things to do.

JH: My brother did that all the time with anything mechanical. He'd take things apart. And then finally my dad was like, "Okay, let's go to RadioShack and get you some kits so you can learn what all this stuff is."

RCH: Yeah. That's what we ended up doing. In Japan, they had a lot of fun toy kits like that, so my mom would give me these little robotic things I could crack open. That was so entertaining to me, and I still love it. My grandfather was a mechanic and a tinkerer, too. He was always building something. He added rooms to the house, and he had a toolshed in the back that he made. He was always working on the car. I was always following behind him and trying to see what he was doing. He let me help sometimes. I loved following him around and just getting into whatever.

JH: Did you sew as a child?

RCH: I started sewing at twelve. One summer, my mom came to Florida to visit. She's like, "You're gonna learn how to sew this summer." I was very reluctant. It seemed like something that was so boring to me at that age. But she took me to the store, we picked out a pattern and the fabric, and she taught me how to make an outfit. It was a vest with some MC Hammer–style pants.

I thought the fabric was so cool. It was this African-style print that I'd found. In retrospect, it was so hideous, but I did it. I thought it was awesome that you can take this flat piece of fabric and create something else that's functional. Putting it together was so intriguing for me. I ended up falling in love with it and started sewing all the time. My grandfather was also a tailor back in the Islands, so he had had an industrial sewing machine at the house. He would always show me all kinds of different things, so by the time I got to college, I knew how to put things together pretty well.

JH: You went to the Fashion Institute of Technology (FIT)?

RCH: Yes, that's right.

JH: What did you major in?

RCH: I started in fashion design and then I switched to fashion illustration. I loved sewing, but it got to a point where I didn't think I wanted to build clothes as my career. When I got to FIT, I realized, "Oh, I don't want to be doing all this sewing." I wanted to draw all the time, so I switched majors, did fashion illustration. That was during a time that [fashion illustration] wasn't in demand anymore. There was no social media. You didn't have any way to show your work other than walking around with your portfolio. I think I got a little discouraged as well 'cause my professors were never very encouraging. They're like, "Well, I don't know why y'all want to do this, but okay, we'll teach you."

It was also tough being in New York. That city will chew you up, spit you out. I don't think I was really sure what I wanted to do at that point, so I started doing temp work to just try and make ends meet.

JH: Did you have student loans or was your family helping you out?

RCH: My family was helping me out. I didn't have any student loans at that point. My family was super supportive. My mother was excited that I wanted to be in the fashion industry. I felt like I had been so exposed to it being around her, being backstage all the time and not just at the shows but at the fittings that she would go to.

JH: You got to go to those?

RCH: Yeah, she dragged me all over the place. I just knew I was going to be in the fashion industry. But it just didn't pan out for me. And I also think I was a little naive and I felt a little too sweet for it, you know what I mean? It's a very cutthroat industry with aggressive people and that's not my personality at all.

Eventually, I moved back to Florida because while I loved New York, I wanted to regroup and figure out what to do next. I had settled into this noncreative life. I got a job at Starwood and was doing HR there, and that's where I met my husband. He was working there in IT. He was doing their web design. I lost his paperwork, and that's how we became friends.

JH: So, he had to come back and fill out more paperwork?

RCH: He had to come back and he's like, "I'm starting to wonder if this was intentional." We just fell for each other. That was in 2005. We got married and moved back to New York.

JH: When did you get creative again during all this?

RCH: I started drawing again and taught myself Illustrator and Photoshop. It was a hobby. I had a Deviant Art account. I'm pretty sure it's still up there. I got a side gig illustrating airbrush tattoo stencils for this company called Air Too. The only reason I know Illustrator is because of that job. I went to the interview and they needed somebody who knew Illustrator. And I was like, "Oh yeah, I know how to use it." They hired me on the spot. I went home and I taught myself how to use Illustrator. I think I downloaded a pirated version.

I fell in love with the app because of all the cool stuff you can do with it. I just kept using it, taught myself how to use it well, and became proficient. Anyways, segueing back to my move back to New York. I had my daughter in 2006. She was such a good baby, and I was a new mom and I was kind of bored. I was in New York; I had had such a dynamic life and suddenly I was a stay-at-home mom. I needed something creative. My husband, Mel, bought me a Canon EOS for Christmas, and he was like, "You should take some pictures of the stuff you sew for the baby. Maybe start a blog or something." Blogs were starting to get popular then, and I hadn't even considered it. I started blogging, posting stuff that I was making for the baby, New York life, and being a mommy. I guess that's what got me to start selling and creating things again. I was trying to fill a void.

You know, I'd had such a crazy dynamic life in New York. I'd worked in a nightclub right after college. I started out in coat check and then I ended up being a cocktail waitress in the VIP room. I had another job during the day and then I would go work at night at the nightclub. And it was fun, 'cause like, you got to make money, also party, and meet celebrities at the same time. You know, Jay-Z, Mariah Carey, Janet Jackson, and all these famous people would go there. It was such a weird transition from this boisterous and young New York life to being a stay-at-home mommy in the same city. Anyway, I started my blog *I Heart Linen* and it started to get popular. It was cool because I had developed my own style.

I loved blogging so much. It was just cool that everyone seemed to have their unique style. Those were the Flickr days—I got to meet so many like-minded people online through that community.

JH: What types of things were you making for the baby?

RCH: I was making her clothes, quilts, little toys, and just all kinds of baby things. I had gotten into the Japanese style of sewing, the *zakka* style. I was discovering all those zakka books. That excited me, too, 'cause I already had such a huge love for Japan and the culture. I discovered this whole other realm of Japanese culture that I didn't even know existed. I think the first time I had seen one of those zakka sewing books was on Flickr, and I started exploring.

JH: Those are back in the days when they were only in Japanese?

RCH: I don't know kanji* very well. I'm still learning that, but I can read hiragana and katakana† pretty well, but that doesn't really help you. I went to a Kinokuniya and started buying those books. I think that helped develop my style and the types of projects that I was creating. You couldn't buy a lot of Japanese supplies either. There were some places on Etsy that were selling them so I had to figure out how to do it my own way with the things that we had here. I got into linen, too, because it is such a versatile fabric. I love how, when it ages, it just gets so soft, beautiful, and buttery. I fell in love with it.

JH: You were blogging and making all these projects, and then you wrote a few books. How did that all come about?

RCH: It was part of my blogging. *Stitch Magazine*, which is no longer around, started because there weren't any modern sewing magazines. The editor contacted me and she asked if I wanted to do projects for the premiere issue and I was like, "Oh yeah, that'd be awesome." I was already posting tutorials and stuff on my blog. She caught wind of my blog and saw that I could do the work. I did a couple projects in their first issue. My husband and I were chatting and I said, "I think I want to do a book, but I'm wondering if I should ask." He said, "Yeah, might as well go for it. The worst they could do is say no." So I reached out to the editor, Tricia Waddell, and asked her. She said, "That's funny. I was going to ask you to do one."

I wrote *I Love Patchwork* in 2009 with Interweave. The book did really well, and then I thought "I want to do fabric now."

JH: That's right around the time that quilting fabric was getting interesting and modern. There were suddenly these big, modern, quilting fabric designers.

---

* Each kanji character represents a word or concept. Each character, borrowed from Chinese, may have multiple pronunciations depending on context, and there are tens of thousands of characters total.

† Unlike kanji, hiragana and katakana characters are meant to convey sound, rather than meaning. Hiragana and katakana are phonetic writing, where each character represents a syllable, and characters are combined to create words. Japanese schoolchildren primarily learn to read and write hiragana and katakana in their first few years of school.

RCH: And a lot of Japanese textiles had started popping up on Etsy, and that was making it more interesting. Spoonflower, too, had just popped up on the scene. People were excited about creating their own designs. I didn't have as much time to illustrate as I wanted because I had two kids and I was busy blogging, writing books, and doing projects for magazines. But I got excited about doing illustration again. I put together a little collection and I reached out to a lot of fabric manufacturers, and I got a ton of noes. The last place I reached out to was Timeless Treasures. I sent them my work and got a response literally the next day. The creative director, Lisa Denney, said, "I can't believe you just emailed me. I just bought your book." That was my first collection, in 2011.

At that point, I had also already started working on ideas for book number two. I had two collections with Timeless Treasures. In my third one, I started to develop my own style and figure out what kind of designer I wanted to be. I think my third collection got a little—I'm trying to remember the exact words the Timeless Treasures' creative director said—but basically, she was just like, "I don't think this group is for us." I shopped that collection to Cloud9 Fabrics to see what they thought. They thought the work was great. I left Timeless and I started designing with Cloud9.

JH: What was the name of that first collection you did for Cloud9?

RCH: It was Tsuru. I was disappointed that Timeless didn't want it. But, I was so excited to be working with Cloud9 because they're such a cool company and their fabric is organic, too. And their design variety is so fun and boisterous. It was a great match. I was super happy with them, and I had a couple of groups with them.

JH: How many years were you with them?

RCH: I think it was maybe two years, so maybe three or four collections. At that point, I had already moved to Atlanta. The fabric designer Melody Miller and I were living in the same neighborhood. We became friends because she had found out that I had moved to the area. Melody emailed me, we hit it off, and have been friends ever since. She tapped me and was like, "I know you're happy at Cloud9. But I have this idea, and I'd love for you to be a part of it." It was Cotton + Steel.

JH: For folks who don't know what Cotton + Steel is, what was the idea behind it?

RCH: First, I would say that it was started because Melody was leaving Kokka Fabrics. She had been there for several years and had several collections with them. But she was ready to find a new home. She went to a couple of fabric manufacturers and got a meeting with RJR Fabrics. She realized that it didn't make sense for her to be the only modern designer for RJR because their stuff was so traditional. She thought it would make sense if they had a whole new modern division instead. In a meeting, she pitched to them the idea of a whole division: Cotton + Steel.

Cotton + Steel was me, her, and Kim Kight, who had the blog *True Up*, which was super popular, your go-to blog for learning about anything fabric. Alexia Abegg had Green Bee Patterns; Sarah Watts had already had a couple of collections, too, with Blend. She was on the rise as well because she's such a talented illustrator. Basically, the premise was to start a new, modern division of all our collections. We used an exclusive palette so that all our groups worked together and you could mix and match them.

JH: How many collections do you remember doing for them? How many years were you there?

RCH: We were going to have our five-year anniversary the year that we left.

JH: Five years is a long time to be anywhere nowadays.

RCH: In fabric years, that's basically a decade.

JH: Now the five of you have branched off and have created Ruby Star Society.

RCH: Yeah, Ruby Star Society. That name came about because Melody had a blog called *Ruby Star Rising*; she'd name her collections some variant of Ruby Star Society. When we were coming up with names, we were all like, "Ruby Stars—we should totally use that. You know, it's like coming full circle after

Cotton + Steel and everything that went down." We were all just happy that we were still able to work together at the end of the day. It could have had any crazy name, and it would have been fine.

JH: One of the things I love about the five of you is that you individually have such distinct voices and you also collectively have such a distinct voice from everything else that's out there on the market. How would you describe your voice, your work, and your style?

RCH: Oh, goodness. I get a lot of influence from my love of Japan and that very *kawaii* aesthetic that they have. That's such a good question. I guess I never thought about that, Jen.

JH: When people ask me that, I don't know how to respond, either. I mean I have an idea. I just find it interesting because when I look at surface design, I see so much of the same. Often, when you come at it from seeing and imitating things you like instead of having your own voice, you're imitating whatever the trends are. But, you're doing something totally different, which is maintaining your voice and doing the design.

RCH: I have to say that that has been extremely difficult for me.

JH: What has? Maintaining your voice?

RCH: Maintaining my voice and not paying attention to trends. With social media, it's so difficult because you want to follow your peers and keep abreast of what everybody else is doing, and you want to know what the trends are as well. But, you have to filter out all that information when you sit down and start doing your own work and just try to come with a clean slate. You put all that over there on that shelf and then you take your stuff down off the other. I think there was a moment where I was like, "Is my stuff starting to look like other people's?" Not that it's bad, but you just really do want to keep it your thing. I had to stop thinking about what I thought people would like, you know what I mean? And kind of just be like, "I'm doing this for me." I'm drawing what I like to draw and what I would want to see, creating fabric that I would want to go and buy. Hopefully, you guys like it too.

JH: In my own work, when I try to design two things that I see out there that I like and I want to not copy but kind of almost mimic that voice and that tone, it always falls flat.

RCH: I agree. I find the same. It's the same for me. You have to keep it organic and do your thing, and stick to that.

JH: Are you drawing every day? What does your creative practice look like?

RCH: I do draw just about every day. Even sometimes if it's just doodling with the kids. With my day job at Google, I do a lot of illustrations. I design icons and things like that, so I'm drawing all the time. But at my day job, it's very regimented. You know, I'm only using these four colors (the Google colors), and it has to be a very tight, pixel-perfect illustration. So, when I get home and I start working on my own stuff, all the extra stuff kind of starts flowing and coming out 'cause I feel in such a tight box in the day job. When I'm home, I'm going to do my thing.

JH: I'm a big proponent of having a day job. I had one for a very, very long time. Why do you have two jobs?

RCH: We live in Sunnyvale, the number one most expensive city in the country! We did not realize how expensive it was until we moved here.

JH: People see the dollar signs for salaries here and they get super excited. I'm like, no, you could actually have more disposable income by staying in, say Chicago, which is still an expensive city.

RCH: It's crazy. We moved out here because of my husband's job. We had his salary and then I was making royalties from my books, fabric, and stuff, which were all doing well. But at the end of the day, it just was not enough. We were just making ends meet, and my husband and I were talking and he's like, "I think you might have to get a regular job." I'm like, "I think you're right." He was working at Google at the time on the Maps team, and one of his coworkers needed an illustrator on her team. He's like, "So, I think I have an illustrator for you. It's my wife!" He connected me with her, and I had to do a design test. I did the test and I passed, so they gave me the job. If we moved back to Atlanta, we'd definitely be able to sustain without the other job, but not out here—and with four kids now, too?

JH: One of the reasons I asked that is, I think what you do is aspirational for a lot of people. People are always surprised when I tell them that the licensing money is nice, the book money is nice, but that's not the core of how I earn a living. This is a really hard way to make a living. Designing fabric is a really hard way to make a living. Most of the people I know who do it have either a spouse who is the primary breadwinner. One, they don't live in California, but two, they either have a spouse who's the primary breadwinner or they make their money doing a whole bunch of other things.

RCH: It's a fulfilling job creatively, for sure. But just designing fabric on its own? No way. You absolutely have to have your hand in so many baskets. I discovered that when I was starting out. You have to do the books, the fabric, something else, and have a shop on the side. I began to realize that there were so many things that I would need to be doing to sustain it, and being a stay-at-home mom, it was too much, honestly, with three kids at that time. We can't do all those things—it's impossible.

THE CRAFTY GEMINI

Interview with Vanessa Vargas Wilson

JEN HEWETT: Tell me about your childhood. Were you always crafty?

VANESSA VARGAS WILSON: I was born in New York City, and then my parents got divorced when I was four years old. My mom moved us to the Dominican Republic, thinking that's where we were going to live. I went to a Montessori school there. They put you in whatever grade level you're at; they don't care about your age. I was in the fourth grade at four years old, and the director called my mom in and told her, "You need to go back to the United States. Your kid is gifted—she'll be able to get scholarships." My mom always pushed education on us, so we moved to Miami. That's where I grew up. I was always really crafty. My dad is an engineer; my mom is a former drafter. The math and the engineering, the creation—I have that brain. I loved math and I was always inventing stuff.

My mom was a single mom with four kids. She worked twelve- to fifteen-hour shifts and we kids stayed home alone. At eight years old, I asked my mom to teach me how to sew. We had a sewing machine in our house, but it was an industrial sewing machine.

A little background: My mom was born in the Dominican Republic—both of my parents were. When she moved to the United States in the sixties as a teenager, she worked in the Garment District, sewing. She got paid by the piece. The faster she was, the more she could crank out, the more money she made. As a teenager, you can imagine she was just hyper and ready to go. She would often sew her finger on those super-fast industrial machines and she had a whole system where she would pass out, lean on the machine, come to, and keep going. She was traumatized by this work experience. She refused to teach me how to sew. But we had an industrial machine at home. I remember when she would be gone, I would turn it on and just floor it. It was so fast. But she would never let me [sew on it]. She'd say, "No, it's too dangerous." Meanwhile, I'm stitching by hand, inventing board games, and screwing pieces of wood together outside in the shed.

So, that's how we grew up in Miami. Just chillin', a big Latin family. Most of my mom's siblings and my cousins grew up in Miami. My grandmother didn't sew, but my mom started hand-sewing little doll clothes when she was eight. When she moved to New York, she liked to sew, so that's why she went that route.

When she was home with us as babies, people would bring her patterns and fabric. She would take their measurements because they couldn't find work clothes in their sizes, and she would make them clothes. Sewing was a little side hustle that she would do while she was at home with babies.

Then I went to college. I didn't know what I wanted to be really. I changed my major eight times. I'm super hyper and I can change my mind from one second to the next as to what I want to do. I was in the student sports management association and we had a sports agent and a sports attorney come and tell us about their jobs. That's when I started thinking, "Oh, maybe I'll go to law school. I kind of like what this sports lawyer does." I started looking up law school and learned it doesn't matter what your major is, you just have to have good grades. I decided to do something I actually liked. I changed my major finally to anthropology. I got straight As and then I applied to law school. I went to law school, but I hated [law school] from day one because I never wanted to be a lawyer. In my second year in law school, I was super depressed. I hated every second of it. I just wanted to leave, but of course, I can't quit something that I start. I was looking for some type of creative outlet and I was looking for a coffee shop to study for finals.

In a college town, all the coffee shops are taken up by undergrads. You know, when you're in grad school, you're like, "I ain't trying to hang out with these undergrads." I was driving around looking for another place to study at and I pulled into a plaza. I saw a shop that said "sewing classes." I was like, "This is a thing?" When you grow up with it and your mom or your grandma does it, you just always assume that it's taught by them. I'm the queen of research, and it never crossed my mind that this was a business and a thing that people actually taught. The next morning, right when the shop opened, I was there.

They told me about their classes. I took the flyer, called my mom, and said, "Listen, I'm twenty-two. I think I can keep my fingers away from the needle." She found me a 1966 Singer sewing machine at a yard sale for ten bucks. She taught me how to thread it. I was like, "Okay, now what?"

She said, "Stitch a thousand straight lines. There's nothing more important than sewing straight." I will never forget that. I wanted to make stuff. This thing is threaded. It's ready—let's make something. When she left, I took an old pair of jeans that no longer fit and I hacked off the legs. I made a purse out of that, and I will never forget—I literally sewed the wrong sides together and was like, "Let's try it again." And that's how I started. I feel like I'm a very practical, very resourceful person.

Listen, I would roll up to law school study sessions with, like, a Christmas stocking. And I was like, "Look what I made!" During my second and third year of law school, after I'd discovered sewing and quilting, I did not buy books. I would sit in the back seat of my classroom and I'd schedule my classes at the quilt shop so that I could leave [my law school classes] ten minutes early and just sneak out the back and get [to the quilt shop] on time. My friends would say, "You're the only person I know at twenty-two years old that is skipping law school classes to go quilt with grandmas." I was like, "Yes, honey. And I love every second of it."

There was a lady that worked at the shop who was amazing, and she taught classes, too. She saw me make a pillow cover and a Christmas stocking and she said, "You're a perfectionist. I really think you should try quilting." I remember asking her, "What is quilting?" I heard the word "quilt" for the first time in my life when I was in law school at twenty-two years old.

JH: You're in law school, you're going to quilting classes, and you finished law school?

VVW: Yes, I did.

JH: And, you decided not to be a lawyer?

VVW: That's right. At first, I mean, there's a lot of pressure from family-friends, and, of course, classmates too. Everybody's studying for the bar. I clerked for an immigration attorney for three and a half years, and he paid for me to take the bar because he wanted me to be a practicing attorney for his firm. When I took the bar, I was in my first trimester, pregnant with my son, and when I'm pregnant, I sleep for sixteen hours a day. I definitely failed the bar. My friend was trying to wake me up. I fell asleep in the middle of the whole thing. I tried, but I still failed it. I wrote a blog post on that called "Why Failing the Bar Is the Best Thing I Ever Did." I know that because of the way that I was brought up, if I'd passed the bar, I would've become a lawyer.

There was a lot of pressure from my mom for grades. I used to get straight As, but if I got one B, I mean, she would take my report card, highlight that shit, and say, "B equals good. I want excellent." By the time I got home, she wouldn't have to do nothing to me because I'd been crying all day in school. I was just so hard on myself. I went to the University of Florida in Gainesville. When you grow up in a diverse city like Miami, it's so different; when I got to college here in rural North Central Florida I did not understand why in my first semester everybody kept asking me if I was mixed. I was like, "What the hell is mixed?" One football player gets off the bus, and he asked, "Hey, are you mixed?" And I'm like, "Okay, you are going to explain to me what this 'mixed' thing is."

To me, he looked Dominican, but he was half Black American, half white. Where I come from, we don't have "Black Americans" and "white Americans." Everybody's from somewhere. The whitest guy in [my high school] school was named Ryan Schneider, and he's Cuban. My friends are Pakistani/Venezuelan. My youngest sister is half Croatian, half Dominican. Everybody's from somewhere. When I would meet a Black person in college, I'd ask, "So, where are you from?" And they'd name some town in Alabama. I realized that they're just from here. For us, you know, I'm like, Bahamas, Jamaica—like where do you come from, from? Because where I grew up in Miami, everybody comes from somewhere. Coming up here was a huge culture shock for me.

JH: Yet, you're still there.

VVW: You know, you find your niches. It's a huge school too. You have your minority organizations and people that you relate to. You join those kinds of things and stuff like that. But then I went to law school here again, the best school in the state. I had scholarships, I had grants. I had assistantships. It just made sense to stay because also the cost of living here is low.

JH: How do you make the leap from not being a lawyer to doing what you're doing now? Because those two are night and day. You're taking quilt classes, but a lot of people take quilt classes and they never think about making this their professional life.

VVW: Even in law school, I was making little projects and people were buying them from me. I made Obama tote bags. I turned the logo into a whole applique thing and put it on a black tote for my laptop and people wanted to buy it. That was back in '08. I sold like ten of those bags.

After I graduated from law school, I took a job at the same university as an admissions officer. Well, when I took that job, the man who would become my husband had been an admissions officer there for two years. He was looking for other jobs, traveling around the state, looking for other positions. And he ended up taking one at the community college that's in the same town as the university. He took the new job, walked into my office, and asked me out to lunch. So, I was like, "Okay." I met his parents and four months later, we were married. We stayed because the cost of living here is low. We got married and had our first kid that next year. Once I found out I was pregnant, I quit my job because it was really stressful. I was like, "I'm growing a human. I need to relax. No stress. I'll just sew."

[My husband] had bought me a longarm. We had a second room in our house, and I set up the longarm there. I started teaching private group classes, doing little projects. I was pregnant and all my friends were having babies around the same time. I would share on my personal Facebook page, "I just made another dozen cloth diapers for my baby." And my friends would say, "Hey, my friend's having a baby. Can you make her some cloth diapers? I want to gift them to her." To help my husband out, 'cause he was the only one working, I started making stuff and posting it. But then, everybody wanted the same thing. I told my husband, "Listen, I like to make stuff, but I only like to make it once for the challenge." He said, "Well, why don't you teach classes?"

I started teaching through the community education program at the community college in town. I taught sewing, beginning quilting, and little classes like that. Everybody wanted me to teach the same class over and over again. I'm not even making the stuff and I'm dead bored. My husband said, "Let's videotape you doing the project. That way you only ever have to do it once. There's YouTube—you can put your videos up there for free."

JH: This is what—2009?

VVW: Yup.

JH: There wasn't a lot on YouTube.

VVW: I didn't even use YouTube for searches, so I didn't know how it worked. All I remember is people sharing cat videos, and that's what I thought it was for. My husband said, "It's a free platform—just put your videos up." Oh my gosh, genius. I only have to make it one time. I started doing that, but we were dead broke. We had our family point-and-shoot camera. I had a memory card for that camera that had 256 megabytes of memory. I would film my tutorials in fifteen- to thirty-two-second clips, take the card out, dump it onto my computer, reformat the card, go back and film the next clip until it maxed out, take it out, and dump it. I don't even know how I got through tutorials doing that. But that's all we had and that's all I could afford.

JH: You're such a good teacher, and you're able to break things down into very concise points. I wonder if only being able to do fifteen to thirty seconds at a time really focused the way that you did it.

VVW: It definitely did. In the beginning, my husband would hold the camera for me, but then I couldn't see what he's filming right until I went to edit it. I would see half of my hand pointing to something that I'm showing here and I'd see his toes. I fired him after the second or third video. Then I thought to myself, "Well, how am I going to show both my hands and hold the camera?" I bought a little tripod for $2.99 on eBay and I screwed it to the bottom of the point-and-shoot camera. I tucked it into my sports bra and tilted it forward. Because, as a teacher, I want to show the view of the maker. I want them to be able to pause the video and say, "Okay, she's folding the right-hand side this way" and copy the exact way that I'm doing it. I would just tighten my chest up and just barely move my arms.

I posted videos on YouTube like that for a year and a half. People would write to me from all over the world and say, "Oh my gosh, your tutorials are so great. Can you do a video on this?" I remember getting an email from a lady in Germany saying, "Hey, I don't even speak English well, but I can understand your video in English a lot better than my German counterparts that are making similar videos."

After a year and a half of that, I went to do a search on YouTube. YouTube, at the time, was emailing me to tell me, "Hey, this video has 50,000 views.

Would you like to monetize it?" I'd say, "Sure." You know, I thought that you'd have to wait until your videos had a certain number of views to monetize them. I never looked into monetizing them because that didn't even cross my mind. But I remember looking for something on YouTube one day, and a video popped up from a girl with a sewing channel. The video said it had eight views, but there were ads playing on it. I'm like, "How this girl got ads on a video that just has eight views? Let me do a little research." I start typing in "monetizing YouTube videos." And I see "Partner Program." I was like, "Oh, okay, let me apply." Well by then, I had videos with a ton of views.

Within twenty-four hours, they accepted me into the Partner Program and I was able to start monetizing all my videos. One day, I was searching for something else. This video pops up—it's a YouTube contest. I click on it and YouTube and Google are looking for the top twenty-five upcoming YouTube stars who basically can grow their brand, who are going to be the next big thing on YouTube. I'm watching the video and I'm thinking, "Please don't let this thing have expired. I need to get in on this." I looked and I had four days. At the time, my husband had just sold his car 'cause we were looking to save up money to buy a farm, a little homestead.

He says, "Well, when we sell this car, I'm going to give you some money. I want you to get a real camera and some real editing software, 'cause I think you could do something with this." In those four days, I ordered a new camera, new editing software, and a new laptop. I had four days to come up with a genius audition video, film it legit with the right settings on the camera, and teach myself the editing software. At the time, I had a belly out to here with my second kid and I had a fifteen-month-old running around. I handed the kid to my husband and told him, "Take him for four days. I'm going to be up day and night. But if I can get my audition video in, I know I will win this 'cause it's twenty-five people. My chances are great!" I ended up winning one of the spots. I was a part of YouTube's first Next Up class. They gave us each $35,000 to grow our brand and our channel. Of the twenty-five winners, I was the second or the third from the bottom with the least number of subscribers. There were people there that were musicians that had already played on the *Conan O'Brien* show. I had maybe over two thousand subscribers. They flew us to New York for a week and I was featured in the *New York Times*. I was on *20/20* because of the story—pregnant mom leaves her law degree; she's starting a career on YouTube from her dining room table, teaching sewing tutorials.

JH: You can't pay for that kind of publicity.

VVW: The [YouTube] marketing girls were like, "This is straight out of central casting." I mean, imagine a mom sitting at home watching that thinking, "Wow, maybe I could do that, too—have a side gig from home while I'm watching these kids." You know? They gave us some money to go to B & H Photo Video in New York. They had people helping us, which was genius because you had a private shopper with you. They would ask, "What kind of videos do you do?" I got a brand-new iMac, new editing software. And we bought our homestead; I bought a separate building, which is what I'm in right now. It's a 12-by-28-foot workshop building. I had it finished. I did the installation, the drywall, and the lighting system. This has been my work studio for the past seven, six years or something.

JH: That's amazing. So, the basis of your business, the very beginnings of it were essentially YouTube, and then you've been able to branch out from there.

VVW: You have to. A lot of people don't realize that, unless you have constant viral videos, which is super hard to do, it's really hard to build your audience through organic search and organic growth to make an income where you can support your whole family. Early on, we started trying to figure out, "Okay, how can we monetize this growing viewership that I have?" I started reaching out to companies whose products I already used and loved and started inquiring. I had drafted my own contracts and agreements for sponsored videos. That was good. They take you a little more seriously.

JH: That law degree is working for you.

VVW: That's really the only place I use it. I tell people all the time that what makes me good at what I do is a mixture of stuff that I'm naturally good at and what I love to do. That combination where those two meet is where it is. Most of this is common sense I've had since I was five. It's not no law school. But you know, you have a little bit better understanding of the background, liability situations, legalities, and stuff like that. So, of course, it's helpful.

JH: You went out and you talked to all these people, or these companies that you were interested in working with and they said yes?

VVW: A lot of people said no. People would write to me and say, "We don't know for sure what the ROI is going to be." I'm like "ROI on an evergreen video that you're going to pay me $250 for once and it's always going to be there? I got your name down. Don't worry. Don't ever holler at me, either." When those same companies that tried me back in the days try to reach out now, I'm like, "Oh no, honey. I remember you." My husband calls me "Petty Crocker."

My husband suggested I try some networking things. I talked to a couple of people that I knew online that were in the industry, and one of them recommended going to Quilt Market, scheduling my appointments ahead of time with companies that I wanted to work with. I went to that first Quilt Market. Some of those companies told me to my face, "I don't think our demographic is the same demographic that you reach." Oh, okay. Let me pull out my analytics real quick for you. You know, at that time, 50 percent of my viewership were women fifty-five and older. I was like, "Is this not the demographic that has the dollars that you would like to reach out to? My demographic doesn't look like me. That's not who I'm reaching."

JH: Who did they think was sitting at home and watching YouTube videos about quilting all day in 2010, 2011?

VVW: Listen, when they would see those numbers, they were like, "Huh?!" Oh, so now you want to have me write a book for you? No, honey, I can do that by myself. That's why over the years, I started dropping off companies because you get to a point where people want to own you. I've had companies reach out and ask me how much they can buy *The Crafty Gemini* for. I'm The Crafty Gemini—you can't buy me. I like my freedom. I like to be able to do my own thing, you know? I know I'm running a legit business, I'm helping tons of people, and I'm not going to work with companies who are going to hurt the reputation that I've built up over these years. All I have is my word. I'm the face of this entire brand.

JH: Okay, so you have YouTube videos, you also have the clubs, and . . .

VVW: After moving up from the sponsorships, where we were charging $250, then $500 and $1,000 and then $1,500, my husband was like, "All this time, you spending for these little dollars working for somebody else. You could be putting that into your own thing." I was still coming from that mentality of like, "This is secure money." I knew if I did this work, this is exactly how much I was going to get paid for it. Little by little, I started just winging it. What's the worst that can happen? I could be right where I'm at right now and I'm making no dollars, so let's try it.

A friend of mine is in a different niche. She told me, "Hey, I read this book, I launched this thing and it did amazing. I think for you and your following, you would kill it." But I hate reading. I got the e-book—it's called *Launch* by Jeff Walker—and I sent it to my husband, asked him to read the book and give me the gist of it. He reads the book. He's like, "Yeah, the guy gives you the formula in here, but I can't break it down for you. You need to read it." I was on a plane; I had my iPad on me. I read it on one flight. I was sitting there, taking notes and making my outline of how I could apply the formula he's talking about into what it is that I do. As I was going through the book, "I'm like, I'm doing all this stuff already." I just needed to put it together into this package. In the two and a half months after reading that book, I launched my first online quilt club. And it was a huge hit. We retired my husband from his job two months later.

JH: How many people were in your quilt club?

VVW: Over 1,300. Paying $17.99 a month, or $107 for the year if they got in at the early bird sale price. We launched the last week of December. I saw these sales coming in while we were at a Christmas party at my mom's house, and I was looking at my husband like, "Yo, my battery is dead off these PayPal notifications." On YouTube, I never got to see the monetary value that people were placing on the content I was giving them. The people who were subscribing to my quilt club were paying money up front and they hadn't even seen the content yet. That's what my husband had been telling me for years, but that's when it really clicked for me.

JH: They trust you because they're seeing you on a regular basis on YouTube.

VVW: Exactly. And they know the quality of the stuff. If you're paying for one of my classes, it's a whole other level than the YouTube videos. If you think you like the free stuff, you're gonna love the for-pay stuff because I have to bump it up, because what's going to be the difference? With my husband home to watch the kids, I was like, "Oh, it's gonna be poppin'." I've got all the ideas and now I've got all the time." We ran that club for two years. It had a lot of weekly tips and tricks, videos, weekly live chats with everybody, monthly projects, block of the month, things for the whole year. I mean it was a lot. We ended the quilt club, and then after that, I started with the same club idea, which people really like because you build community, but it kind of gives them a push to get these projects done. Or if they can't, it's no big deal because the videos are archived forever.

I have ladies who buy everything of mine. They're like, "I'm retiring in twenty-six months and then I'm going to sit down and make all the things." We started doing clubs that were six-month sessions. I would do handbag clubs that were for six months. You'd get a different handbag video course and a PDF pattern per month for that period of time with some bonus live chats thrown in. We sold kits for the projects. We did several Bag of the Month clubs with video courses. That hadn't been done before. We jumped into garment sewing. Now, I'm doing these online video courses for specific garment patterns that we sell, plus the fabrics and the materials they need. So, that's been great for us, too.

JH: Do you still have the brick-and-mortar store?

VVW: I do. For the past two years, I had just a little studio space about 750 square feet, just for classes. I only taught classes; it wasn't a retail space. Then we up-sized to include classroom and retail space. It's almost 2,400 square feet.

We hired an assistant to handle all our shipping, our customer service. I'm getting ready to hire somebody else to work in the shop. It's cool because 80 percent of the customers that come into my shop know me from online. They're not locals. These people come from everywhere. "Hey, I'm here from Pennsylvania. I'm here from Chicago. We're vacationing in Florida. We're from Wisconsin. You know, I'm here from Alabama 'cause my grandson lives in Orlando and I came to his graduation. I told my husband, we got to stop on the way up." [The shop] is a destination spot. I never know who's walking in the door because they could be from anywhere.

JH: That's great. I think that one of the hardest things for people to do is to build up a loyal audience without losing a sense of themselves. I think that people who try to be everything to everyone often fail. But, you have a very clear personality, have a very clear aesthetic. You have a very clear message and it still applies to a broad range of people.

VVW: It does. There's certain things in there that could take me one way or the other and make me lose some followers. I don't just be posting about the whole political thing. I don't [usually] get into that. But when it's something that fits into the realm of what I normally share already and it happens to us personally, I'm gonna post about it.

We had an event two years ago—a big quilt show in Paducah, Kentucky. It was our second year vending there and my husband and I already knew what we were in for. There weren't very many brown or Black people in the building. Everybody was looking at my husband like he worked there. They would wait at the door with their boxes like he was going to open and hold the door for them and help them with their stuff. We had to bring our own stuff inside to setup. They just couldn't believe that we were actually vendors, too. The feedback from vendors the first year was ridiculous. I had some vendors coming up to me asking me, "How did you even get this booth?" Someone told me in the past you had to do five of the smaller shows and then get on a wait list to get a booth at Paducah. I'm like, "Honey, they called me because I did really great at another show." I had one vendor ask me the first day, "How did y'all do today? It's going to be really tough for you at this show if you only have that one ruler to sell." I was like, "Girl, I made all my money back by lunchtime. From here on out, the next four days are like icing on the cake. How about you?" After that first year. my husband was like, "All the drama aside, it was good money. Let's go back."

That second year, we rented an Airbnb. We were eating breakfast one morning and I asked my husband to go to the car and get me my external hard drive. It was 7:15 a.m. He went out front to our rental car and I quickly got a call on my phone from the Airbnb owner. She said, "Are you parked out front? I would check your car because the tenants from upstairs said there's a really sketchy guy suspiciously pulling stuff out of a nice car out front." So, I looked outside and I'm like, "Nope, not us." I mean, it didn't even click in my mind. As she continues to talk, it hit me. I was like, "Are you serious? That's my husband." As I was hanging up with her, two police cars were pulling up fast. That's when I was like, "I don't post this shit, but I will today because this happened to us at a quilt show." Really? A Black guy with dreadlocks "suspiciously?" How do you "suspiciously" do anything to a car that you're not breaking into?

I was livid. Told my husband, "Pack the car—we're leaving." My husband's like, "Relax. We about to come in here and make this bread and go." Now, the police officers are looking at the car checking it out to see if it was broken into, so I come out and ask, "Is there a problem?" He said, "Well, we got a call." I said, "Yeah, the Black guy right there is the one that you got called about. My husband, who had the key fob for the car 'cause he went to get something for me." That officer was so like, "Oh my God, I'm so sorry."

Of course, I posted about it on social media, and the fans came out in full force. "You should be happy that somebody called the police. If somebody was really breaking into your car, you would've been thankful."

JH: Yeah, that statement: "You shouldn't be worried if you're not doing anything wrong." Have you been watching the news? Are you watching a different channel than I am? Oh, you are.

VVW: They were posting screenshots of neighborhood watch manuals. "They did exactly what they were supposed to do." First of all, it's not a sketchy neighborhood. It's a plush old vintage house. It's an Airbnb. Everybody that stays there and looks different is from somewhere else. Oh yeah, girl, I was mad. And when I posted that, I mean, people were like, "I'm unsubscribing." Honey, go ahead and unsubscribe. But when you need that free pillowcase tutorial, you know you're going to go right back to mine. You ain't going nowhere.

I was like, "I'm sharing this story, 'cause that was personal to us and it happened in real life." I tracked the numbers and I lost like fourteen followers that day.

I stopped going to quilt shops years ago because they would follow us around. I'm like, "What do you think he's going to steal, a fat quarter? On a Saturday morning?" Whenever we walked into a quilt shop, they look at us like, "Are you lost?" I'm like, "I'm lost on a Saturday morning at 10:15 with my husband just walking into a shop. Really? I look that out of place?"

JH: That is the story that I hear most often in the survey responses. Almost everybody has that story. They go to a local yarn store, they go to a quilt shop, and those are the experiences they have over and over and over again. Someone will post something about their experience, and a white lady will say, "I've never seen that happen and that's never happened to me. Maybe you were just misreading it." We are telling you about our lived experience and you're not believing it from one person, but maybe when you read a book and there are 280 people saying this is their experience, maybe you'll actually pay attention. Probably not.

VVW: I had that experience almost everywhere. People ask me, "Have you been to this shop?" I'm like, no, I'm not going to any shops in rural Florida. I've had great experiences with some shops up north. I was like, "These people are actually nice." And then the Denver one for sure—Fancy Tiger. That's my spot. I spent a week up there filming and I went to their craft night on a Tuesday night. I told some of my fans to come through 'cause I was going to be there. Everybody was super nice. And those knitters, they didn't know who I am. They were just like, "Hey, what are you working on?" I was like, "Oh my gosh."

JH: Thing is, it comes from the owners, right? The owners set that tone.

VVW: You could tell. I mean, that was like the most welcoming spot ever. I mean, they have all decals, "Anybody's welcome here. This is a safe space" on the outside. I was like, "Well, okay, we coming in here, let's see."

A lot of these shops in Florida run by ladies that were retired, they're closing down left and right. They're not doing anything to get new fresh talent. That's why I started the chapter of the Modern Quilt Guild here in town ten years ago. There were maybe a handful of quilters at our local traditional guild that were nice to me and that took me under their wing, the type of quilter who wished that one of her kids would've liked quilting. They saw me as a daughter. But not the majority of them. I had brought a friend with me once to one of the meetings. I always had stuff for show-and-tell because this was when I was pregnant with my son. I'm like making all the baby things, you know, bright colors, fun things.

My friend sat in the back and was like, "Girl, they were talking so much shit about you back here. They were like, 'Here she go again with her show-and-tell.'" I would get up there with like a picnic quilt and they'd raise their hand and ask, "What kind of applique is that?" I'm twenty-six, all excited, and I tell them it's fusible. They just rolled their eyes. "Who did the quilting?" I'm like, "Me, I have a longarm." I was their webmaster for a while. Working on the website and email newsletter list. I did all that stuff for them, and I just got tired of the looks and treatment. Why am I pulling teeth over here? Getting treated every kind of way just because I'm looking for that group of people that speak my language. I was like, "No, forget this. I'm gonna start my own thing."

JH: In so many ways—and this is really important for women who marry men—you're really lucky in who you chose as your husband because he's been super encouraging of you all along.

VVW: I get a lot of women who cry and tell me, "My husband puts down my crafts, tells me I'm wasting my time, I'm wasting money." But my husband is the opposite. He pushed me to do all this. Everything we've done since the beginning has been his idea. Because of how I am and how I was raised, I would have never done this on my own, thrown a law degree to the side? Nope. I'm super resourceful and I am a risk-taker, but I don't take risks on myself. I just didn't have that level of confidence to have done this by myself. So he's like, "At least you come around, it only takes six years of me telling you the same thing every damn day and then you finally come around." It took me like seven years to believe that yeah, [people] actually like me and the way I teach. It's a struggle, and if I didn't have him, I would not have done all of it.

JH: As a woman who is not married and pretty much has to do everything on her own, I think of how nice it must be to have someone who has rearranged his life in benefit of you and the family, rather than expecting you to do it all.

VVW: Absolutely. He does all the grunt work because there was a time where we were building, building, building the business, and I was trying to create and be creative, and then cooking and cleaning the house and trying to watch these kids. I can't do all this. He said, "Give me all the grunt work. I'll do the customer service emails. I'll do the shipping. Give me all the shit you don't want to do so you can create." That's been a great help. I do dishes, but he does all the laundry, the cleaning, all this extra stuff. A lot of guys ask, "How is your husband okay with having you be the main breadwinner?" They ask that all the time.

JH: I admire you immensely because you're a full decade younger than me and you've built so much. You are the master of all your content and your projects, and it's rare to see that.

VVW: I need to learn how to delegate a little bit better. But when you build something, you're the face and you're the brand. You worry that if something goes wrong, it will tank the whole thing. I feel like I have to have my hands in everything. If you hire somebody, they're not going to care about it as much as you do. It's not their business, you know? So, that's hard for me, but I'm getting better at picking and choosing good people.

When you get to a certain point, you have this following. Companies can't pitch to me no more like it's for exposure. I'm like, "Honey, I will give you exposure." I would tell companies back in the days like, "Thank you for your offer—here's my agreement. Feel free to look through it if you want to pay for a sponsored video." Some would offer up fabric in exchange for the video. I couldn't pay my mortgage with a fat quarter bundle. This is a business. At the time, I had like 200,000 subscribers. I'm not doing stuff for free no more. It's evergreen content. It's there forever. It's also about knowing your worth. I've worked for companies before on sponsored videos where people would message me and say, "I was doing laundry when I watched your video and I had to stop and run out to the store that you just told me to go buy that item from." A TV commercial cannot even do that for you. Who can do that? I can. You gotta pay for that. That costs bread.

SURVEY PROFILE

Raquel Busa

Age: 35
Location: Howard Beach (Queens), New York
Profession: Office manager and the illustrator and sewist behind the brand Máquina37

What types of fiber crafts do you engage in, and how many years have you been engaged in each?
I currently sew cloth dolls, quilt, and embroider. I have been doing each of these crafts for eight years.

How do you self-describe/identify yourself?
I am a Hispanic woman. I am a lesbian, wife, daughter, sister, aunt, cousin, and friend. I am also a creative. I don't like to label myself as one type of artist because I love expressing myself through art in many different ways.

I was born in New York to immigrant parents. My mom is from the Dominican Republic and my father is from Puerto Rico. I identify as Hispanic, but when people first meet me, they think I'm Jewish or Moroccan. They are surprised when I speak Spanish. I was made fun of in school for speaking English well. Kids said I was trying to be white. That's not the case at all. I love being American. I love being Hispanic. I embrace both of my identities.

When I was growing up, I had many heterosexual examples of "happily ever after." So, I thought being happy was tied to getting married to a man. I was also taught that being gay was wrong. So, that could never be me, right? Well, in my late twenties, after much heartache, depression, stress, and anxiety, I embraced my sexuality. I am a lesbian. I am married to my amazing, strong, and powerful wife. I have found my own version of "happily ever after."

I have a huge family with many nieces and nephews who come in all different colors. I want each of them to know that they are beautiful just the way they are. I want to spare them from some of the craziness I had to go through.

So, in a way, my business was inspired by them. I want to use my artistic abilities to help people celebrate diversity and individuality.

What's the first thing you remember making?

I remember drawing and coloring as a kid. I loved drawing people. My favorite memory of my young artist self was when I was about five years old. I got a big box. It was big enough that I could sit inside of it. I cut a window into the box. I took all my drawings and crawled inside of the box. I taped the drawings to the inside of the box. I even wrote prices on the backs of the drawings (five cents, ten cents, etc., depending on size). Then I called my family over to see if they wanted to buy anything. I guess it was my first exhibition.

What are you making now?

Currently, I am making look-alike dolls. Customers send me pictures of their loved ones and I make cloth doll caricatures of them. Then with all the leftover pieces, I make quilts, baby doll keychains, and embroidered cards.

The cards are quickly becoming a favorite with my customers. I embroider positive messages on scraps of fabric and sew them onto paper. I also make the paper. I use paper that is on its way to the recycling bin and mix it with bits of thread and fabric. I love the paper-making process as much as I love the embroidering and sewing.

What's your favorite thing you've made?

I made a look-alike doll of my wife. The little doll has her salt-and-pepper hair, a T-shirt, some jeans, and flip-flops. It also has ten tiny embroidered tattoos. When I was making it, it made us laugh. Years later, it is still an awesome conversational piece. I guess because it was made with such love and joy.

How and why did you learn your crafts?

I remember always being creative and making things. My brother is an artist, and I found him amazing to watch as he drew assignments for art school. My father was always finding ingenious ways of fixing things with whatever was in the house. My mom took me to the factory when she worked as a sewing machine operator and that experience always stuck with me.

I went to college for painting, but left because I was afraid that I could never make money as a painter. I enrolled in college for art history instead.

The entire time, I continued making art. I even had a few exhibitions. I thought I wanted to go into art conservation, so I traveled to Egypt and lived there for two years, studying art and chemistry.

After Egypt, I came back to New York and had to find a job to pay the bills. I fell into human resources and hated it. Finally, I found the courage to be happy and turned to art once more. That's when my mom gave me my vintage sewing machine and taught me the basics of sewing. I love sewing and embroidering. I love making art that people use and touch and that makes them happy.

Does anyone in your family practice this craft, too? Are your pieces similar or different aesthetically?
My brother still paints. His work is very different from mine. He is inspired by Latin American Indigenous cultures. However, his paintings are bright and colorful—in a sense, that fearless use of color runs in the family.

Tell me about your creative community. You can define "community" as broadly or as specifically as you'd like.
For a long time, I found it difficult to believe that people wanted to be part of my life. I have PMDD (Post Menstrual Dysphoric Disorder). One of the many symptoms of PMDD is self-deprecating thoughts. I thought people were just being nice but that deep down, they didn't really want to be part of my community. These thoughts and the idea that some part of me was wrong (my sexuality) made me isolate myself.

Once I embraced my sexuality and started confronting and treating my PMDD, I started building my community. First, I started with my close friends and family. Then I expanded into new communities. I started meeting new people, which was and still is at times very difficult for me. I am slowly expanding my circle, but feel comfortable with what I have now.

When have you felt like an "other" within the context of your craft?
When I lived in Egypt, the Egyptian Revolution erupted. I left the country, but went back weeks later. The art scene had exploded. I was invited to exhibit alongside Egyptian artists. I felt like an outsider then, as an American, but I loved experiencing art with people who had been censored for so long.

I'm usually the only artsy or creative person in my circle of family and friends. I am often asked to help with tailoring or DIY projects in their homes. I don't mind. I like being able to contribute.

When do you feel recognized in your craft? Who recognizes you and how does that feel for you?

I love it when my work makes my customers happy. I love getting positive feedback about how my work enriches their lives. It makes my work worthwhile.

During one of my markets, a family came to my table. A white family with a mom, dad, and baby. They asked the baby to pick any baby keychain he wanted, and he picked a Black baby. The parents purchased it. I loved that moment. There was no judgment, just love and encouragement. It's the basics of teaching our kids to celebrate diversity.

Are there aspects of your work that you feel are misunderstood?

Sometimes people think my dolls look like voodoo dolls. At first, I didn't like it. But then I looked into voodoo dolls and how they are used in many cultures. So, I thought, "Why not embrace that as my brand celebrates diversity?" I now offer custom voodoo dolls.

Do you engage in these crafts for income or as a hobby?

This is my second year of seriously running my business. Last year, I broke even. This year, I hope to make a profit, so legally, it's not considered a hobby.

If you sell your pieces, who are your customers? How long have you been selling your work? Do you employ other people to help you create your work? What challenges have you faced in building your creative business?

I had an Etsy shop between 2011 to 2020. I sold many different things during those years. In October 2017, I quit my HR job and decided to devote more time to my business. I was able to focus and develop my brand. Since then, I have published two coloring books for children: a bilingual coloring book about sewing and a coloring book about LGBTQAI+ terms.

I do everything by myself, but my mom and my wife help me with little things here and there (stamping cards or putting keychains on little dolls).

I have also illustrated coloring books, cards, and apparel, which I outsource to get printed.

Figuring out who my customers are and reaching them have been my biggest challenges. I thought I would be making mostly dolls for kids, but I have discovered that people love them as gifts for many age groups.

Do you exhibit your work? If so, where? Tell me about those experiences.

I used to exhibit my painting while in college. I curated group and solo exhibitions in New York, Uganda, Italy, and Egypt.

They were mostly grassroots exhibitions, if you will. For example, I curated a group show with my friends in a community center in New York. The proceeds from that show went to fund an art therapy program in Uganda, which I designed and implemented. The program ended with an art exhibition. The program in Uganda has continued and they have repeated the art exhibition.

Looking back, art has been a way for me to experience other cultures. It's been wonderful to find this common language.

Do you have an artist statement or any principles that guide your work?

I just want to make art that makes people happy. I want to make pieces that help people express love and care for each other.

When you were younger, were you exposed to other people who looked like you, or who were from similar backgrounds as you, and who engaged in this craft?

I lived in Washington Heights, surrounded by Latin Americans. But I was usually the only artsy kid. It wasn't until college that I found like-minded individuals. But because of my introversion, it was difficult for me to stay connected.

What colors are you drawn to and why?

It changes. Right now, I love mustard, blush, navy blue, seafoam, and burnt orange-pink. They are happy colors that remind me of the sun on my face.

Where do you get your materials?

I love buying organic fabrics from Organic Fabric Company on Etsy. I also buy secondhand clothes for special doll projects.

How do you choose your materials?

When I am replenishing my fabrics, I typically pick out colors and patterns that I am drawn to. I try hard to listen to myself, which I had stopped doing for so many years. The results have been great and customers respond to them.

When I pick out fabrics for custom dolls, I work closely with the customer. I want to make sure I pick out fabrics that are close to what their person is wearing in the picture.

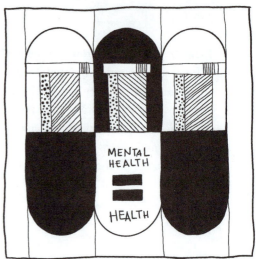

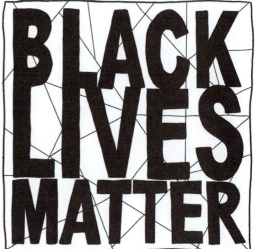

Craft Is Political

< A few of Social Justice Sewing Academy's 2020 Blocks of the Month

QUILTING DEPTH

Interview with Chawne Kimber

JEN HEWETT: Tell me about young Chawne. Who and what were your early influences?

CHAWNE KIMBER: It is key to know about me that I'm Southern. I grew up in Florida, but my family's from the Deep South. My dad's from Alabama and my mom's from Charleston, South Carolina. I grew up in Tallahassee, Florida, which is the capital, but it's right on the Georgia border. On vacations, I went even deeper, into Alabama.

My parents were always doing something with their hands. Both my parents were psychologists, so I'm just talking about what they did around the house. My dad liked fiber arts. My mom can crochet like nobody's business. She would come home from work on Friday afternoon and by Monday morning, poof, she'd have made a whole blanket. She'd watch Westerns all weekend and just crochet away. There was always a sense that one ought to be industrious. But I didn't really ever fix on a particular craft of my own. I played around with just about everything, and my parents encouraged that.

My godmother in Kentucky, which is where I was born, repairs the embroidery on church vestments for the Episcopal Church. People from around the country send her historical garments, and she repairs them. She came to visit us in Florida and was absolutely astonished that I had idle hands, so she took me to the local TG & Y (a local five-and-dime) and bought me this tiny cross-stitch kit. It was a snowman (which was of course very relatable to a Florida girl) and she taught me how to cross-stitch with that kit. There is something just really nice and meditative about cross-stitch. So, I made this snowman and I sent it to her for Christmas, and she sent it back with notes about what I'd done wrong.

My godmother and I have had this forty-eight-year correspondence. She still has letters I wrote in kindergarten. I would write to her and ask questions and she would explain, for example, why you make all the top stitches go in

144

the same direction. I'd try it and could see how her advice improved the way the thing looked. That built into me this sense of workmanship, and also the discipline to start and finish a project. I went from there to sewing garments in high school. I took a class in school where we all had to make a pair of pants and a collared button shirt.

And then I made all my formal dresses. Again, I lived in the South. You've got three or four formal events each year, and my mother was never going to buy me a new dress for each one. I got one new dress per year, but you can't wear the same dress to every event, so she would buy me a bolt of satin. One year, she bought a bolt of black satin, so I made three black satin dresses. And then the next year, the satin was pink. I could mix in the dresses from the previous year, but I was slowly developing, so I couldn't reuse three dresses from year to year. That was kind of fascinating for me to learn, this sort of topography of the human body, how fabrics respond to stretching and growth.

After high school, I didn't do anything creative until I applied for tenure. That was a good ten-year stretch, except I picked up cross-stitch near the end of grad school again because I started getting stressed and needed some sort of outlet. I was then doing a lot of French samplers. When I applied for tenure, my sister sent me a $50 Brother sewing machine and I went out and bought the book *Quilting for Dummies*.

I made every single project in the book just to learn the skills—butt-ugly and ridiculously stupid projects. But I knew I wanted to make my own things, eventually. I made ten quilts in my first year of quilting because I had applied for tenure and everything was out of my control.

After I got tenure, I didn't make another quilt for two years. I came back to it because my dad passed away, and again, I kind of remembered, "Oh wait, this sewing thing was a good place to put my feelings and my anxieties." That's actually when I started doing political quilts because it felt rather meaningless to be making, you know, the just plain old geometric stuff.

My dad had worn a tie every day. He traveled a lot and would always "forget" to take his tie so that he could buy a new one. I inherited his collection of five-hundred ties. His death was a huge surprise to me; it came out of nowhere. But we had already been talking about me making a quilt from his ties. So, he had gone through his collection and sent me like thirty in the mail that he had chosen for me to experiment with. I knew that I needed to make these tie quilts. I gave them to my sister and brother.

I still haven't made my own tie quilt, but I still have five-hundred ties, so I will get around to it. That was the first time I made a quilt that actually was meaningful. My mother had also secretly been collecting old clothes from all the people in my family, people in Alabama who worked on the farm. We're still on the land where my dad's family was enslaved. She got old jeans from them; she got khakis from cousins in Michigan. And, this box arrived on my front step one day. I was like, "You know, I probably shouldn't open that. I have no idea what it is." She hadn't put a return address on this mystery box that weighed a thousand pounds. It turned out to be the biggest treasure chest ever.

JH: I think one of the things that makes your work—I don't want to say "transcend" craft because craft is its own thing that doesn't need to be transcended—but that makes your work art in addition to being craft is that it expresses very complicated and often really uncomfortable messages. You clearly have technical skills because the work that you do requires you to have technical skills, but what is it about quilts that you felt made them a good receptacle for the messages you're trying to get across?

CK: Two things. One is that my great-grandmother made quilts and we grew up with them on our beds. My dad told a story about when he was five. When you do the giant quilting bee where you've got the whole quilt stretched on a giant frame, and you're quilting into it, you can't reach underneath to catch the needle. So, my dad, at five years old, was under the quilt pushing the needles back up through the quilt.

And if you're quiet, the ladies will forget you're there and they will gossip—and you get power. This is my father in a nutshell: super smart and devious, to some extent. He was treated like an adult growing up. It was a great way to grow up. If you're going to be on a farm in Alabama, you need this extra stimulation. He took the quilts with him after my great-grandmother passed away. I didn't really know her. She died when I was two. But I do know the farm. I know the shack where my dad was raised. It is a dirt-floor shack in the middle of Alabama, and it's made out of old wood branches.

So, we had these quilts on the bed in the house and they are absolutely one of the things that are embedded in my memory. I mostly remember the texture because she made them from threadbare clothes and then would need to put patches on top of her patchwork as the fabrics continued to wear out. There's always been something about those quilts. Even when I was spending all that time making dresses in high school, I desperately wanted to make a quilt.

We all associate quilts with a mother or grandmother. It's a very kind of homey, cozy, protective sort of object. I think it's just a wonderful venue and a large enough canvas to open up other questions. People get pulled in by the geometrics of what you're making. They get drawn in and then you hit 'em with an issue to think about. I think it's partially a bait-and-switch kind of thing—you take advantage of the shock value. People expect one thing, and you give them another. I also think, by the way, that you can't talk about race, which is mostly what I'm talking about in my quilts, without talking about cotton. For me, this cotton was made into clothes that were then made into quilts. So, it's a long process, a sustainable process that we seem to have abandoned. That's the connection for me.

JH: While I was doing research, I read interviews with people about the modern quilt world versus the traditional quilt world. And there are even all these divisions within the modern quilt world, of people who see quilts as something whose function is to be beautiful and comforting, but they don't want that mixed up with a political message. They just want to admire the quilts, and they don't want to be shocked. They feel like this is their safe space. How do you respond to that?

CK: I say, "Welcome to my life," right? There's not a moment of my day that isn't a political statement, right? I'm a math professor. I'm a woman math professor. That is already a challenge to anyone's notions of normalcy, and I'm a Black woman. You know, come on, let's forget it. I live in an area that's predominantly white. Going to the grocery store, choosing what time of day to go, who I talk to there—everything is a political choice, but it's often not a controversial choice. But I cannot escape politics and adversity in my life. And so, my quilts welcome people into the space in which I dwell. I don't have the privilege of turning off politics because every moment of my life is fraught with danger. I guess that sounds dramatic, but I think it's true.

JH: It's not dramatic to me.

CK: Right. And so, especially in shows like the show "Quilts of Resistance" for instance, which I'm not part of, you hear, "Why do I have to see these things?" A lot of us cannot turn these thoughts off. And honestly, modern quilters, by making modern quilts, they're also making a political statement. I think they're just not considering the full complex context of things. But also, you know, you don't have to look and you don't have to comment.

JH: I think I have a certain level of access because there are a lot of things about me and my work that check a lot of boxes that white people are comfortable with. You and I are both middle-class, educated Black women. So already, we can kinda slide into that world. I make work that is pretty and fairly happy, and I get asked sometimes, "Why don't you bring your Black cultural heritage to your work?" And I respond, "What is not Black about flowers? What is not Black about having a garden or being attracted to beauty?"

CK: I have problems with African print, by the way. Someone asking you to access your African heritage, they already have this sort of image in mind of what you're going to produce and it's going to involve zebras . . .

JH: Or mud cloth, which I love. But why am I the person to do that?

CK: It's not your heritage. I had my 23andMe done. The results gave me this big region of Africa I could potentially be from. I'm not rolling up saying, "Hey, I'm home." I'm not buying African garb and starting to wear it and saying, "This is who I am," because that's not who I am. It's them trying to make you fit their mold for what a Black person's allowed to do.

You reminded me that I have been told that I don't make Black quilts.

JH: I read somewhere that you asked, "What is really a Black quilt?" Because everybody looks at Gee's Bend quilts as if this is the Black language, that it's impromptu and it's scrappy. But there's a whole continuum. We can do—and have done—really detailed precision work, but someone's decided that Gee's Bend quilts are what "Black" quilts are. How do you respond to that?

CK: I mean, often it's not being asked by a person who wants to have a serious conversation. I don't need the label. Many Black artists have for years been pigeonholed and rejected because they don't fit into some category. There was one person who was really, truly trying to tell me that I wasn't living up to their expectations. And I'm not sure I care, but what do these labels mean? I want to break free from the labels, of course. I said, "Well, you don't make white quilts."

JH: Are your colleagues aware of the work you do outside of work at all?

CK: Yes. I was extremely careful about it until I was promoted to full professor. When you're in a male-dominated profession, you want to kind of tamp down your femininity, and what could be more feminine than making Grandma's quilts? It turned out that I didn't need to worry. My students saw that I was making "fuck" quilts, so it wasn't anything that needed to be hidden. I work with a great group of guys, and I might have underestimated them. In June 2019, I will have my first solo exhibition at my college gallery on campus. I did my first local exhibition in 2018 in a gallery downtown and many of my colleagues stopped by and were very impressed. They actually said, "I didn't know this is what you meant by a quilt." That's often the comment that I get—that they didn't know quilts could be like this. In that exhibition, the first quilt you see just says, "bitch," and I'm like, "Welcome to my life here, and let's talk." So, for this upcoming exhibition, I'm doing all political, word quilts.

I thought of going soft on them and making my work all just geometrics. But now I think I'm going to go all in. If I'm going to show them I'm an artist, I'm going to show them quilts that might show them who I am because a lot of them have never thought of me as a person with a life and depth. As sad as that sounds, it's true. A lot of my colleagues, not in my department but beyond, just project onto me their assumptions about who a Black woman is. I'm also in this very strange zone where I can't talk about the research that I do as a mathematician because even the mathematician in the office next to me doesn't know what my nouns mean. And so, I cannot go out and pontificate in ways that make you respect me as a scholar because honestly, you have no chance of understanding what I'm talking about.

So, that means that people tend to assume that I don't do research or tend to assume that I don't have that intellect. They assume all sorts of shallowness on me instead of talking to me. I'm in a highly segregated environment. Black and white people don't hang out together. That's not universally true. I do have friends who I reach out to, but that segregation is pretty much the rule. I work at one of these very high-tuition, highly selective institutions. So, in a show like this, I am putting myself out there. There is some risk of mis-reading, and I'm prepared for that. But it's also going to have consequences. At a regular gallery show in, say, Chicago, I'm never going to see those peo-ple again. But after my show here last summer, I developed new friendships with people I had known for twenty years but who had never bothered to find out who I am, what I think about. And they were open to knowing me after that. That's my hope. I mean, there will be detractors and I don't really care. I think my work communicates that pretty clearly. There are people who will see that and understand, "Oh yeah, she doesn't give a fuck what I think." And then there are people who are going to see it and just think, "I need to tell her everything that's wrong with her work anyway."

JH: There will always be those people.

CK: I'm okay with that.

JH: You had written a few years ago that "there is sense in a sense of math-ematics that I'm still trying to prove myself, but by virtue of making some-thing, I am an artist." Which I have to tell you, as an artist, I've found it's often the other way around for me and for a lot of the artists I know. Often, being an artist is the hardest thing to claim even when you are actively mak-ing art because there's a lot of insecurity and baggage tied up in that word. Have you always been, as long as you've been making work, really confident calling yourself an artist?

CK: No. What I was referring to there, and maybe I didn't make it explicit when writing that, but Rachel May wrote a book, *Quilting with a Modern Slant*. She interviewed me and a few other people. She put together a show of a select few of the quilters from the book, in Boston. I decided to go to the opening. It was my first opening. I landed and was picked up from the airport by a sculptor who's pretty amazing. We went to lunch, and I had a conversa-tion with this woman, and she talked to me like I'm an artist. There was just no question: she had seen the two works I had in the show. One was a Trayvon Martin quilt and the other was a sharecropper shirt that I had turned into a log cabin quilt. I didn't have to prove myself. Maybe I had already proven myself ahead of time with my work. In math, I've published articles. But every single day, I have to renew this argument with people about my right to be there. You know, I'm not your average mathematician as a person. I have a personality, and I also do not fit the description of the other people in the room. And so, some of it is me projecting on them my own imposter syndrome about being there. But at the same time, I am honestly testing them on the same level that they're testing me. Math is all about just verbal argumentation. So, that kind of trickles out into what it means to interact as mathematicians. It's a combative sort of zone. People often truly wonder whether we're angry at each other sometimes, because it's intense. You're thinking quite deeply to build your argument. You're listening to them to assess their argument.

There's a level of vulnerability to the whole thing as well. You know, I worry about saying the wrong thing. If you say something wrong, you'll be assumed to be an idiot for the rest of your life. That's part of that imposter syndrome thing. But as an artist, I have never been in a space where someone has challenged my work in a way that meant they assumed I knew nothing, that the thing I was making had no meaning. There are all kinds of questions that I still need to have answered about what the pursuit of art is, right? Because for me, art needs to have meaning. Obviously, that's not the case all the time. But that, that's to me like a quilt, not every quilter is an artist, I'm sorry . . .

JH: No, and most are not. I think many are technically savvy. But, they're working with fabric they've bought and patterns they've bought and they were told which colors or color values to use . . .

CK: But they find it an insult if they're not called an artist. I don't know where that comes from. I need to be known as an artisan first. To me, the craftsmanship and the quality of the engineering are high on my mind. I thank you for saying that we don't need to transcend craft. Craft is still very important. I don't know if it's just that I have the wrong expectations for things, and that's just my lack of experience in the art world, so maybe it's just that I'm meeting all the right, nice artists who are treating me kindly and respectfully.

JH: Or that you really are an artist.

CRAFTING A MORE EQUITABLE WORLD

Personal Narrative of Chi L. Nguyen, as told to Jen Hewett

I GREW UP in Vietnam, and my family history is very tied up in the Vietnam War. Half of my family on my mother's side lived in the North and the other half lived in the South. There is a saying in Vietnam that when you go to the battlefield, you may be fighting someone in your family. So, the trauma is deep. Sometimes, people try to get over it through humor or by not talking about it at all.

In my family, we were much more encouraged to study math, science, or literature; art was something that we were encouraged to do as a hobby but not as a livelihood. If you are doing what we would consider crafts, people would say, "Okay, yeah, you can knit, but you'd better sell that, and it must be wearable. It must be practical."

So, no, I didn't do any art at all as a child and never thought of myself as being particularly good at it. Throughout my mom's childhood, she had to knit and crochet products to sell with my aunts and grandma. It's how they made a living during the war.

My grandma on my mother's side was a nun before she met my grandfather. She met him, fell in love, and moved to the countryside with him to work on the family's land. He was already married at that time, but he fell in love with my grandma, but his family did not like my grandma at all because she was the second wife. Later on, when my grandfather joined the Northern Vietnamese army against the French government and left the South, my grandma was left behind. She didn't have any family except for his, and they didn't accept her.

Eventually, she left town without any money. She got on buses and bikes and walked from the South to the North, trying to find him. Because he was in a secret army, there was no way that she could find him. She didn't have an address for him, but she heard that there was a town up north where a lot of people in the secret army were.

She finally got to that town and sat down in front of a house because she was just tired. When she looked up, she saw a pair of boxers that she had made for my grandfather and thought, "I know that's my husband's. I handmade that. I embroidered his name on it. That's my husband's." So, she went inside and was told that he wasn't there. She said, "I know he's here, so I will just wait."

She then joined the army and later on ran the textile factory in our hometown. She had long hair that fell down to her ankles. Her hair was so long that my grandfather would wash it for her. A lot of my work has to do with that history of trauma and war, these acts of love, and the long hair and hair weaving—a lot of that comes from my grandmother, my mom, and my aunt.

I came here to the United States with my mom and my eighteen-year-old brother in 2003, when I was thirteen. We moved directly to New York City with six cardboard boxes. My mom restarted her life here, and my brother and I learned English here. Unbeknownst to me, my parents had already been separated for many, many years.

My mom had worked for the United Nations in Vietnam and got a job with the United Nations in the United States. She wanted my brother and me to get a better education. In Vietnam, there is only one test that you can take to get into college. Many students don't get in, which prompts a lot of depression, and there is a high suicide rate. My mom didn't want us to go through that.

We moved to Roosevelt Island, which has a high Vietnamese and UN-worker population. Many kids on the island had moved there from somewhere else and kind of grew up knowing that they might not be there forever. It was nice to be with people who knew that we were new there. However, I didn't know English at all and I went to public school. The first year of that experience wasn't the nicest experience. I couldn't understand what people were saying. I was bullied for my accent and for not being able to participate.

After finishing high school in New York, I got into the CUNY Macaulay Honors program. I got into a few other colleges that I really wanted to go to, and my mom, who was a single mother, couldn't afford any of the other schools' tuition. She asked me to go to Macaulay, which gave me free tuition and a scholarship. I was so upset at that point, thinking that I wanted the American experience of the college towns and campuses I had seen in movies. But, I'm grateful that I went to CUNY because that's where I became more aware of racial and economic justice because of the professors who I had. They taught me about the Civil Rights Movement and gave me the language to understand my identity, gave me the language to understand a lot of the context in which CUNY existed and why. That made me the person I am today. Without CUNY, I would have become a very different person.

I wanted to be an art major, but my mom said it would be very difficult, making money off art. My mom is a beautiful writer who has written books and novels, but to support the three of us, she still holds a full-time job. That's why when she asked me to major in two things, I decided to major in political science and art.

I took a class about the Civil Rights Movement in college and was surprised to learn about Asian American activism that was inspired by the fight for racial and social justice led by African Americans. Indigenous people and people with disabilities were also fighting on the front line for equal rights and equal access. There were many movements that I hadn't learned about in high school, so that class was important to my understanding of American history and my interest in American politics. That's where I learned about practices of globalization and how it fed into the economic system in Vietnam. That's also where I learned about the Vietnam War through a completely different lens than what I grew up learning. The way that I learned about it in Vietnam was, "Look at how powerful we are. We are a tiny country. We've fought the Americans—we beat the biggest, the strongest, best country in the world. Our people died for us to have this freedom."

But the US narrative was, "This country is so backward. They're communist. We tried to save them, and they didn't want to be saved. Look at that. Now we have to bomb them, so we can save them." This inconsistency triggered me to sit down with my mom, my dad, and my aunts to ask them about their lives growing up during the war. That's how I learned about my family history. Then, I reached out to the group Vietnam Veterans Against the War. The veterans were kind enough to send me their letters. They talked to me over the phone. They let me interview them. At the age of nineteen, they entrusted me with their stories.

A veteran sent me his medals and he said, "I don't want these in my life anymore. These are for you." I turned them into an art piece for a college class, where I was working a lot with performance art, video art, and Vietnamese textiles. I took a traditional gown that Vietnamese women wear and projected images from the war on them. That was my first piece of merging political context and art.

Right after I left college, I was so afraid that there wouldn't be an outlet for me to create. My mentor, who was also my professor in college, referred me to the Textile Arts Center (TAC). I went from painting 6-by-6-foot canvases to a residency at the TAC where everyone was very textiles-oriented. I was the only person there who did not know anything about textiles.

TAC took a chance on me. I used to hate knitting, I used to think it was such a bore. I hated sewing—I hated all of it. For me, everything about textiles was so practical in my own history that I couldn't understand how it couldn't be. When I got into TAC, the teachers and community there taught me how to weave. They taught me everything that I'm working on now. It was really amazing to start knitting. My mom would come to my studio and she would say, "Hey, you're knitting the American way. Here's how to knit the Continental way" or, "You're sewing the wrong way. This is how we thread the needle." That was fascinating. It was so cool to see that part of my mom.

When I go back to Vietnam—I visit often—we all sit around knitting together, and my aunts say, "Oh my God, you knit so slowly. How are you going to ever sell this? Why are you taking so long? Who would buy this? It's too wide. It's inconsistent."

That year at TAC, I spent so much time in the studio alone. I was twenty-three and I needed to figure out a lot about myself. I was going through a lot at that time, and having a space to explore that through art was wonderful. I think I was also trying to fight the textiles a little bit. In college, I had painted on canvas, which was so tough and could handle so much. Painting was sturdy because the frame was sturdy and the brushes were sturdy.

With textiles, everything is just lovely, and a lot of people at the TAC make lovely things, things that are so beautiful. And I never thought my work was beautiful in that way. My work was always rough, it was never even, it was never bright, and it was always so moody. Because I didn't know anything about textiles, I was happy to experiment with whatever. So, when I went to the hardware store and saw a roll of steel wool, I decided to spin with it. As a durational performance, I spun steel wool for seven hours every day for months to knit into a larger piece.

The steel wool was a lot about—I wouldn't say punishing myself, but probably there is part of that there out of guilt. That process was about exploring queerness and finally dealing with that and then figuring out, "Okay, what are the materials? And what way would I want to use them to say that?" When I was sixteen, I fell in love with a girl and I couldn't be honest and say that I was in love with her or say that we were together. So, every time people asked, I would just say that we were friends. She was already at the stage in her life where she was ready to come out. She was very open and she didn't want to hide it.

A lot of things were said between us that I regretted. Then after we broke up, a year later, she died from suicide. For me, for six years straight, I never said a thing. I told myself, "This is my fault. I didn't see the signs—it's my fault because I couldn't come out. This is my fault. If only I could've been honest." So, that steel wool period was very much about exploring that and then finally saying, "Okay, maybe I punished myself enough and now I can let it go."

It's the physical manifestation of that pain that I think I needed. It was a durational project, so I could count it by days and by hours, count how much I had already done, the thoughts I had as I was doing it. So it's like, "Okay, can I bottle that up? Can I just manifest it and then move on?" Of course, I did not move on because a lot of my work was still about her.

5.4 MILLION AND COUNTING PROJECT

I was working at the Center for Reproductive Rights in 2016 when the Supreme Court heard arguments for and decided on *Whole Health Health v. Hellerstedt*. In 2013, Texas legislators had passed HB2, a sweeping measure that imposed numerous restrictions that could shut down nearly all abortion clinics in the state and prevent 5.4 million women of reproductive age[*] from accessing the health care they need. The Center for Reproductive Rights filed a lawsuit on April 2, 2014, challenging the ambulatory surgical center and admitting privileges requirements.

At the Center for Reproductive Rights, we were doing a campaign around the case called "Draw the Line." In digital campaigns, we sometimes ask people to share a graphic or message online, but I wanted to have a different way for people to participate. I thought about how some people were very afraid to

---

[*] Chi writes: "I believe the average 'reproductive age' is considered between twelve until late fifties. We were thinking of reproductive age in many different ways, like assistive technology when it comes to giving birth. That was part of our account. One thing about this experience that I always regret, it's very women-centric and the language doesn't include transgender and gender nonbinary people."

put their names on a petition or be out and loud about abortion access. And, I knew that I had a community of people who can draw lots of lines but in a different way.

I said to my team at that time, "You know, I think we can get 5.4 million lines embroidered." When I first suggested this project, some people were doubtful that it could be done, so I approached the TAC and they were like, "Yeah, you know what? Let's try it." We put out the call on Instagram, we created a web page for the project, and we asked people to embroider swatches with each line representing one in the 5.4 million people whose reproductive care was at risk. We asked people to host stitch-ins at their homes and public spaces.

I'm very involved in community organizing around reproductive justice. One thing that we always talk about in community organizing is how to build movements that can be mobilized outside of us. If the movement ends with us, then we have not done our job. I was committed to sending people fabric or embroidery materials if they couldn't afford it, so I created tool kits containing these items. I wanted to make sure that everything would be free for people to participate. If people couldn't ship their swatches to us, I would send them the stamps.

I wanted to get rid of any kinds of barriers to participating in the project. It started with an Instagram post and a website, and then it grew and it grew and it grew and it grew. We were hosting a lot of stitch-ins, and then all of a sudden, more people were asking about hosting their own stitch-ins. It was incredible. It was an amazing feeling to all of a sudden see the textile community on Instagram rally behind the project, and people started posting photos of it. We started getting so many envelopes that the mail delivery person was like, "I don't know what you're doing here."

Every day, there were buckets of embroidered fabric sent to the TAC. It was an amazing feeling on the day before we went to the Supreme Court the first time. We had to ask volunteers to come into the TAC to help us sew the embroidered fabric into a quilt because we had received so many of them. We sewed for fifteen hours straight.

At 3:00 a.m., the morning we were leaving for Washington, DC, Kelly, who is now the CEO and director of TAC, and I were like, "Oh my God, this is exciting. We are done." Then we lifted up the quilt—it had been sewn by accident into an L-shape instead of a flat shape. I thought, "Oh my God, it is 3:00 a.m.—we have to hit the road at 6:00 a.m. I'm so exhausted." But, we made it. I think we literally stuffed the quilt into the car and left.

ON "CRAFTIVISM"

If you look online, craft looks very white. The group of crafters I know do not look like the group of advocates I know. When I'm doing political organizing, the people who show up are mostly people of color. However, if I'm doing craft or art as political organizing, the reverse is true. I believe that this is both a reflection on me to make sure that my work is as inclusive and accessible as possible—and a reflection on the barriers that exist in the craft and art world.

With 5.4 Million, I really wanted to do stitch-ins in different neighborhoods in Brooklyn and Queens. I wanted to go to Philly. I wanted to make sure that we provide all the materials, so every community can be a part of this quilt.

A lot of the time when I'm asked to speak, I'm asked to speak on art as activism and that's where I try to bring in history and say, "Hey, people of color have been doing this for a very long time." If a person with disabilities creates craft, it should not be looked at as, "Oh, how nice. This is for their mental health." This is more than that. We need to look at their work as art pieces that they've created." So, I do get to use my platform in that way, but usually, I'm speaking to a very white group of listeners.

ON THE SUSTAINABLE FASHION MOVEMENT

I think the whole conversation about sustainability and textiles is not very nuanced yet. It's very much, "Oh, this country is making it. It's automatically bad." Being from Vietnam and knowing a lot of people in production in Vietnam influences the way I look at sustainability.

Organizing around reproductive justice, disability rights, and immigrants' rights has taught me that we cannot build a sustainable future without creating a foundation for marginalized communities to continue to survive and thrive. In our current model of sustainable fashion, can a factory worker afford the final product, a shirt, or jacket that they spend time making at market price? Who is behind sewing sustainable fashion and who gets to wear sustainable fashion?

With visible mending, it can be read as expensive or low-income based on a person's skin tone or the kind of job they have, due to unconscious bias. We need to actively address racial inequality and economic disparity more pointedly within the sustainability movement.

I've thought about writing a piece on the sustainable fashion movement, but I need more time and research to better understand and verbalize what it is that I'm uncomfortable with in regards to the movement.

WHAT ARE YOU MAKING NOW?

1760 hand-embroidered Robe à la Française.—TANYA HUGHES

I am currently repairing my nephew's thirty-year-old cloth doll so that he can give it to his newborn daughter. I've also created a pair of black and white stockings and two dresses for the doll plus a sweet little outfit for the baby made from leftover fabric from some of my handmade garments.—LISA WILLIAMS

So many things: a scarf, a throw, a poncho, a sweater, and a pair of socks all currently in various states of completion. A couple of pillows and a bedspread are beginning to form in my mind!—CHARNITA BELCHER

SURVEY PROFILE

Virginia Johnson

Age: 45
Location: Cambridge, Massachusetts
Profession: Costume designer for film, and owner of gather here, a craft store

What types of fiber crafts do you engage in, and how many years have you been engaged in each?
Sewing (40 years), knitting (39 years), quilting (40 years), embroidery (40 years).

How do you self-describe/identify yourself?
I am a maker of things. Through making things, I craft visual stories, be they on the screen or on my own body.

What's your favorite thing you've made?
My prom dress, followed by my daily uniforms of button-up shirts.

How and why did you learn your crafts?
My paternal grandmother, Nita, taught me so I could be useful and we could share in her expertise. She didn't have any daughters and had taught my father to hand-sew, but she had been raised with two sisters and craved sharing her love of fiber art. I became a costume designer because I didn't want to be a doctor. And, I loved reading scripts and being a part of the theater. I didn't even know it was a job until I was in college. I had a job in the costume shop, stitching, and this really opened up the profession to me.

Does anyone in your family practice this craft, too? Are your pieces similar or different aesthetically?
My mother sewed when we were children, mostly clothes and curtains. And, she used to crochet totally crazy doilies that she stiffened in starch, like sea creatures. She also created massive embroidered pieces with pineapple cloth

and velvet. There was a giant bull fighter in our living room my entire child-hood that she had made. My sister sews for her son and her wife is an avid knitter—we both knit socks.

Tell me about your creative community. You can define "community" as broadly or as specifically as you'd like.
I opened up a craft store because I missed having a creative community beyond my film community. In film, many of the crew think of it as "a job." And it can feel that way. I only had a handful of friends who wanted to make things outside of work. When I traveled to other locations, I always sought out a yarn store or a fabric studio where I could check out what other folx were making. Oddly, I never clicked with a shop in Greater Boston. And honestly, even after opening my store, I don't have a ton of interaction with area yarn store owners—I have been made to feel like an outsider, an other. When we first opened, we were excluded because gather here was not "established" and I wasn't "serious." Then, it was that we weren't on a train stop. And then, it just got awkward—perhaps it was because I was younger. Or not white enough. So, opening gather here has meant meeting other crafters that look more like me. That's been awesome because I have made real friends. And, I don't think it's a coincidence that two of our other instructors are Latina, that our book club leader is Native American, our machine technician is Haitian American, and that we have four queer employees. We are still located in a primarily white, upper-middle-class neighborhood, but we reach beyond the neighborhood to spread our message of inclusion.

When have you felt like an "other" within the context of your craft?
Well, I'm from a tropical country, so people don't understand that I knit and crochet. My Filipina grandmother, Christina, was in love with crocheted lace. Because the people who come to gather here are primarily white, they don't expect to hear that craft is part of other cultures too. Same with quilting. And, as someone who is highly educated, I've noticed those specific communities also don't "get" that making my own clothes is part of me using that education.

When do you feel recognized in your craft? Who recognizes you and how does that feel for you?
Well, the first quilt show I organized for Squam. I organized a show and

reached out to some really "famous" quilt designers and artists to see if they would loan a piece of work to the show. And everyone said yes. Everyone acted like they knew me, they appreciated me, and they wanted to be in a community and a space *with* me. I guess that was a moment where I felt like I had made some kind of mark. I get notes sometimes from other women of color that see me. And know that I see them. That is important to me.

Do you engage in these crafts for income or as a hobby?
Oh, it's my *job*.

If you sell your pieces, who are your customers? How long have you been selling your work? Do you employ other people to help you create your work? What challenges have you faced in building your creative business?
As a costume designer, I'm contracted per project. Sometimes, the pay is ridiculous and I'm overwhelmed with how lucky I am. Owning the store, everything I make now is part of the store—it's literally advertising. If I make a shirt, I can then sell the pattern, the fabric, and the workshop.

Do you exhibit your work? If so, where? Tell me about those experiences.
I have exhibited my quilts in shows. I often choose the most "traditional" fabrics and motifs, which I think is surprising for people when they learn that it's made by me.

Do you have an artist statement or any principles that guide your work?
Sustainability, Accountability, Affordability. I do not want craft to be only accessible to the wealthy and the elite. I also want it to be meaningful and to be created for a lifetime of use and enjoyment. And, I want what I make and what I carry to be held to the highest standards. "We Are What We Make."

When you were younger, were you exposed to other people who looked like you, or who were from similar backgrounds as you, and who engaged in this craft?
The weird thing for me is that the nannies and the cleaning ladies at our home in the Philippines did crafts. But, the wives of my uncles were more interested

in magazines and shopping. Same with the navy base. I don't remember other aunties crocheting or sewing. But I do know my Lola sewed and crocheted.

Who do you look to for inspiration today?
Michelle Obama and Jenny Han.

What colors are you drawn to and why?
I love *all* colors. I used to just love red. But now, I use them all in every way I can. I have to be careful not to look like Punky Brewster. As a visual storyteller, I'm painting with textiles, silhouettes, and colors. It's hard to pick just one.

Where do you get your materials?
From my shop. Gather here strives to support creatives and distributors who are committed to issues that we believe are paramount to the survival of textile arts—racial justice, climate change, gender equity. So, I feel pretty good about what we carry and what I use.

Are there aspects of your work that you feel are misunderstood?
I think there are moments when I feel like maybe the greater population doesn't grasp that I'm actually really angry about discrimination and the craft industry. My "You Belong Here" project wasn't made to make people feel better—it was a rallying cry, a scream—that we see you, we stand with you, and we will not let you fight alone.

ART MADE ON AND
BETWEEN BORDERS

Interview with Tanya Aguiñiga

JEN HEWETT: You crossed the border between Mexico and the United States every day for fourteen years during your childhood. Why?

TANYA AGUIÑIGA: My parents didn't have a babysitter, and my grandma had moved to the United States. Because my dad worked in the United States, he would just drop me off [at my grandma's house] on his way to work, and then I enrolled in a school by my grandma's house. Then, I just kept trying to figure out how I could stay in school in the United States, first using my grandma's address and then, when my grandma passed away, using my different aunts' addresses.

When my aunts got tired of my parents not taking care of me, or my parents not giving whoever I was staying with enough money for my breakfast, for taking care of me, then I would have to find another place to stay. From an early age, I learned to hustle adults so that they would provide me safety.

I ended up staying with best friends, best friends' grandmothers, and other random people. It was a really weird, very nomadic childhood that was constantly overshadowed by fear. Because I was always in public school, I couldn't tell anybody that I lived in Mexico because I would get kicked out of school because I didn't live in the district. So, I couldn't make close friendships. I had a couple of friends, but it wasn't until I was in high school that I was able to be out about the way that I'd lived.

A lot of that was because I also didn't have a phone. In Mexico at the time, in the eighties, it was really difficult to get a landline. Even if I trusted someone enough to share my experiences, I couldn't talk to them after school. They obviously couldn't visit my house. It was a really different way of growing up than what US kids experience.

I have a five-year-old now, and when she had her first playdate, I was crying because I realized, "Oh my God, this is revolutionary for my family line."

To be able to even have somebody visit your house and it's your actual house, you know? To even be able to call your friends, I could never do anything like that. So yes, it was a strange way to be a part of two societies. At night, I would come home to Mexico. I had friends in Mexico, but my school experiences were so different than theirs.

JH: What was crossing the border itself like?

TA: Pretty horrible. I think people tend to exoticize the experience, saying, "That's fascinating. You must've loved getting to experience two cultures." I respond, "It kind of sucked." It takes a long time to cross the border. If you're lucky, maybe you'll get across in an hour. But most of the time, it takes more than two hours. On the weekends, it can take up to six hours. [The border crossing] is a space that's really weird because everybody's defensive. You have a duty to protect your space so that nobody cuts in line. Everyone's super pissed off because they're in their cars. If you have an older car, you're constantly scared that your car's going to break down or overheat. You can't get out of your car, especially if you're by yourself, to, say, go to the bathroom. You're kind of just trapped.

Nobody talks about the experience of actually crossing the border, which is always difficult because nobody knows what the rules are and what the Border Patrol has jurisdiction over. But the Border Patrol itself also doesn't know. The way that you get treated varies all the time, but most of the time, you're interrogated every time you cross.

I was lucky that I'm a US citizen, so they couldn't deny me entry. But every time you cross, you're scared that you're doing something wrong, so you say that you went to Mexico to do something random. "Oh, we went to do laundry. Oh, we went to visit family. Oh, we went to go shopping. Oh, we went to . . . " whatever other random reason my mom could come up with. Every day, we told a different story about why we were crossing. My mom had a green card, so she actually had reason to be scared of getting her green card taken away. So, it just makes you really scared all the time.

You don't speak unless you're spoken to. You can't advance to talk to the Border Control agents unless they wave you over. Otherwise, you get in trouble. You're constantly afraid of being detained, being searched, or being sent to secondary. It's a stressful experience, and nobody talks about the stigma of living in Mexico. Nobody talks about the hardships of enduring this every single day. "Why would we have to do this every single day?" Because there's not a lot of economic opportunity in Mexico that allows for people to have the same type of living that they can have if they earn US dollars.

Nobody talks about the fact that everybody crossing the border is at work on the US side but lives in Mexico, is paying taxes to the US government but not benefiting from any of those services that taxes provide. You're not an active participant really on either side [of the border]. You're just kind of constantly living under the radar. You're constantly living in a liminal space.

JH: You talk about liminal space a lot in your work, and the border of the liminal space as well. Your project, the AMBOS (Art Made Between Opposite Sides) Project, addresses this idea of liminal space. Tell me about the project.

TA: I had done work with the Border Art Workshop in the nineties, so I had already done a lot of work on the border and had seen what community-based art on the border can do. I already had a framework for how I wanted to engage the community. So in the beginning, I focused just on the community of transnational people, the people that go back and forth between the United States and Mexico. I thought about how much that impacted my life and my parents' life. I wanted to check in with the transnational community people and ask them how they're feeling with all the political rhetoric that was going around about Mexicans being rapists and drug dealers. Originally, I just wanted to make sure everyone was okay by talking to them individually.

In the first year of the project, the AMBOS Project rented a stall at the border crossing in this little triangle of vendors that has been at the border crossing since the eighties. It's the only area of any border crossing in Mexico that has private space. That area was going to be demolished, so I wanted to be able to use it while it was still there, as a space to have different types of programming. Then, I collaborated with artists from San Diego, Los Angeles, and Tijuana to do activations at the border.

The activations would get us to think more about our transition into the United States, or our roles in both societies. I collaborated with radio artists, sound artists, photographers, and filmmakers. The project engaged the community in a multisensory experience. We had a film series that was projected on one of the billboards at the market. People could tune in on a private radio station and hear the audio that accompanied the films. It was like a drive-in theater. The films showed different macro and micro issues of borders around the world, then it narrowed in on the San Ysidro border crossing.

In the beginning, I was just thinking about how to activate the space in that community. I didn't really think of it as going beyond that, mainly because of funding. I had written grants for four years and couldn't get any funding. It was also before the 2016 presidential election. So, I just wanted to capture this one moment in time, thinking the election wasn't going to go the way it did. Then when the election went the way it did, I thought, "I need to do this for the rest of the border."

I went from a myopic perspective, from engaging only the transnationals, and that stemmed from the knowledge that a lot of us are US citizens—taxpayers, people who are a part of civil society in the United States but whose opinions and experiences are ignored because of biases. That first year, I was thinking of it from a perspective of how can the United States see our experience and how can we become more engaged in the experience of being a US citizen.

But after that first year, I realized we also needed to include people who had been deported, people who are affected by larger issues of migration. We need to include people who are like all the migrants who are still trying to cross, all the migrants who have crossed, all the migrants who are stuck in Mexico who were a part of the United States for a long time.

Then as the years went on, as the political situation changed with every trip, the scope of the project was widened. This last year, we worked a lot with the migrant caravans, the racism that exists within Mexico against migrants from other countries, how a lot of the ways that Mexicans get treated by the United States, and how Mexicans then treat other migrants the same way. It's been this crazy, eye-opening experience that's taken a lot of difficult emotional labor on behalf of myself and my teammates.

Every person who's part of the AMBOS team also had a really specific connection to identity, politics, or issues of migration. We didn't know until we started going on the road the first time that one of our team members had walked from Guatemala to the United States alone when she was seventeen to be reunited with her mom, who had left her and her brother in Guatemala when she was two, so that she could work in the United States to get enough money to pay for her brother's medical care. So, a lot of things would keep resurfacing as we would go on the road to these different sites, and each of us connected to the sites in really different ways. It was three years of three people doing full-time work, researching, coordinating, and planning everything out. I think it required five different grants over three years.

Having worked on the border since the nineties, I knew that the way to understand this space is to not understand it through our own lens but to be guided through the different issues in each community by people that are from the community so that we're not imposing our own views onto it. All these liaisons were artists who we developed relationships with so that we could have safe passage into their towns and be shown what the issues are in the town. What the art is that's made in the towns, what are the issues that the art is bringing up, and to see if there was any dialogue between both sides, on either side of the border to see . . . how artists navigate their own border issues regionally.

JH: Logistically, I just can't even think that through, but I suppose if you were a person who grew up having to deal with the logistics of your own life from a very, very early age, maybe this is just a natural outcropping. Taking it back to your childhood though, were you always this creative?

TA: I was, and I just didn't know. I think it's one of those things where unless you see yourself mirrored in positions of power, you don't know that it's an option for you. And then socioeconomically, knowing how hard my parents had to work, all the different jobs they had to do, everything they sacrificed to provide us with the life we had in Mexico. I also had a lot of class guilt behind allowing myself to be an artist. So even though I was always artistic, I was always super entrepreneurial, as a lot of people in Mexico are.

You know, you just kind of figure out, "I need money. Oh okay, I'm going to make a bunch of quesadillas, sit outside, and see if I can sell them to make money to buy candy." You know? Constantly like, "All right, what do I need?" It's how a lot of systems work in Mexico, it's really analog. You don't have a prescribed path for getting to anywhere. You have to ask a lot of people questions, be self-motivated, be ready to experiment and fail, and not let it get you down.

So, I was always creative. I just never knew that I would be making art a career.

JH: Tell me more about the class guilt. Tell me about how that played out in your own life. You are an artist. How did that happen?

TA: I was never formally exposed to art. My dad would take me to the swap meet and sometimes to car shows. My exposure to art started with looking at low riders and car culture. Then, through going to check out stuff like that, I was exposed to murals. Then, we were introduced to Mexican muralism and ideas about socialism and revolution.

I worked through high school at a Hispanic marketing research firm, and I was a project manager by the time I was sixteen. I was in a situation where I was severely sexually harassed. I was locked in a room while a dude pulled his pants down. But, I didn't want to speak out about the sexual harassment because my aunts worked there and I knew that one of my aunts had a hard time getting jobs because of her skin color, her height, and her weight. I knew I could get further than she could—because I'm white-passing, because I had an education, because I could speak English without that much of an accent, stuff like that.

I didn't want to complain because I didn't want my aunts to lose their jobs. When I finally complained, I was let go, but I didn't know what to do next. I didn't have money to take the SAT. I was in all AP classes, but I didn't have money to take that AP test. My college path was different than people who are . . . "American."

I thought, "Well, I've always liked art. Maybe I'll go to an art museum and apply for a job." I went to an art museum and I applied for a job, and then two hours later they hired me. So, that was my first experience with formal art, working at this art museum and spending time in different galleries. I then fell in love with Josef Albers's work and Robert Irwin's, all these different people. Then I thought, "Oh, maybe I should try to study art." In community college, I started taking some art classes, and then through them, met my mentor Michael Schnorr, who was one of the founding members of the Border Art Workshop. I started talking to him about crossing the border every day and my experience with having to constantly experience seeing thousands of migrants, mainly men, risking their lives to jump over the fence, constantly dying on the road that my dad and I would traverse every morning.

So, he brought me onto the Border Art Workshop, and I started working heavily on migrant rights, specifically using art as a way to bring attention to Operation Gatekeeper, which was the strategic reinforcement of the border. I grew up a few blocks away from the border fence, so that also had a lot to do with how I saw the border.

Through meeting this one professor, I started getting more involved in art . . . I had never painted before until he gave me some paintbrushes and some random paint. I was like, "All right, I'm going to start trying to paint." He showed me, "Oh, this is how you hold a drill. This is how you hold a hammer." I didn't know any of that stuff. So, through trial and error, through building a community center with him, and doing arts programming in this community, that's how I got my start in art. It was through one amazing professor.

Oh. I just remembered what your original question was.

JH: I don't even remember what it was.

TA: It was about class guilt.

So, my family and I didn't think that I was going to ever make a career out of art, but then through the projects that I was doing with the Border Art Workshop, I was able to travel to Mexico City—I think I was nineteen at the time—and do this massive installation against Operation Gatekeeper in the Zócalo* across from the Presidential Palace. At the time—I don't remember if it was during the first or the second installation that I had done in Mexico City—Pope John Paul II was visiting Mexico. I was on the list of people for him to meet, so that was what made my family okay with me doing art. They were like, "If the pope's cool with you, we're cool with you."

They were like, "I don't know if you're going to make any money off this, but that's cool. That's nice that you're actually doing stuff." You know? Help our community. Once I started traveling and getting more attention, they saw that money isn't always—shouldn't always be—the goal. Being a good person has value, too. Then everybody was like, "Okay, that's fine. She's doing her then."

I felt like I had to do functional art and focus on things that were real-life skills, education-wise. Otherwise, it was like a slap in the face to all the generations of hardworking people who helped get me to the right opportunity.

JH: One of the reasons I wanted to talk to you, and I think this probably plays into your background too, is just that you don't deride craft at all in your art

---

* Zócalo, meaning *base*, is the common name of Mexico City's Plaza de la Constitucíon, the main public square in the city center.

practice, where a lot of artists are like, "Nope, not craft." You allow both to exist within the context of your work.

TA: When I started taking classes in craft-based techniques, from the beginning I understood that it [craft] was a really important part of maintaining tradition. Culturally, we have so many ties to materials, way beyond anything that we can understand, because I truly feel like some of the stuff is intuitive because it's been passed on through generations. For me, it's about connecting to a different consciousness. The more I traveled and the more I learned different techniques and things about different materials, the more I fell in love with how craft-based materials give so many people an entry into thinking about larger issues.

For me, it's been this really beautiful, democratizing way of working. I've managed to figure out what I like working with because craft allows me the flexibility of working without tools, working without electricity, working without water, working with everyone from children to elderly people. Working across different genders. I connect with so many of the different processes that craft covers because it doesn't have to go by Western ideals of what success is or higher education and stuff like that. You know? Craft is just a really beautiful way of breaking down hierarchies and making space for everyone to participate.

JH: I love that. Why textiles? You work with a lot of fiber in your practice.

TA: For me, fiber is such a gendered thing, and especially in the United States, it feels like such a gendered thing. I mean, in other places it's not so much. In different parts of Mexico, the weavers are men. In India, there's a bunch of amazing men who are silk weavers. But for me, it has a really beautiful connection to the domestics sphere here and offers a way for me to infiltrate those ideas and expand on how we can carve out our interior spaces, and how we can be more subversive with cloth and things that we wear every single day.

With the AMBOS Project, I wanted to do something that was fiber-based because I knew that everybody has a connection to fiber because we wear it every day. But, it's something that's so connected to labor that people don't usually think about. Working with fiber was a really good way to start, but then it also gave me options to think about decolonizing that practice and going back further and further to find some type of common denominator that could be a start for children all the way to the elderly.

The whole project was just asking people to make a knot. At first, participants were like, "I don't know how to do this." You know? I'm like, "Dude, you tied your shoelaces this morning. You know how to make a knot."

We asked people to make a symbolic knot of their experience on the border, so then people could start to think about that experience a little bit more. The project was based on the quipu. It was a way for us to also visualize our experience and visualize our connection to one another as a community.

JH: Explain the quipu. It's a counting system, right?

TA: Yeah, it's a counting system. It's an organizational system of knots. It looks like an abacus with a lot of knots that are all connected to one main horizontal string. People don't know exactly what they were for—if it was a calendar, if it was like a language, if it was like a counting system.

JH: What's next?

TA: Right now, we're doing a project at the New Children's Museum project and then the next really big thing that's coming up is I have a big solo show at the Armory in Pasadena, which is going to include a lot of more performance-

---

When you have a good community around you, and you know that there are a lot of incredible people willing to help, and they just need a place to put some of their energy, it makes it easier to get involved and to give people an opportunity to be involved.

---

based stuff. And, just working through what happened in the AMBOS Project. A lot of the work at the show will be glass. It's interesting to keep playing with different craft-based media and to see what the possibilities are of the different materials.

JH: You are so busy, I don't know how you do it all, and you have a child.

TA: It's crazy. There are three of us in the studio, but it's hard not to get involved in everything. I just heard on NPR that they're shipping a bunch of people from Texas to San Diego. A bunch of asylum seekers. I have to also figure out when they're coming and how we can get involved. So, you know, there's plenty of stuff to do.

JH: The work never ends, does it?

TA: No. But here's the thing—when you have a good community around you, and you know that there are a lot of incredible people willing to help, and they just need a place to put some of their energy, it makes it easier to get involved and to give people an opportunity to be involved.

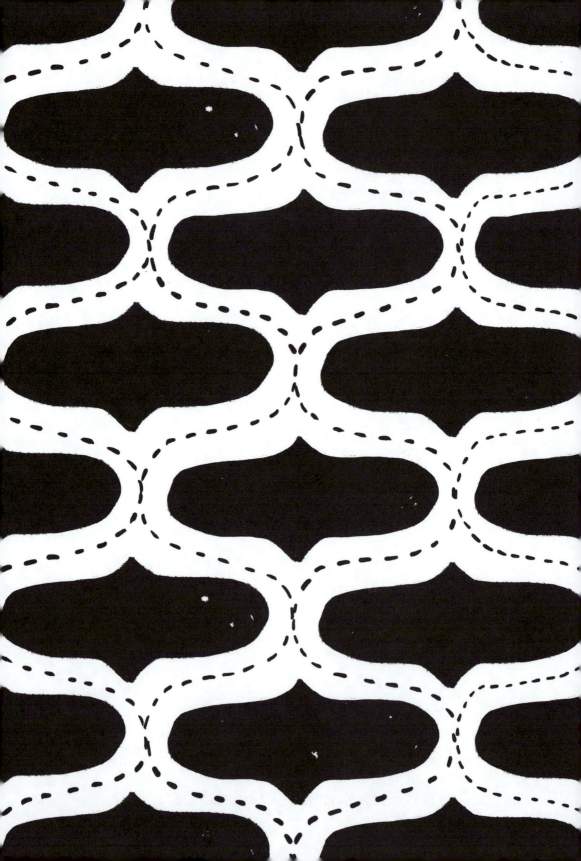

Handmade Past
and Present

< Seema Krish's ogee pattern

BRAIDING THE SWEETGRASS

Essay by Jenna Ruth Empanayv
("One Who Tells the Story" in Creek) Wolf

FOR AS LONG as I can remember, my grandmother Geraldine worked with her hands; shelling nut meats from the pecan trees behind the farm she was raised on, rolling red clay that dots the landscape of eastern Oklahoma into ornamental items until it dyed her nails deep orange, and honing pieces of turquoise to create wonky, silver rings in attempts at jewelry making. And of course, drying and braiding the sacred sweetgrass for ceremony and restoration.

Whenever I visited her as a child, I studied her hands. "Do mine look like hers?" I'd contemplate.

Her hands are delicate, but used. They are well cared for despite all that work. She is deeply satisfied with what those hands can produce and therefore treats them with utmost care, constantly trimming and filing her nails, rubbing oils and creams into the creases of her skin.

"Would mine one day hold the history hers do and still look that good?" I'd hope as I cataloged the detailed turquoise rings that were her fingers' constant companions, even as her joints began to bend in advanced age.

One holiday season when I was small, she took me on an adventure to collect red clay. We meandered along the dusty, desolate roads near Dustin, Oklahoma, clawing our fingers through the roadside dirt, scooping up and storing piles of clay. "Dig harder, get your hands into it," she demanded smoothly, as we repeatedly bent down to collect the riches of a landscape afforded us through the Dawes Act of 1887, which broke up tribal land and parceled it to Muscogee Creek families willing to adopt European American style subsistence farming and forms of property ownership.

The controversial act essentially forced my ancestors, who managed to survive relocation from southeast Georgia during the Trail of Tears, to register with the federal government and quantify their "Indian Blood" to receive land. As Oklahoma neared statehood at the turn of the twentieth century, the Creek tribe lost more than two million acres of land to white settlers and the US government as part of the Dawes Commission.

As we walked those roads collecting clay, I was reminded of the sacrifices my family made to create a life they could be proud of in Oklahoma, a land that wasn't ancestrally home. But, my grandma taught me how her family made it home, cherished it, nurtured it, and used the land to create, molding the red clay for useful items and nourishing themselves through their resourcefulness.

Later, in the farmhouse kitchen that smelled of leaky propane that my grandmother called home as a child, we created a sliver of space on the counter to roll out thin sheet after thin sheet of clay. We centered the space with a burning of sweetgrass that my grandmother dried and braided. On that day, we created tree ornaments for our extended family; small Christmas stockings, sacred turtles, stars, and snowflakes that glistened after we fired them in her oven. She gave me a delicate wooden pick to carve my name in each ornament.

"You'll want everyone to know you made these by hand, Jenna Ruth," she told me, her voice liquid, an emphasis on lengthening certain words anyone with a Native grandmother would recognize. "Uhhuh, like that," she said as she guided me.

I remember never wanting to clean my hands. To keep that reddened, hardening clay under my nails for as long as possible; a reminder of what we created, together.

As a child, I wanted so desperately to feel close to my grandmother; distance was the largest chasm between us. At the same age, I had been contemplating all the details of Grandma's hands and the work they had seen through the years. She was sent off to Chilocco Indian Agricultural School in north central Oklahoma. She was a young girl about to live away from the farm for the first time. It was here she learned to work with her hands in new ways: tailoring, ironing, laundering, and other assorted domestic duties.

Chilocco was one of the five non-reservation boarding schools established by Congress in 1882 to "civilize" and "Americanize" Native children. Just three years prior, Captain Richard H. Pratt delivered a speech that would be central to the creation of these boarding schools when he said, "The only good Indian is a dead one . . . all the Indian there is in the race should be dead. Kill the Indian in him, and save the man."[*]

---

[*] Richard H. Pratt, "The Advantages of Mingling Indians with Whites," in *Americanizing the American Indians: Writings by the "Friends of the Indian" 1880–1900*, ed. Francis Paul Prucha (Cambridge, MA.: Harvard University Press, 1973), 260–71.

This is how America has seen, throughout history, my fellow Indigenous people. My grandmother Geraldine. The countless other Native grandmothers who have created some of the finest art with clay, fiber, natural dyes, and other gifts from our landscape. And in this gaze, what has emerged is a long-standing belief that Indigenous people no longer exist—that we are in the past, long gone.

This collective consciousness has a way of braiding itself through every aspect of the making traditions today. Non-Native crafters, who have been systematically taught that Indigenous communities are no longer thriving, tend to make through this lens; their appropriated work is presented as a new discovery, with their experiences at the center, negating the existence of those originally tied to the processes, skills, and even the land itself. What is often produced is work that romanticizes and appropriates Indigenous design, eliminating the need to see, recognize, and appreciate work produced by Native people—work that continues today.

Our making traditions are often warped to particular trends. The past decade of crafted creations has sniffed of Indigenous origins—woven wall hangings with vaguely Native-inspired geometric designs. Hand-stitched sachets to protect smudging sage. A major crafting house publishing a cross-stitch pillow kit called the "Idaho" featuring a Diné (Navajo) Yébichai, using its likeness for profit without the permission of the Diné people or an understanding of its meaning within the Diné universe.* What's more, pattern collections inspired by the places most sacred to Indigenous peoples fail to mention the original inhabitants—then and now—and how Native people have ultimately influenced their color palettes and designs.

As these trends continue to take shape unchecked, their celebration in the crafting community causes deep harm to the communities who not only hold these ideas sacred but who also often rely on their designs and creative outputs as a source of livelihood. In a world where crafters and artists can easily expose audiences to their work, Indigenous artists are experiencing deeper isolation and ignorance of their work. Non-Native makers creating crafts that blatantly rip off Native designs have access to a wide audience;

---

* The author expresses that the meaning of the Yébichai to the Diné people is theirs and theirs alone. It is not defined here nor should it be used as a symbol or aesthetic by and for any non-Diné audience.

their work tends to be more palatable to white audiences simply because it conveniently celebrates the artistry without actually having to celebrate and include Indigenous creators.

Recognition opposes erasure. But, to acknowledge the work of my fellow Indigenous makers would mean a reckoning with what has happened here—and continues to happen here—to Black and brown bodies on this "free" land.

As my grandmother Geraldine focuses on drying and braiding the stalks of sweetgrass, she tells stories of the riches of what it means to be Indigenous: the pride of creating something through your own sweat and hard work, and how to use and understand the land around oneself not only as a tool but also as inspiration.

Each year at Christmas, I reminisce on this time with my grandmother as I place each of those red clay ornaments on my own tree in a far-flung city, a reminder of family, time, and place. A reminder of why I continue to make things, to consider history, culture, landscape, the sacred way, and to ultimately make it my own, too. Because that's how we grow and shape the future.

When our elders walk on, we younger Indigenous creators are tasked not only with teaching the next generation as we have been taught but also with reminding this country that we still exist. It is of utmost importance to our continued creation, evolution, and recognition. And, it is ultimately for our survival as a people—we are still here, humbly and mightily, in large part because of what our grandmothers have taught us.

SURVEY PROFILE

Soukprida Phetmisy

Age: 30
Location: Chicago, Illinois

What types of fiber crafts do you engage in, and how many years have you been engaged in each?
Sewing: I've had an on-off relationship with sewing since I was around twelve or thirteen; I have been sewing steadily for the last four years. Knitting/crocheting: about two years in now

How do you self-describe/identify yourself?
Asian American/Southeast Asian American (specifically of Laotian and Vietnamese heritage; LaoViet), bisexual cis-womxn, US-born citizen to Lao-Vietnamese immigrant-refugees who has benefited from settling on stolen Native and Indigenous land and is temporarily able-bodied, a first-generation college graduate (Savannah College of Art and Design alumna), caretaker, coming from a low-income background/presently middle class, sister, auntie, and daughter.

What's the first thing you remember making?
An "Ugly Doll" knockoff back in the early 2000s. I remember my mom trying to teach me to make something useful, like a pair of socks or maybe shorts, but what I remember actually making for the first time—like, an actual completed project—was a version of an "Ugly Doll." I remember intentionally not asking my mom to buy me one, even though I wanted it so badly. I could tell she thought it was a frivolous purchase, so I decided to just make a knockoff and felt so proud of it. I made it out of felt and a pair of my dad's old boxer shorts that were ripped up. I don't think I have it anymore.

What are you making now?
My own clothes! My big projects this year included a coat and a pair of wide-

leg pants. I finally got over my fear of making jeans and have made three pairs already. Being able to make clothes that fit my body shape has been so fulfilling. Given the push toward more inclusive sizing in the indie-pattern community, I actually feel more confident in being able to dive in and make things that weren't options for me before (like pants, actually). Being afraid of making pants was more about my internalized fatphobia than it was about being afraid of learning how to do a "full tummy" or "knock-knee" adjustment. I had learned through all the messaging I got (unrealistic "beauty standards," mostly) that needing a "full tummy" adjustment was a bad thing, when actually that wasn't true. I had internalized this idea that I had to be a certain size to make certain types of clothes. I don't think I would have realized that and begun to unlearn it if I hadn't found more folx in the community who were talking about body image, inclusivity in sizing, and the like, who had similar body shapes to mine and were owning it.

What's your favorite thing you've made?

My Sapporo coat, a pattern by Papercut Patterns. I really took my time with this coat and it is the first coat I've ever made. I wanted it to be something that would turn into a staple in my wardrobe (as part of my capsule wardrobe project) and also something I would be able to hand down/pass on to future generations. I own a few of my mom's clothes that she made herself—many are traditional Lao dress—and I've always kept them close to remind me of her. This coat was the first item I made with the intention of carrying on the tradition of passing down a beloved garment and giving it new life. This is why it's my favorite handmade item thus far.

How and why did you learn your crafts?

My mom always had a sewing machine around, and I think I picked up the talent from her. She used to tell me this story about how she would be able to knit a pair of socks in under an hour because of the sheer pressure of having to make these socks for soldiers fighting during the Secret War in Laos. It made me think about crafting in a completely different way.

When I started making clothes for myself, I wanted to do it for a couple of reasons. I'd always felt the itch to make/create, and I think this comes from my mom's value of being someone who used her creativity in very tactful ways (making socks for soldiers, for example). I saw her using her hands a lot when I was growing up, and she was always able to make something out of nothing just using those hands. I think that instilled a sense of determination and creativity in me.

The other reason making and craft feels salient to me right now is the relationship I was able to cultivate and nurture with my body. It had started to change shape over the last couple of years and I was starting to find myself not being able to engage with ready-to-wear clothing because nothing fit right. It made shopping stressful. At the same time, I had so many visions in my brain about things I wanted to wear—full-on outfits—visions of how I wanted to present myself in terms of my identity to others. So, the combination of not being able to find an item that spoke to me, fit me right in ready-to-wear options, and matched what I envisioned pushed me to start sewing more intentionally and regularly and to also start asking myself, "How do I want to show up in the world?" I watched a lot of videos and tutorials, got involved in the sewing/making community on Instagram, and started pushing myself to bring this skill back into my daily practice.

Tell me about your creative community. You can define "community" as broadly or as specifically as you'd like.
I've been seeking more of a community virtually, especially a community that looks like me—looking for more representation (Asian American, Lao, queer, not "straight-sized," for example) because right now, my creative community feels pretty small and pretty white. In Chicago, I've got a lot of folx within my circles who are creative (acting, visual arts, broadcasting, musicians, etc.) and I tend to draw inspiration from them when I think about what a creative community is.

When have you felt like an "other" within the context of your craft?
Many times, actually. A lot of times it's mostly when I am online and trying to engage with virtual communities, like on Instagram, where I've felt little to no representation. It takes a bit of effort on my end to find makers who look like me and who are also doing the same craft. I've had to purposefully and intentionally seek out folx who look like me because otherwise, my feed becomes pretty whitewashed. I am trying to move away from whiteness more these days as I grow to understand my own identity more and am looking for that cultural affinity with others.

Other times, I've felt like an "other" is when I see big-name brands culturally appropriating traditional garments/dress from my community. For example, the recent Max Mara line that plagiarizes the Oma people of Laos has particularly been on my mind. I posted about this on my Instagram stories and received many messages from folx I didn't even know who were white/ white-presenting, telling me I was incredibly sensitive and "taking inspiration from a culture is not cultural appropriation." It made me feel gaslit to be told that what I knew was cultural appropriation of my own culture was deemed not so by folx in my own maker community. Given my work as an activist and anti-racist/anti-bias educator, I've had many experiences where my worldview clashes with those I follow and with what I see being amplified in the crafting community grids. However, I am glad for the openness and dialogue happening.

When do you feel recognized in your craft? Who recognizes you and how does that feel for you?

I've let many of my colleagues and friends know I'm on a journey to rebuild my wardrobe with pieces I have made where I have intentionally thought about the sourcing of material, the labor involved, and the way it allows me to present myself how I want to present. After telling them this, they've made it a point to ask me about my clothing in a way that is less transactional and more about holding me to account for the things I said I would do and the things I say I value. I also feel recognized when my mom, who is a maker herself, sees the work I am making and asks me to make her similar garments because she's proud of me.

Do you engage in these crafts for income or as a hobby?

This is definitely a hobby, but mostly a labor of love. Labor of love because it has helped me begin to love myself and my body *and* because I've been able to share this craft with some of my friends and family friends who also have a hard time finding particular garments, such as the abaya, in ready-to-wear settings.

If this is a hobby, how much of your time and money do you estimate you spend per year on it?

Oof. Probably something close to the tune of $300–$500 a year.

Do you exhibit your work? If so, where? Tell me about those experiences.

Just on Instagram (@soukprida) and as a way to connect to more makers, but especially makers of color. One post I shared was about a pair of pants I made.

I wanted to share my reflections I had while making this pair of pants because a lot of what I was reflecting on was the fact that in the thousands of images on the hashtag, I could barely find anyone who looked like me in shape/size, but also in identity. It made me feel slightly discouraged about whether or not the pants would even look right on me or if I was even a part of the target audience the designer had in mind when they designed these. When I ended up sharing the pants and my reflections, I wanted to also connect it back to why this was such a moment of joy, learning, and accomplishment for me because as I was making the pants, I had to unpack/face the internalized messages about body image/beauty standards that kept creeping in at every stitch. I wrote about how I was unpacking the ways white supremacy would have me think about our beauty standards and what size was considered "normal," what bodies were considered beautiful (spoiler: it's not bodies that were browner, fuller, softer, and that needed many "fit adjustments") . . . and when I wrote that reflection out, I got so many messages of affirmation and love, coupled with white/white-presenting folx seemingly annoyed/angry/confused with me about naming white supremacy, as if I was calling them out individually for perpetuating it—which, I mean, we all do sometimes if we go forward without examining our own biases or socializations.

It was strange to be in a place where a post where I was sharing a personal reflection was not immediately believed as a truth about my lived experience. It became a post where I felt like my identity was put out there vulnerably, but the response back was one of defensiveness where people were trying to prove me wrong about something I felt and lived every day. It was a bit tiring and I didn't post again for a while because of it.

When you were younger, were you exposed to other people who looked like you, or who were from similar backgrounds as you, and who engaged in this craft?
You know, when I think about it, the folx who looked like me and who engaged in this craft were a part of my family. So, of course, they looked like me. Some of the craft is part of my family history and traditions, especially when it comes to traditional dress in Lao culture—many of those skirts and dresses are handmade by people who could be my aunties, grandmothers, and elders.

When I think about commercially or through spaces outside of my family unit and community, I don't think I was often exposed to folx who looked like me or were from similar backgrounds unless I, myself, intentionally sought them out. I spent a lot of time Googling phrases like "Lao sewists," "Lao knitting community Chicago," and then would move to the more general terms like "Asian American" to then "people of color," etc. I knew I always wanted that connection to a group of folx who looked like me because I wanted to be affirmed in the craft and feel a sense of cultural belonging and warmth.

What colors are you drawn to and why?
I am drawn to muted colors and jewel tones because many of these colors have symbolic meaning in Lao/Vietnamese culture. I also just want a neutral colorway for my own closet—earth tones are the softer tones I find myself leaning toward every time I look in my closet. For me, it's easiest to mix and match a uniform when nearly everything is the same colorway.

MY LOLA, MING GUIHAMA

Essay by Ava Guihama

WHEN I ASK my Lola how sewing has influenced her, she says simply, "Sewing is my sanity."

Born in 1931 in Takas, a small neighborhood in Iloilo City, Philippines, Herminia Guihama first became interested in sewing when her own grandmother came to visit. "My grandma used to do embroidery. She came every weekend to the house. I was not even going to school yet, so she watched us. She did her embroidery there. Like bedspreads and pillowcases—anything, you know. One time, she turned around and saw that I cut the pillowcase and put a string on it to make my skirt. I got scolded because this embroidery is for a rich family. They give her material to do the embroidery, and she got paid for that. I cut that, and I made my skirt! After that, one after the other, I just learned to sew."

From there, sewing became an integral part of her life. "Nobody taught me," she says. "But my aunt owned a big shop. Dressmaking. And I stayed with her during school days because she lived close to the school. When one dressmaker got sick, I sat down and did her work." Once she found a job that paid, she spent her first paycheck on a sewing machine. Even in college, while she studied to be a nurse, my Lola found time and reason to sew. "I used to make party dresses for all my friends in the dorms. Later, when I moved to Chicago, when my friend got married, I made her dress at the desk in my dorm room."

After finishing school in Chicago, my Lola returned to the Philippines, where she married my Lolo, who she'd met in high school. They had two daughters in Iloilo—my mother, and her older sister—before my Lolo relocated their family from Takas to Los Angeles, California. There, my Lola took a job as a nurse at a large hospital, working the evening shift from four to midnight. She had a third daughter and worked to put each of her children through Catholic school.

Sewing played a role in her career as a mother, too. "If tomorrow is their birthday and I forgot, they'd say, 'Mom, tomorrow is my birthday!' Then I'd rush, get material, and make them clothes for their birthday. All occasions, even picnics, I would make clothes for them."

From the number of times my Lola has made dresses for me, I know she's choosy about her materials. She refuses to shop at large stores like JoAnn Fabrics, instead insisting on traveling all the way from her house in the San Fernando Valley to downtown Los Angeles to visit retailers there. "It's cheaper," she explains, "and you have a better selection." When I asked if the quality is the same, she nodded. "I like material that if you wash it and wash it and wash it, it still looks the same." In fact, she often makes the argument that fabric from retailers from downtown is better.

As a devout Catholic, mother of three, and nurse, my Lola has always lived a life of service. When I asked what she struggles with the most in sewing, she brushed me off.

"I know I can design any gown. I can make any gown. The only thing I can't do is make a business out of it. I don't know why I can't make money from sewing. I usually instead do charity."

My Lola has found that sewing is one of the main ways she connects to people. How many wedding dresses has she made for friends? "Too many to count." How many party dresses? "Any. For anyone of my friends who asked." As for her inspiration, she focuses more on what the recipient of the piece wants rather than her preferences or the trends of the time. "I sketch, I ask them, 'Is this what you like?' And then I make it."

Not only did she make wedding dresses for all of her daughters' weddings but she's also made wedding dresses—free of charge—for friends of friends. "I usually have two wedding dresses a year. I do three fittings, and I usually have the material three months in advance. Especially if it's expensive." At times, the jobs are too big to undertake on her own, so she enlists help. "Once, I did a wedding where the bride wanted embroidery and beads for all of the bridesmaids' dresses. Six of them. Some lived in Canada. So, I called a lady in Canada to do the measurements. I can't do the beadings on my own, so I sent it to the Philippines. I made the form and sent the materials, and once it was done and they sent it back, I finished the dresses here."

Sewing is how Herminia Guihama connects with others, but more than that, it's how she takes care of herself. "There's always time for me to sew.

If I cannot sleep, I go down and finish something. I figure things out—like your mom's wedding veil. Or her wedding gown. She wanted a train. So, I put a train, and then her veil, I said, 'What kind do you want?' She wanted a long veil. So, I wake up at two o'clock in the morning, I stay there sewing, and I made her veil."

Now that my Lolo is struggling with dementia, my Lola's ability to prioritize herself has diminished. "I have so many half-finished projects," she admits. "Because, well, I'm so busy taking care of him all the time." As I interview her, my Lolo sits on the bench outside the door, swatting flies and watching the dog in the yard. A few years ago, he stopped driving. A while after that, he stopped going out at all. Soon after, the two of them moved into a small apartment unit behind the house that my parents, brother, and I live in. Adjusting from having a room dedicated to sewing to having to put her machine on a tiny table shoved between the front door and the television has been hard on her.

I'm leaving for college in the fall, and I've heard my fair share of "I'm turning your room into a yoga studio/craft corner/second office/game lounge" jokes from my parents and brother. But, if my room is converted into anything, it should become a sewing room for my Lola to use. After all, as she says, "I don't know what I'd do if I couldn't sew. Go crazy, I think."

MAKING HAPPINESS

Interview with Youngmin Lee

JEN HEWETT: I was just listening this morning to your interview with Kristine Vejar and Adrienne Rodriguez on their podcast, *Reverberate*. My favorite part of the interview was when you said that you had a box of scraps of fabric when you were a kid, because I did too. Did you always like fabric?

YOUNGMIN LEE: I did. I do not know why, but I kept all the scraps in the box. Sometimes, I used them to make something, but most of the time I just opened the box and admired them or touched them.

JH: I did the same thing. My mom doesn't sew, but my grandmother (my dad's mom) did. She always had fabric around. I would cut little pieces of fabric and put them in a box, and I would never use them.

YL: Too precious to use, right?

JH: Yes, too precious! What interests me about *bojagi*, because it seems like every culture has its own textile culture, is how it uses scraps of fabric. How we use fabric is both the same and also very different, depending on where you're from. Could you explain to me what bojagi is and how it plays a role in Korean culture?

YL: Bojagi is a wrapping cloth. That word covers so many things—it's a name used for so many different things. Bojagi is used for covering and wrapping, carrying and storing things. Some bojagi is just a simple square or rectangular shape of fabric that you can use for wrapping, covering, or storing things. Sometimes you see patchwork bojagi, which is called the *jogak-bo*. Jogak-bo means "pieced or patchwork" bojagi. That is one way how people recycled fabric. Bojagi can be found in daily life, a special occasion, or a religious ceremony. There are so many different names of bojagi, depending on its construction, how it was used, who made it, who used it, and the color design. But mostly, bojagi is something that you use to wrap things. Not only objects— Korean people believe that they can cover or wrap happiness too. In "bojagi," the "bo" sounds similar to the Korean word for happiness, *bok*. When people make bojagi, especially jogak-bo, or *subo*, which is embroidered bojagi, they often think about their recipients' happiness or well-being while they're making it. If it is a stitched bojagi, those stitches are the wishes for happiness, and if is an embroidered bojagi, then those embroidery stitches are also a wish for someone's well-being.

JH: That's just lovely. I love the idea of a wrapping cloth that is as much a gift, if not more, than the gift.

YL: It's a part of the gift. You can add a little bit of your wish for someone's happiness, and give a present at the same time.

JH: You also have to think about the present itself because the size of the bojagi needs to be the right size for the gift I suppose?

YL: Right. Most of the common projects that I teach in my classes are *yemulbo*, gift-wrap bojagi. That's bojagi to wrap a gift, and it is not that big—around 13-by-13 inch—big enough to wrap a small card, letter, or a small object. In our tradition, bojagi can be as small as that, or way bigger. It depends on what you wrap, what you cover, what you store. Bojagi can be bigger and can contain more pieces. For example, you can wrap your clothing or bedding in a bojagi and then store it in the closet. In that case, you need to have big bojagi to wrap and tie those objects. There are records about the size of bojagi in the past. The smallest one is 30–35 centimeters square, and it can be bigger and bigger.

JH: So, do you reuse gift bojagi? If so, how do you reuse it?

YL: You can reuse it. When you get a gift wrapped in that gift-wrap bojagi, the bojagi is part of the gift, so you don't have to return it to the sender—that's yours. You can keep it, or you can reuse it when you give a gift, too.

People ask that question a lot. In most cases, when I say you don't have to return it, that you get to keep it or reuse it, they say, "No, I'm going to keep it."

JH: I'm curious—is there a right side and a wrong side of the bojagi?

YL: Bojagi can also be defined by how they are constructed. Sometimes you see two-layer bojagi, the seam stitches and seam allowances are covered with another layer. In that case, the pieced side is the right side and the other side is the wrong side.

Sometimes when I make bojagi, I use a special technique called Ssamsol that is very similar to flat-felled seams. In that case, the front and back are the same. There's no raw edge with that finished bojagi, and it's hard to say which side is the right side or the wrong side. You can use both sides.

JH: You said that your grandmother did this, but she didn't teach you. Is that correct?

YL: Right. I saw her making it but, well, I never had the chance to learn from her. I was young and I could have learned from her, but that thought didn't occur to me then. I missed that chance.

JH: How and when did you learn how to make them, then?

YL: Even though I had a box full of small pieces of fabric, I didn't do much with bojagi until I went to college. I majored in clothing and textiles, and I pursued my dream to be a fashion designer. I went to grad school and did a master's in fashion design. Maybe in my junior year of college, I took a class on Korean costume—history and construction—and as part of it, I had a chance to learn how to construct bojagi.

JH: You were already in your twenties when you started doing this?

YL: Yeah. Right.

JH: Is it still customary for people to make these themselves and to use them for gifts, or is it an older tradition that people don't engage in?

YL: Luckily, nowadays many people make them. They want to learn how to make bojagi. But when I was young, I didn't consider bojagi a precious thing because it was so abundant. Bojagi was everywhere. There are simple boja-gis that you can take to the market and put groceries in, and make into a pouch to carry them. There are some jogak-bo that people use for covering a dining table or tea table, or covering food, or decorating furniture—things like that.

But to go back to your question, when I was young, bojagi was everywhere, so I didn't value it that much. I think other Korean people didn't value it much either because everybody was interested in doing Western-style things in our daily lives. Fifteen, twenty years ago, all of sudden, people started to revalue and recognize the old traditions. They think it's important to keep the tra-dition of bojagi and to know how to make it. So nowadays in Korea, you see many people are making bojagi not only for practical purposes but also as their art form.

JH: I like your work so much because it's abstract in many ways. There's a rhythm to the color in your patchwork that you don't necessarily expect. Is that particular to you? Or is that traditional?

YL: Well, I think it is partly a characteristic of jogak-bo and partly it is me. I love to play with fabrics, and I love to arrange shapes and colors and lines. So, it can be part of me because there are many different types of bojagi construc-tion. But, my main bojagi construction is sorting by color and type of fabrics, putting those right next to me, and thinking about it a little bit. I start with two pieces of fabric, and then from that moment, everything is expanding. It's a very organic process. It's not a thing that I plan ahead of time; I could, but I have a hard time planning and then following my plan. I'd just rather just get two pieces of fabric and start from there.

I am working on a bojagi right now using silk fabrics. This fabric has a story. A friend of mine who also does bojagi and does natural dyeing is not making bojagi that often anymore. She said, "Why don't you take them all and then make them into something?" She lives in Japan and travels to Korea. She has collected a lot of fabrics and she dyed them with natural dyes. At some point, she said, "I think you will use them better than I can," and she sent all her fabrics to me.

JH: After she already dyed them? That's nice.

YL: Yeah, it's nice. She sent me a list of what kind of dye she used, so I'm thinking of this as a kind of friendship bojagi.

JH: I like that idea. It's almost like how people do the quilt block swaps where everybody does the same block ten to twelve times.

I grew up in Los Angeles just on the edge of Koreatown, and so I saw a lot of bojagi when I was a kid, but they were all-white. It wasn't until I saw your work that I realized that they can be done in color.

YL: Those white bojagi or just one very light color—pale pink, white, or pale yellow—those are the ones that people use for wrapping presents, or for wrapping things in daily life. When I started making bojagi, I thought of it as a canvas for me, so I could play with all different colors and pieces of different fabrics. The bojagi that are made out of many pieces of silk fabrics are called jogak-bo. I think people in the twentieth century didn't have much time to make jogak-bo.

Before that, in the old days, people collected fabric scraps and made them into something useful and pretty at the same time. But by the time you and I were growing up, we probably didn't see much jogak-bo because people didn't have much time. My grandma made it because she wanted to use her scraps. Nowadays, we see more jogak-bo and elaborately designed bojagi in more than just one color because people want to make pretty, beautiful things.

JH: I think a lot of people forget that only fifty to one hundred years ago, fabric was really expensive. So, if you had fabric, you wouldn't waste a single bit of it. Fabric was expensive. Clothes were expensive. It's only been in the last twenty to thirty years or so that fabric isn't so expensive.

YL: Right. Clothing, too. Nowadays, we have so many inexpensive, fast-made, goods, right? Not only clothing. We don't consider them precious things anymore.

Korea has been a fast-changing country for the last fifty, sixty years. My parents' generation went through three wars. People didn't have the ability to get much material back then, whether you're poor or not. When you're building a country, there are so many other things that you have to do. People focused on making more money, constructing more buildings, and developing a country. After thirty, forty years, when they can think about what is important in life, what is tradition, and what they have missed while they were busy with different things, Korean people started to think about traditions, and other things too. Bojagi is a part of that.

My story is a little different because I moved from Korea to California twenty-two years ago. I chose bojagi to express myself. Like other Korean people, I was missing my tradition. Maybe that's why so many people started making not only bojagi but also started being involved in other extra traditions that they didn't value much when they were really busy. Now they think, "We need to focus on old traditions."

JH: I read that you chose bojagi when your daughter was born and you needed something to do.

YL: That's right. We moved to the Bay Area when my daughter was six months old. My husband got a job here, so he said, "Why don't we move to California and live there maybe five years?" It didn't work that way. At some point, I knew that I would live here for longer than five years. I was busy raising my daughter, she started school, and I had to learn a new language. Everybody was busy for a while, and when she started elementary school, that's when I felt "Now, I have some time."

We moved to California right after I had gotten my master's degree. I had to stop pursuing my career because I was in a different country with a young child and I was living in the suburbs. I couldn't just say, "I need to go to the city and pursue my dream." I had to compromise for some time. When I finally got some time, I thought, "Yeah, fabric and textiles are my thing, and I need to do something."

I hadn't intended to do bojagi. It just came to me and all of a sudden. It was so comforting for me. Then people started asking me questions like, "What is that? How do you make it? Why do you make it? How do you get the materials?" I thought, "Oh, maybe I can do this for longer."

JH: How were you sharing your work in those early days?

YL: Well, let's see, this was around 2003, 2004. I was doing it, and people around me asked what it was, and how to do it. I would go to the Asian Art

Museum in San Francisco quite often. I had a friend who worked at the museum, and she knew that I was making bojagi, so she invited me to a special program at the museum. It was a public event, called "Asia Alive." They invited local artists, and I was there for a month, to share and demonstrate and talk about bojagi.

JH: What year was this?

YL: I think it was 2004. That was the first time that I had brought all my bojagi outside of my house to show. After that, the Asian Art Museum asked me to teach a workshop, so I taught workshops there. From that, I taught at the Oakland Museum and art centers like the Richmond Art Center and Mendocino Arts. Other places asked me to do either public events, demonstrations, or workshops. Textile people are drawn to textiles. I often have conversations with quilters because they stop at my table and we will talk for a long time. They want to introduce me to their guilds so they can learn new things from me. Once I started meeting people, well, you just need to meet one, and that leads to another chance.

JH: Now, you teach pretty regularly. You also teach kids, too?

YL: I started teaching bojagi to kids in 2012. There is a public school in San Francisco that offers a Korean immersion program. Every year, I go there for eight to ten weeks, depending on the school schedule and my schedule. Each grade has a different project. So, we start with just putting two pieces of felt together using a very thick needle, and gradually, we move to smaller needles and threads and different materials. This year is the first time I've introduced real silk fabrics to the kids. They made wonderful projects. At the end of this month, Oakland Asian Cultural Center offered me a gallery space over there, so I'm bringing all the things that we did this year and showing the children's work there.

JH: What do you like about teaching?

YL: Whether I'm teaching children or grown-ups, teaching is fun for me. I'd rather say that I'm sharing than teaching. I'm sharing what I love to do. I was just thrilled when people started showing interest in bojagi. So that's how I started, by sharing bojagi. Teaching gives me a lot of joy. Not only teaching techniques or how to construct things but also talking about philosophies, traditions, and culture. For example, when I use Korean silk, it has lots of patterns woven into the fabric. So, I can talk about the auspicious symbols, the longevity symbols. For example, bats can be a symbol of happiness.

The word for "bat" sounds the same as the word for "happiness" in Korean. Adding a bat decoration can be an act of adding more happiness or wishing for more happiness. So, when you see bojagi, you often can see lots of bat images.

Things like this can connect people with me, and we can talk about so many things in culture and tradition. Sometimes people say, "Yeah, we have similar traditions or thoughts." That's when I feel really happy because I can connect people to the things that I know or I can share. So, in that manner, teaching just gives me joy. I just love teaching people, meeting people, and talking about what I love and what I do.

JH: Where does your bojagi go after you've made it? You probably give some as gifts. Do you sell others or have them in shows?

YL: I've done several group exhibits in the Bay Area, and some other places. And bojagi can travel to festivals.

JH: Is that why you're going to the United Kingdom this summer?

YL: Yeah. I met this friend who lives in Brighton in the United Kingdom. She and I both have an interest in bojagi. We met at a bojagi forum in Korea. We became friends; social media helps us keep in touch. Last summer, she got a bursary to learn bojagi because she wanted to write a book about bojagi. I recommended a couple of teachers in Korea, but she said, "Can I come to you and learn?" So, instead of going to Korea, she came to my house and stayed at my house. We visited the Asian Art Museum, which has the biggest bojagi collection in the United States. She got an exhibition opportunity at the Festival of Quilts in Birmingham, so she asked me to participate. I'm going there with my bojagi, and I will be teaching over there.

JH: You've taken your bojagi all over the world, and now you're teaching all over the world.

YL: It's a joy that bojagi is giving me a chance to travel, to meet people, to teach classes, and to initiate conversations with people. I just love it.

JH: That's so wonderful. What a gift that this craft has given you!

YL: Yes. When I make bojagi, I wish for someone's happiness. And bojagi is maybe wishing for my happiness, too.

WHAT ARE YOU MAKING NOW?

Weaving Hair and incorporating talisman/healing objects, which is part of my ongoing project called "Buhok at Anting Anting—Hair and Talisman." I also started a series called "Totem Poles." Also, my ongoing series of "Cocoons," partnering with other artists so they can give me their waste, which I reweave into new cocoons.—CYNTHIA ALBERTO

Dyes/pigments from my yard and dyed cloth for classes/demonstrations, and future work. I have some pieces in dye pots as I write this.—CECILE LEWIS

I'm currently working on a tapestry weaving that is inspired by an aerial view of a beach.—ASHLEY HUGHES

Making Your Place

< A selection of handmade knits (clockwise from top left): Brandi Cheyenne
Harper's Allay Jacket (pattern her own from *Knitting for Self-Care*), Jenna Wolf's
Rug Sweater (pattern by Junko Okamoto), Candice English's Assonikinakii Cowl
(pattern her own, for Sister's United), Shanel Wu's Druid Circle Sweater (pattern
their own), Dana Williams-Johnson's Glass Ceiling Sweater (pattern by Heidi
Kirrmaier), Mia Nakaji Monnier's Valdres Hat (pattern by Kate Running)

TRAVELING MILES

Personal Narrative of Kenya Miles, as told to Jen Hewett

I WAS A HIGHLY nurtured, highly loved child, which was really important. My parents knew each other from high school. They went to school in Richmond, Virginia, together, and subsequently reconnected. They got married pretty young. We spent a lot of time with our family in the country. My grandparents lived in a working-class/poor neighborhood. That was my dad's family. My mom's family lived in a middle-class neighborhood. I got to see these two very different sides of the tracks. My dad's whole family is from Charles City, which is in the country.

My great-grandma, my Big Mama, was a hog farmer. I remember spending a lot of time on the hog farm. She had a double-barreled shotgun. She didn't fuck around. She had an outhouse; there was no indoor bathroom. We spent time there, and those are really strong memories for me. Now that I'm doing this work, my dad said, "Oh, your grandparents would be proud of you." I never really even thought about it in that way. Even with textiles, my mom passed when I was young, but while she was alive, we would make dresses and stuff together for dolls. She was a voracious knitter, but she never actually passed on any of those skills to me.

To come into textiles in a certain way without that legacy connecting me in an actual acute way is sort of special. I've seen that in some other artists and their practices creating, where they have family and they may not have had time to learn the skill that they did, but somehow that crept into their narrative as well. I find that to be special and those are sort of the roots of that.

My dad was really big on the Black Arts Movement, back-to-the-land, and all of that. We grew up very sort of steeped in that energy. We didn't eat pork or beef. It was kind of this progressive thing. My father aligned with Dick Gregory's teachings; Malcolm X was his mentor. He used to read those books to me as a young child. Records were also a really big part of my childhood. We (my brother and I) had an old-school Fisher-Price record player, which now my son has, which is great.

I used to listen to a lot of Nikki Giovanni records. She would do a lot of LPs. I would listen to all these Last Poets records before bedtime or my dad would read me poems. I had a lot of early support in my creativity, in my art, and in the way that I saw the world. I was seven or eight, and I was like, "I'm an artist." I was very clear about who I was and what I wanted to be. My uncle (my mom's brother) was also a painter. He is an amazing painter.

He moved in when my mom got sick. Then when she died, he lived with us for a while. He turned the guest room into a studio. I would just sit with him and watch him paint with oils. He had journals and sketches all over. Those kinds of interactions supported me in acknowledging that this is viable. I mean, I never asked like, "How much money do you make, Uncle Van?" But I was like, "This is a possibility." All these people in my life are sort of foundationally connected to arts and creativity. My father was an architect who couldn't practice, due to issues with not necessarily segregation but just a very limited amount of work was available for Black architects at that time. He ended up going into human resources, and really, his trajectory of who he is was to take care of his family. I think he just poured all his creativity and love into me, specifically. I think he tried with my brother, but my brother and I are very different people. At some point when I was twelve or thirteen, he built me an art room in the basement. He took out his old drafting table and he set it all up for me so I had this little room in the basement that I could use. That was my art studio. I would have friends come over and do sittings for me. They would come and sit for me. I always felt like that's what I was going to do.

FROM FILM TO FABRIC

I went into art school thinking I would do computer art and rationalized it by saying, "Well, I can take the illustrations and I can put them into the computer. Then I can make them move and it'll be just like being an animator or a cartoonist." I went to school in New York at the School of Visual Arts. The first year, our foundation was all the painting, all the photography, and all the drawing—I loved that.

The incoming chair of the program was so annoyed with me. He was like, "Whatever it is you want to do, as long as your core classes are completed, I don't care. Whatever, if you want to take feminist theory, take feminist theory. If you want to take anatomical drawing and illustration, just take it. I don't know how any of that stuff is going to make you a better computer artist."

When I got out of college, I was one of five people or so in the program who was able to get a job. I could make storyboards, I could write stories, and I could frame things in certain ways. I don't think that teaching someone just to be a technician was actually a round enough sort of education. I'm trying to achieve a goal. The goal is to nurture and nourish all these parts of myself that find stimulation in a creative space. Once I got out of college, I was working in computer art and doing motion graphics work. I was able to find good work by doing assistant editing. I was not sure that I wanted to do it very early into getting a job, but I was excited about documentaries. We never really had the access to TV. We could watch *The Cosby Show* and *A Different World*, Thursday nights. And we watched PBS.

I always loved PBS. I was like, "Oh, this is maybe more of what I want to do." They didn't talk about that stuff in college. A good friend of mine had a friend who had worked on this documentary called *Eyes on the Prize*. That was a huge documentary. She introduced me to the producer, Anne, and Anne took me in and was like, "If this is something you want to do, we have a Black documentary collective."

I would go up to Harlem in one of these brownstones and sit and hang out with all these people who had worked on things that were mind-blowing to me. One of the women who was there was pitching the Shirley Chisholm documentary, and she ended up later getting funding from Oprah. I just remember being inspired by these people. In turn, while I was doing that, I took on a documentary that I had found on my own.

It was me and another guy who were editing the documentary. I would go to work at my day job from 8:30 in the morning until 5:30 at night. Then, I would get off work and I'd go to Stephanie's at 7:00. I would stay there until 2:00 in the morning. Then I would do it all over again every day. Youth is a beautiful thing. You have energy and drive and enthusiasm.

It was amazing. It gave me the insight and I realized, "I don't know that documentaries are the thing that I can make." People had spent so much time and they saw so little gain from it. I just couldn't put my mind around spending ten years of your life on this thing and still trying to get distribution.

I started working on the first iteration of *Queer Eye for the Straight Guy* as a motion graphic artist and an artist for the company that was running them, Scout Productions. I was making a lot of money at twenty-three and just was like, "Yeah, I don't want to do this anymore. I'm ready to go. I'm not feeling it." I was a little bit tired of being in New York and being in that.

One day, the art director, Aleta, handed me a book that was in the Fab 5 loft and said, "You're always talking about old ladies and textiles and making baskets and whatever. Here's this book." The book was called *Oaxaca*. I looked at the book and thought, "That's where I'm going to go. That's where I'm moving." I essentially spent the next year saving money and decided that I was going to pack up my apartment in New York.

I got a one-way plane ticket and moved to Mexico. I decided that I was going to learn how to weave. I didn't know what any of that meant. That was in the spring of 2005. I call that my landmark, my point of departure. What Mexico gave me in the year that I lived there was probably more than any experience I've had quantifiably to this day, other than having my son. I remember feeling that very specifically like, "Oh, this is who you are. This is the person that you are." Immediately, once I got there, I was very clear. I didn't have any questions. I think the questions that came up later were "How can you do this for the rest of your life? How do you move from this experience that you've learned so much from and make it last?"

I had taken up weaving while I was there, while also trying to learn Spanish. There was a woman, Silvia, who owned a store in town. She was helping to do a revitalization of old traditional techniques, embroideries, huipiles, etc. I asked her one day, "Hey, I want to learn how to embroider. I want to learn how to weave. I want to learn how to do these techniques. Can you help me find some people?" Right there, she called up three women and they all agreed to take me in. I learned all these different traditions in these women's homes and in their spaces. The woman I honor as my weaving teacher, Monica, gave me more than I could have imagined.

I lived in Teotitlán del Valle with Monica and her daughter Wendy two weeks out of every month. I would weave that whole time. That village is a traditional rug-weaving community of people who are Zapotec. Depending on what generation they're in, most people are trilingual and can speak Zapotec, Spanish, and English. But some of them just speak Zapotec. There was a lot of quiet for me because I didn't know what anybody was talking about. My teacher could speak some English, but I preferred her to speak in Spanish. If I'm not going to know what's happening, I might as well try to figure it out in some other language. I wove rugs for that year.

After that, I decided to continue to travel and continue those types of experiences and practices in different countries. I went to South Africa, Europe, and the Caribbean. I spent a lot of time traveling and kind of trying to replicate that experience. I think what I have come to understand is that my time in Oaxaca was just a very unique thing. After traveling for two years, I didn't have the same amount of time to give or savings to support myself. I went back to New York and I worked on a movie to give the city and production one more try. I left New York after that.

I decided, because of the arts and crafts movement in Northern California, that it would be a place that I would feel better aligned. That's how I ended up there and slowly started this trajectory of working back in computer art. I kept freelancing, figuring out what things were not things for me. But, I still always kept a freelance job in Northern California. I would take a sabbatical, live some other place abroad, and kind of try to redo the same thing that happened in Oaxaca. When I was turning thirty, I took two months and I traveled to fifteen or eighteen different cities in six countries. By the end, I was pretty burned out. I don't enjoy living out of my suitcase like I used to. I got my own apartment in Oakland, which was still really affordable at the time.

It was a magical time. I had a good friend, Kori, who had lived in the Bay Area for many years. He's a painter and had a studio and a loft. He let me take part of that studio, and that's the beginning of my practice in a permanent space. Before I had been practicing in different countries or living in different places. I couldn't make big work and I couldn't take it back on the plane. Having a permanent space drew me into a different kind of community of people. I started applying to different things and trying out different projects and ideas.

A NATURAL DYE EDUCATION

My friend Barbara, who was from El Salvador, and I decided to enter a bag competition in New York. We entered in the eco category. I went to the Antique Faire in Alameda and collected a bunch of scraps and old leather bags that were being resold. My friend suggested we dye the pieces in indigo because a lot of people do indigo work where she is from in El Salvador.

Neither of us had ever done that before. I had never done any natural dyes. I'd seen people using it in Mexico and other countries. But one thing that is standardized around industrial production is that people are making things with chemical dyes. Even if those communities were once steeped in a certain tradition, they are trying to figure out how to make money and how to connect to their consumer. Capitalism insists that turnover is important.

I got focused and spent months trying to figure out how to create an indigo bag. There were no tomes. Not like now, where people have written books about their natural dye practice. Back then, I would find these ten-page leaflets about Nigerian Adire or these small little things from a 1970s *Better Homes and Gardens*, *Craft Horizons*, or dyeing in the preindustrial age. I spent a ton of time trying to figure it out. I was able to get these beautiful blues, and I was doing wax printing on things just based on whatever I could figure out how to do.

I still even have some of that fabric because I took the bag apart in the end. I kept the bag for many years, and then I was like, "I don't need this bag. I just want the actual fabric on it." We did well in the competition, but we didn't get a prize. That was exciting for us.

I would visit my friend Isabel in Vancouver every couple of months. There is a textile school and store called Maiwa on Granville Island. I saw that they had a textile symposium. The symposium is a mixture of all these different techniques in textiles taught by all these different instructors from all over the world who come for two months. The class I took was an immersive natural dye course that was four days long. It was the first one they had taught. I was like, "I'm in." I think it was just this really important experience for me. But the truth is that I went back home and never did any of that. It took me years. I would try some things, but I was still into my indigo.

STEWARDING AN URBAN NATURAL DYE FARM

My family and I moved to Baltimore in fall 2017. I decided to forgo all my computer art work and try to make a go of my art. I had just turned thirty-eight and I had a two-and-a-half-year-old. I think I was just feeling ready. I was ready to stop pretending, I was ready to stop hiding. I was invigorated by the year before when I had made a textile painting every day. I set up a studio in the house. I wanted my son to remember me as a person who was making things, not as someone who just talked about making things. In November 2017, I was teaching a workshop at a place called Neighborhood Fiber Co. in Baltimore. A fibers professor and the department chair from Maryland Institute College of

Art (MICA) unknown to me were participants. During the lunch break, they came to me and said, "We have this project that's around natural dyes and we'd love to talk to you about it more."

They invited me to be an artist-in-residence. All these things just sort of kicked off from there. There's an urban farm three blocks from my house that I had said when we moved to Baltimore, "Oh, I want to do a dye garden there." When I met the folks at MICA, I told them I wanted to do a dye garden." They're like, "Oh, that's great. We literally just talked to the woman who started Hidden Harvest Farm because we want to do one there too." The Baltimore Natural Dye Initiative is an eighteen-month collaboration between the Department of Commerce, the First Lady (the governor's wife) Yumi Hogan, and MICA where they have grant funding to do this natural dye project. They wanted to farm some land in West Baltimore. A lot of red flags came up around who was going to do the farming, how the farming was going to be done. A lot of that looked, again, like a sort of white and Black relationship, where people were not necessarily being mindful or thoughtful about a lot of the histories of agriculture and enslaved peoples in America. Indigo also being one of the reasons that—that and rice—that people were enslaved and brought over, and land was taken from Native Americans.

That's also a part of what I'm interested in looking at in this project—conversations that don't happen in this artisanal resurgence space where people are like, "We're just having fun." I want to have fun, too. But I also want to honor all the people who spent all the years of their lives or lost their lives or lost their traditions because of industrialization, colonialism, and enslavement. Even just the decision around what plants are the best plants. Dye plants that are considered historically the most highly lauded have been chosen for a myriad of reasons including workforce, labor, transport, colonies, control, etc. All these people are doing all this work and they're like, "I love . . . This is the most viable of this color." The only reason that this is actually a premise is because somebody decided that they could have bodies work on it, that they could have a certain amount of it grown, that it could grow in the West Indies where they had a workforce. All these things. It's like, even that, the fallacy of that is overwhelming sometimes. I feel like just thinking about those things, this project has allowed for a lot of that to happen. There's a class at MICA based around this project that allows for these discussions. No one wanted to farm the land because the RFP was set up in ways that held the farmer to task remediation and soil amendment, infrastructure, equipment, and harvest on their own. Working with Rosa Chang, who is a supervisor under the Maryland State Arts Council and a fellow artist-in-residence at MICA, on the dye garden at Hidden Harvest was inspiring. Rosa and I were talking about it and saying, "Yeah, we should do it together. We should farm the state land." She's also been a liaison for the First Lady. In March 2019, they took the First Lady over to see another space that offered to host the dye farm because the original site was going to be Coppin State's land. That land was raw: remediation, having it amended, and all these things was an impossible task for one farmer; to then later get paid at the very end of the project is essentially a sharecropping model.

Parks & People took it on and said, "We'll do it." They're in West Baltimore, and they have a relationship with the community there and the First Lady to feel comfortable that they had enough space and land to do it. They're also a white institution (as is MICA). I mean, all these institutions are white institutions. But part of it is, what do you do with those resources and that access? Nobody's asking you not to be white. We're just asking you not to be neocolonialists. I think that in the end, those conversations are what separate this project and why it's so critical to present these ideas outside of academia. Rosa sent me a text one day that said, "Everything's set. You're going to do it." It's funny—look at what happens when you say something. Look at what change is affected, what involves, and what moves when you open yourself up to the universe.

I've been in Baltimore a year. To move to a place and have there be a government-funded natural dye project, to then be the person who is not only an artist-in-residence but to also be one of the lead farmers on the project to be growing this indigo, cultivating it, working on harvest in the late summer and the fall—I mean, that's an honor. That's a gift. There's nothing that I could have ever imagined that would come up like this. I had this moment where I was in the city and I was driving and a lot of things have happened. Throughout the struggles that I've had, with family and other things, I've still thought, "I'm supposed to be here." There was no evidence of why I'm supposed to be here. There wasn't a lot of money or work coming in.

But in the end, to have this opportunity come up, this really amazing space where all the experiences that I have had, all these years of work, all the things I wanted to work on . . . Or just even these conversations. I never had time to have these conversations outside of my community of people because I'm trying to make work, I'm trying to make product, I have a son, I'm trying to get paid. I need to take care of him. I had thought about going to grad school when we moved and I looked into what it costs to go to MICA. I was like, "Oh, no."

The interesting part about deciding not to do that, being invited into an academic institution, and then being given the opportunity to do research and study my work, that is all the universe. I don't have any doubt about that. This didn't magically appear for no reason. It's like, "This is for you. This is supposed to happen. You are supposed to be here at this time."

EMBRACING THE CONSTRAINTS

Interview with Windy Chien

JEN HEWETT: When I started talking about writing this book, you were the first person to be super excited about it. I wanted to ask you why.

WINDY CHIEN: It's because of the milieu that we're in, right? A few years ago, I was showing at West Coast Craft, and that's almost all white crafters. I started thinking, "What is this world that I have consciously chosen to join because I wanted to make tangible objects?" But when you look at the community, how much privilege is here, and how much of it is acknowledged, or how much are people aware of it—that kind of thing. And now that I make fine art, who are the folks who are furnishing their gazillion-dollar homes?

They're rich white people. Or they're companies like startups. Of course, we have so many startups here in San Francisco that need beautiful office spaces, and who gets venture capital start-up money? White men. So, it's just interesting to look now at the world, the various communities that I'm a part of, and notice it. There's something very precious about the way that white people—or maybe all of us—treat craft. So, yeah, I was like, "Oh my God, finally someone's going to say something about this."

JH: I think that there's something about in the art world, artists of color are becoming a lot more prominent than they have been, even though art education in a formal sense hasn't been accessible to a lot of us until the last generation or two. Whereas, in craft, it's very, very white, but craft is actually something that was done in this country largely by people of color for centuries.

Your work is both art and craft, and I'm fascinated by that. I know you don't think of yourself as a textile artist, but you use rope almost exclusively in your work. What is it about rope that interests you?

WC: I didn't go to art school. For me, rope is a utilitarian object that we all use, whether we're artists or not. So, it seemed like the most nonintimidating place to start. Of course, I quickly got to the point where I was like, "I want to elevate what I can make out of this humble material and the humble objects that I'm making, which are knots themselves." We all tie our shoes every morning, you know—they're humble objects. I want to elevate them. And if I have communicated via my art what I think is beautiful and ingenious and intelligent and historic about knots, and if my viewers see that, then I will feel that I have been successful. That's a long answer to that question.

JH: That's a fantastic answer.

WC: That's why it starts with rope. Rope is also a beautiful way to draw a line. You can draw lines in 3D space with rope without creating too much weight. There isn't bulk attached to it. You can draw outlines. You can draw volumes in space without it. So that's another thing that I like about rope.

I could talk forever about why I like it. Most rope, not the rope that I use, but most rope is that twisted structure and it's made of three pieces that are twisted. The three pieces are strands. Three strands make up the rope. What makes up the strands are the yarns, and what makes the yarns are the fibers. I love knowing that stuff. I love geeking out on it. I like what you said about making the distinction and the overlap between craft and art. The way that craft comes into my fine art practice is that I take a craftsperson's approach to the materials.

I've often thought about how a designer sits in front of a computer and imagines something and only then figures out how to make it. That's the opposite of how a craftsperson works: what we're really interested in is knowing our materials backward and forward, knowing exactly what they might want to become, how they will behave, and how they won't behave. With those interesting constraints, then making something. So, you're more in harmony with your materials when you understand them and you begin with them as the starting point. I think that's the craftsperson's approach.

JH: I hadn't thought of it that way, but that makes complete sense, like how fashion designers can't always sew. And you have a whole team of people who can put things together. I think, in many ways, to be a successful artist who's also got the craft aspect, you have to have both the visionary aspect as well as the purely functional, operational aspects. That's a rare combination.

WC: I guess it is, I don't know. It comes early and I understand that to be part of my work now. I liked that. So maybe, maybe I'm one of the few who are actually both. I don't know.

JH: Let's back up to your early years. Were you always creative? You said you were a musician at one point.

WC: I'm a child of immigrants. My parents immigrated to the United States, and my father joined the US military. I come from a long line of Chinese generals, so the military has been in my family's blood. I think it does make sense that when his mother immigrated him and the rest of the family to the United States that the military was the path that he chose. My brother's in the navy. I'm the black sheep.

What I'm trying to point out with that is that my parents were so busy assimilating; my mother was learning English and figuring out how to be part of this society. Art seemed like the most foofy, unpractical career path. We were never encouraged to do anything creative, except for typical Chinese parents stuff like learning how to play the piano, which is not very creative because you just learn how to play Chopin, Bach. It never turns into "What kind of music would you like to make?" It never feels that way. It's performative. So yeah, not a very creative childhood.

The only person in my family that was creative at all was my grandmother, who was a widow. She had her mother, her three children, and a full-time job. She would do petit point at night. She was a painter as well, but she was a week-end warrior type. Art was never valued as something that was a valid career path in my family at all.

I did just typical things. I would draw, and my mom taught me macramé back when macramé was a thing, in the seventies when all housewives were doing it. We made a double plant hanger, and I remember loving it. So that kind of stuff. But you would never call me the arty kid. I was the straight A student in school.

JH: I had the same thing, too. My dad had trained as a draftsman, but jobs in architecture and drafting were very rare if you were Black in the sixties and seventies. He worked in and eventually managed factories. My mom had immigrated to the United States from the Philippines. My parents were working their butts off so my brother and I could go to private school. It was great for me to take enrichment art classes, but I was always actively told that art was not something I could do professionally.

WC: Yeah. Enrichment. Like so you can be more well-rounded and get into a good school, of course.

JH: What did you do for college?

WC: I decided that I would study film because I didn't know what I wanted to do. I thought maybe something creative was the right thing to do. This is because when I was a junior in high school, my parents sent me to the fanciest high school in Hawaii that they could afford. My father was stationed in Hawaii. I fit in well there, but we were still military kids. I looked like I belonged, but I didn't belong, in a way. They sent me to the fanciest high school in Hawaii, which is the same high school that Barack went to. He was called Barry then.

I went to Punahou, and because I had transferred there as a junior and was just such a weird misfit, I started hanging out with all the misfits. Before that, I always fit in—straight A student. Junior year in high school, I started hanging out with the punk rockers, the poets, and the people who wore black raincoats and went thrift shopping. Very quickly, I realized this is way more fun than anything else, and this is probably who I am. So that's why I felt like when I decided I had to figure out a major for college, I had already taken some steps in the direction of nonconforming. I always say that if I had known that you could major in graphic design or design at that time, I would have done it.

But I did not know that that was a thing that you could do. Filmmaking seemed creative. That's why I chose it.

JH: Did you always live in Hawaii?

WC: No, my dad was in the US military, so we lived in Georgia, Colorado, Washington State, Hawaii, and West Point where he taught Chinese at the Military Academy. But most of my growing up years were in Hawaii at Schofield Barracks, which was the army base there.

JH: On an island!

WC: Which I didn't appreciate, of course, being into punk. I never went to the beach. It's tragic when I think about it. I lived a block from the beach and never went.

JH: So, you studied film . . .

WC: I studied film in school. I always try to be good at whatever I've set my mind to. The film that I made as my undergraduate thesis did well. It played all over the world. It was a short; it played at Sundance, in '92 or '94. But then I realized that I wasn't into it. What I know now, and this is a recent realization, is the reason I wasn't really into filmmaking was because I didn't love the process. It's a super long, drawn-out process. It takes forever to get stuff done. Also, back in those days, there was no iPhone video or even video cameras. It was all film, which meant it was expensive, which meant that I would have to beg for money to make feature films. And I was not into that idea, either.

Now I realize that it was the process of making the films that didn't appeal to me. Of course, I love stories. We all love stories and want to tell them. But that's a realization that came recently as I was ruminating about how much I love my process now and how whether or not I enjoy this moment of making the clasp on a necklace, if I enjoy this moment, then I'm going to keep doing it. If I don't enjoy it, I'm not going to make necklaces, you know? Whether or not you like your process, it is so important.

JH: You also talk about being a punk rocker as a teenager. So, you identify yourself a lot as an outsider. What does that mean?

WC: I've never fit in. There were times, especially in middle school, when you really want to fit in. But I've never quite fit in. I was an Asian kid in the US military in the sixties and seventies, right after the Vietnam War. You should hear my dad talk about his experiences, fighting for the United States in Vietnam, looking the way he did. I never fit in, and we would move all the time. I never got to have a stable set of friends. I always felt like I was just kind of on my own. And then I felt like an outsider because I had been thrust into this very exclusive private high school in Hawaii, and I didn't fit in there, either.

I've never felt like I fit in, but I embraced it as soon as I hit my late teens, college, and definitely my twenties. Because being an outsider means freedom.

It means people don't know what to make of you, which means you get to self-define. Getting to define yourself is what I think so many of us long for, and not to play prescribed roles.

JH: Right. I was thinking about that too, in terms of your career that you've changed careers a lot. You also owned the record store.

WC: I always worked in record stores. It was my part-time job during college—I put myself through school. I didn't get any loans. For me, my entire social scene outside of school was music—going to shows, going to see bands, reading 'zines, and finding my next favorite record. So, record stores were the center of my community. I thought, "Well, that's where I should spend all my time as well. I'll get a job in that world."

JH: Where were you going to college?

WC: I went to San Francisco State—started at the University of Hawaii for a year, and then I went to San Francisco State and spent the rest of my time there. I started out working at a chain record store in San Francisco, but my goal was to get a job at Aquarius Records, which was the coolest record store in the city. I finally got one there and ended up staying for fourteen years, nine of which I was the owner. I bought it from the previous owner, who had had it since the seventies.

JH: How did you even get it together to buy a record store?

WC: I didn't even know that that was possible, but I started mentioning it to some of our regular customers. The store was in Noe Valley, and I thought, "We should move to Valencia Street." But the original owner was not invested in moving to Valencia. He didn't understand why. Valencia had become a thing in the nineties. Some of my regular customers said, "Well, do you need some money? We'll lend you some money." People literally offered to lend me money to buy it. I bought it for $25,000 and moved it to Valencia Street. It was good timing, too, 'cause it was right before the first tech boom. It was right before Valencia Street started changing.

JH: Yeah. Because once it started changing, it just changed quickly.

WC: So quickly. It gentrified really, really quickly. Maybe we were harbingers of that. I don't know. Probably. I think we all are, artists always are.

JH: You had the record store for nine years or fourteen years?

WC: Nine as an owner. It was the best experience. Again, it was about getting to define who we were. We had our own aesthetic. We were very unified as a staff about the things that we liked. We only carried music that we loved. We would not carry music that we didn't love. So, we just championed the things that we loved. It was there that I started honing my aesthetic and getting articulate about why is it that I love this music. What is it that makes it compelling? Is it because it's from Brazil in the sixties and that's amazing? Or Ethiopia in the early seventies in between military coups and that makes that music fascinating and also it fucking sounds great?

Being able to articulate that and understand my aesthetic, and having a finely honed aesthetic, has served me so well in my work now. I've only been making art for five years, but I've been able to make a living from it—which is only one gauge of success, but it is one—very quickly. I think it's because I was able to make work that I felt had value very quickly. And that's because I spent two entire careers before making art, just swimming in the world of aesthetics and figuring out what resonates with me.

JH: When you left the record store, you sold it to your employees. But, you didn't know what you were going on to next, is that right?

WC: No, and that was so scary because my whole identity was wrapped up in the record store. I mean, I was literally "Windy from Aquarius." People knew me as that all around the world. It was about leaving my identity, so it was terrifying. But, I wanted to go because I thought fourteen years is long enough to do anything, maybe a little too long. I just wanted to know how the rest of the world lived. That was about as articulate as I was able to get about leaving. I had no idea what it was, but I somehow found the courage to do it.

JH: But, you did many things for a little bit for that year.

WC: Yeah. That was the year where I started realizing I had to have a résumé and I had to figure out how to articulate what I'd been doing for the past fourteen years. I was starting to be able to think, "What is it that I have?" I'm really good at event organizing, creating community, creating a safe place for people, you know, and running a small business, all of that.

I did things that capitalized on some of those things. I ran the social events committee for a mayoral campaign that was happening at the time. It was a really important historical one. It was the one where Gavin Newsom finally became mayor. I did that and then I got bit by the politics bug. I also ran various parts of Dennis Kucinich's campaign. I did that for a year.

Somehow, I ended up at Apple. If you want a job, think of the companies that you totally respect and admire and go on their job boards. So that's what I did. Go straight to the heart of the thing that is most interesting to you or most compelling given whatever the context is. My dad brought home an Apple IIE when I was a sophomore in high school, and thank God he did and didn't bring home some other computer because as a result, I have been Mac OS from day one. I had every iteration of Apple computers, even before the Mac existed. I loved it. I was a super fan. I looked on Apple's job boards. This was right after iTunes had been invented, and the iPod was already out. You could already burn your CDs and put them on iPod. Apple opened the iTunes storefront where you could purchase songs for 99 cents. They needed music experts at that time to help run the store because iTunes was invented by engineers. I joined iTunes in the early days, music being the connecting factor there. It was great.

JH: You also talk about being able to curate. It never occurred to me that that was an actual skill. But, I look at your work, and so much of it is about having a point of view, knowing what you like and what you don't like, and questioning the reasons you like or don't like things.

WC: Yes, that's exactly right. That's exactly right. It's really about having a point of view. I've never heard it quite put that way, but you hit it on the head. That's exactly what it is.

JH: I see so much work right now that doesn't have a point of view or everybody has the same point of view, and it's kind of boring. I think a lot of times, social media does this to us where people see a trend and they just kind of hop onto that without having the context of the work behind it or the reasons why they're doing something other than it looks nice.

WC: Or it's cool. It makes them feel a certain way.

JH: Which is valid . . .

WC: It's fine. But, it's so much more interesting to go beyond that and go, "Why? Why does it make me feel this way?"

JH: You had given advice in an interview to young artists or aspiring artists. You said, "Embrace the constraints."

WC: Wow. I don't remember saying that, but that could make sense on so many different levels, like briefly what we already covered, which is when you approach the work from a craftsperson's perspective, there are constraints built in, right? Rope is flexible. It's not rigid. Wood is rigid. It's not flexible, and what can I do with that? That's a simple constraint. But, then there were also beautiful ways in which constraints can release creativity or embolden it. For example, when I was making *The Year of Knots*, I specifically wanted to downplay every element of art other than the line. I wanted to downplay color, for example, or texture or scale. The work was about none of those things. It was solely about the line as it travels through a knot.

I removed color from the equation by making all the knots with neutral-colored rope and photographed them on a neutral-colored background. That was a constraint I put on myself. Yet, it allowed me to fully go deep on the parts that I was interested in because I wasn't distracted by these things that weren't important to the work. It was a practical constraint that actually allowed the work to blossom.

JH: Tell me more about *The Year of Knots*.

WC: I had been doing macramé for, I don't know, a year and a half, and I was making the same hippy-inspired, Bohemian wall hangings and plant hangers everybody else was making. It's enjoying a resurgence now and everyone's doing that work. But the aesthetic is always really similar. The more I began to take my work seriously and consider whether I could make a living in this world, the immediate thought after that of course was, "What's my voice, and what am I trying to say with the work? And what is the substance of it beyond looking pretty? My work looks like everyone else's." My next immediate thought was, "Oh my God, the reason all macramé looks the same is because only two or three knots are used in macramé." Pretty much. Just in repeated but different combinations. And that's why it all has this boho look. And it's always symmetrical.

Then, I had a light-bulb-over-the-head moment, standing in my backyard on January 4, 2016. I was sweeping up sawdust, and I thought, "Oh my God, I should just learn more. No, I should learn *all* the knots." I have all those knotting books in my library that I've been collecting since I was a teenager and never even opened up. I just thought they were cool. I had a couple, so I ran upstairs, opened the book, and was like, "Oh yeah, oh yeah, this can be done, this can be done." I still remember that day. It was an incredible light-bulb, epiphany moment. I decided that if I learned one new knot every day, then my work would naturally differentiate itself from everyone else's because I'd be using a wider variety of materials.

It's like a painter who has only three colors. I wanted the rainbow. Why wouldn't a painter want a rainbow instead of being limited to, you know, yellow, red, and blue? That was the kernel of the idea. I approached *The Year of Knots* as a yearlong practice in self-education. I love learning from books. I decided I was going to learn from all my dusty, old knotting books. And that that would be what it was. Amazingly, about two months into the making of a daily knot and photographing it and posting it on social media also daily, I looked at the knots that I had nailed up on my living room wall, and I noticed that they were—I was nailing them up in a growing amoeba-like shape—and I realized, about two months in, that it was going to hold together as a single work of art. By the end of the year, I would have a single work of art.

I did not start out the project thinking that's what it would become. I didn't know what it meant to be an artist at the beginning of 2016, and I would never have presumed that I could make some gigantic, installation-sized work of art. I never would have thought that—I approached it solely as an opportunity to self-educate. And I love that. I approached it with such pure intentions, and then it became this great thing that is interesting on many levels: the level of daily practice and how that can change our lives. The level of how it did change my life. How that becomes a story. How stories are interesting. How each knot has a unique—the line, the rope, which sailors call "line"—the line that travels through each knot is unique in each knot and how fascinating that is—and how we all have unique paths in life. And, it's sort of disgustingly rich in metaphor as well as being this stand-alone project.

JH: I think one of the reasons it holds together so well is because of the constraints you've placed on yourself. It's purely about the knot itself. It's about the line. It's one color for the most part. I think in many ways when you have constraints and you have to stick within them, it makes things a lot more interesting. It's also in some ways a little bit easier if it's going to be a sustained practice to set up the constraints up front, you know, and have your style guide in a way and then everything you have to do already has, it's somewhat of a framework.

WC: Yeah. Because otherwise, you start to experience decision fatigue, right? And you don't want that. You want to be able to wake up every morning and go, "Here's what I'm going to do," and plunge into the work as quickly as possible because when you plunge into the work, then you're in flow, and that's bliss.

JH: I have now had three annual projects. The most recent one I did was a tea towel project. I know I had to have a theme and a look and feel, and everything has to play into that. It's challenging because, in some ways, I was stifled in what I could do, but it was also wonderful because I was allowed to not do certain things, too.

WC: How wonderful is that? It's a principle that I honed when I was at the record store. It was about more, more, more, accumulation, excess, how extreme can people be in their music. So, the idea of constraint began to make itself known to me from my time at Apple. During my time at Apple, I absorbed the lessons of "less is more." And the simpler the object is, the more clearly it can speak. Decoration is only that—decoration. If it doesn't feed into the greater message that the object or the piece of art is trying to communicate, then discard it and see what happens.

What I learned at Apple is that the beauty comes from the simplicity of the functional object. It doesn't need any distracting, decorative elements to make it more beautiful. In fact, its message becomes diffused when there are distracting elements. I learned that at Apple—as weirdly corporate as it sounds for me to say that, I did. I learned it there.

JH: You left Apple, and then you started doing other things. I took your wooden spoon carving class when you were still making spoons.

WC: I did. Well, the first thing that I did when I left Apple, knowing that I wanted to make tangible objects. But having no idea what that might look like, I decided to take classes. Classes were starting to be a thing back then and they still are. I took as many classes as I could in anything I was even slightly interested in trying, which was a really good thing because I took like twelve or fifteen classes and a bunch of the stuff I didn't like. I'm so glad that I took those classes because that's how I learned that it was okay to shut that door.

I took classes in anything I was interested in, and, again, going by the principle of if I liked the process, I would keep doing it. And if I didn't, I would absolutely discard thoughts of going further down that road.

JH: Again, curating and editing.

WC: I guess so. Yes, and you'll understand this. I tried to be methodical about my creative search. I was like, "I don't have time to waste." Within a month after quitting my job, I signed up for all these classes. I have a really strong work ethic, too. It's not okay for me to not be doing things. I've always supported myself. I took all these classes and the only two things that stuck—where I wanted to go further within five minutes of taking the class, I thought, "I love how this feels—the doing it. I love how the doing of it feels"—were wood-carving and macramé. I took a macramé refresher class to remind myself how to get started. As you know, I had done macramé with my mom in the seventies, but I couldn't remember how to get it started. I took this refresher class and within five minutes I thought, "Oh my God, I love this." I just want to keep doing it. Same thing with wood.

I started teaching woodcarving and going deep with that and developing my own line of wooden utensils in a shape that I had never seen before. Already, I was thinking about how can I make my work distinctive and original and went down the product route for a while. I was teaching and I was making products. I was also teaching other people how to make my products, which, today, I question how smart that is. And thinking about if I could make a living doing it and I think that I could have. It wouldn't have just been spoons. It probably would have evolved into something else. But after a couple of years of participating in beautiful, high-end craft fairs, dipping my toe into having an online shop, and starting to wholesale my work at retail stores, I realized that products were not where it was at for me.

I think if you're going to have a product-based business, you are repeating yourself a lot—and I'm too easily bored. The work evolves too slowly for me. Of course, it would still evolve, but it would probably be slower. Also, when you have a product-based business, the challenges that you have are how to scale, packaging, customer communications, having all your work look identical so the customer expectations are met, supply chain stuff—none of which I was interested in. Once I realized that, happily at the same time, I had already embarked on *The Year of Knots* as a way of attaining fluency in this other thing I was interested in, which was knotting. Then, I just sort of went full bore with the rope and with the knots. Very quickly during *The Year of Knots*, I started getting offers of well-paying work, making very large installations out of rope. Ever since then, that's been all I want to do.

JH: I think we have to create the work that we want. A lot of times, people sit around waiting for it . . .

WC: To be invited. . .

JH: That's been the theme of almost everybody that I've interviewed is that they're making things because they want to make this thing and not because they're being commissioned. They start out because they're making the thing that they want to see. Or, they're making the project they want to work on, and then sometimes, it catches on. By doing the work, instead of sitting around and being passive about it, they're setting themselves up for this constant momentum. I have so many people emailing me: "How do I get started?" I don't know. Somebody emailed me a two thousand–word essay talking about all the ways she feels stuck and I thought, "Stop emailing me." The number one way for you to move forward is to actually do something. That something is not emailing me.

WC: Just do it. Hello? It's written on all of our shoes. Do it. How many more times do you need to read those words?

JH: One of the reasons it's important for me to write this book is that I think a lot of people think, particularly women, that you have to have all these things in place to get started.

WC: To go back to the idea of constraints, how might great art spring from that? Maybe not constraints the way you and I were talking about it, aesthetic constraints or material, behavioral constraints. There are so many different ways to approach this conversation. I was being interviewed recently, and at the end of the conversation, the interviewer talked about an article she had read about how statistically speaking, people in the upper-third of income, or kids who grew up with more money, are more inclined to make art. And that statistics back that up. I get what she was saying, but immediately where I went to in my mind was that the greatest American art, which is hip-hop and jazz, and all the stuff around hip-hop, basically graffiti and dancing, all of that has not come out of the upper third of income. It's come out of adversity.

It's come out of constraints, making do with what you have and not letting your creativity be boxed in by the fact that you don't have something. You just start. You literally start where you are. I mean, look at how hip-hop started. It started with DJs, with sound systems on the street. Maybe they didn't have instruments, but what did they all have in our living rooms? Turntables. So, it was DJs and sound systems on the street. That's how reggae started in Jamaica too, with DJs and sound systems. The best turntables in the world come from Daly City. Filipino kids had turntables because their dads had them in their living rooms. They didn't go out and buy guitars or have drum sets or room to put up a drum set even, but they all had turntables. So, not having the materials that you need or not having an invitation to do something—none of those things are necessary to make great art. In fact, sometimes, the opposite is true.

JH: I agree with you. We're talking about art that arose within communities. I think that community is often downplayed as a really important part of being an artist. That if I didn't surround myself with women who are far more successful than I am or who are also doing the work, I don't know that I would see the possibility or have the continued energy that I have to see it out there to know that it's possible.

A friend was visiting a few years ago. We were in Golden Gate Park and we walked by the band shell. There was a yo-yo competition. Have you ever seen a yo-yo competition? It's essentially a bunch of b-boys who are too young to go into clubs with their yo-yos, dancing. It was the most amazing thing to see. They would do these break dancing moves with their yo-yos. I had never seen this before, but there was this whole community around it that I didn't know about. This work is evolving out of a community. They were all competing, but they were also all cheering each other on.

WC: That's beautiful and very apt in terms of what we've been talking about the past few minutes, where adversity can become a glue. When you're all suffering from similar conditions, whatever those conditions are, then there's a way to self-identify through the things that you make. Once those things have become established as "this is the thing that we make," then there's a lot of pride in and evolution of that thing that we make and create. It's not just an art form anymore, but it becomes a culture. That's really beautiful. It's so nice to talk about community in that way. You know, I get asked the question, "Who's your community?" a lot. I always feel so dumb being like, "Well, I've met some women who are all trying to do our thing," and that's not ever a potent answer and it doesn't get to the heart of what I think we're talking about, which is really like how does culture come out of community? How are those connected? Especially when we think about craft, Indigenous cultures, and how much of that has been taken or co-opted or evolved or whatever we have, we as Americans have done with it.

JH: Is there anything that I haven't asked you that you want to talk about?

WC: Yes. Most of my work, especially the big-ticket stuff, tends to be large installations in commercial or hospitality spaces. However, as my work has progressed and my career has progressed, I'm having a lot more private collector commissions, which is wonderful. What I've noticed is that at least half of them now have been from Asian women. I never would have thought because I did think my private commissions were all going to be from rich, white women. But it hasn't been that. About half of my private commissions have been from Asian women of means. I live in the tech mecca of the world, so they're involved in tech and are creating their dream homes. I've talked about this in terms of race and gender with only one of them, and she said, "Your work is totally stunning, but what sealed the deal and what enabled me to approach an artist," which was something she had never done before, was the fact that I was an Asian woman. I was like, "Thank you so much for telling me that." I don't know how unusual that is. Maybe you can tell me from having spoken to so many artists, but for me, it was major to realize this and to get to have that conversation.

JH: I know how I get a lot of purchases from other Black women mainly because there aren't many who do the kind of work that I do. I've had people tell me, "I saw you on the cover of your book and I didn't know who you were, but I had to buy it because you were on the cover of the book."

WC: It just . . . it felt really good. I guess I just never had anticipated that a demographic that I belong to would seek me out for my art. The fact that it's interesting to me may be a sign of how cynical I am. I never would have expected that someone who's rich and was going to spend some money on art is gonna care enough to seek out someone who belongs to their demographic as well. I never thought that anyone would do that. Yet, why should I be surprised? I mean, when I spend lots of money on clothes, I buy from female designers, most of whom I know. I'm okay with spending a little bit more money when I know the woman who made your clogs.

It's just nice. At the level of fine art, it was like, "Wow, that works at that level too." Awesome. Hell yeah. I'll take it.

SURVEY PROFILE

Lisa Woolfork

Age: 50
Location: Charlottesville, Virginia
Profession: Associate professor, African American literature and culture, University of Virginia
Avocation: Creator of the group Black Women Stitch and the *Stitch Please* podcast

What types of fiber crafts do you engage in, and how many years have you been engaged in each?
Sewing and quilting for about twenty-five years.

How do you self-describe/identify yourself?
I love to sew. Sewing is a creative outlet, a therapeutic process, but also a practice tied to my family history and liberatory practices in general.

What's the first thing you remember making?
I recall making free-form Barbie clothes as a small child.

What are you making now?
Right this minute, I am making peace in my sewing room by organizing patterns and fabric. Under the needle, I am sewing pajamas for my husband, loungewear for my sisters, and a bralette for myself.

What's your favorite thing you've made?
A raincoat and matching umbrella. Though, I love making men's shirts, baby shoes, and 90 percent of my own clothes.

How and why did you learn your crafts?
My mother and grandmother both sewed. My mom was a fourth-grade teacher. In the summer, she would sew school clothes for me and my sisters.

She would set up her sewing machine so she could sew and watch us while we played outside. Later, in graduate school, I took formal classes in quilting and garment construction as a stress release from dissertation writing. Later, I apprenticed with a master quilter. My passion comes from my family legacy. My skills were formally acquired, and I've built upon them in the decades since.

Does anyone in your family practice this craft, too? Are your pieces similar or different aesthetically?

My grandmother, who passed away at the age of 104, was a couture sewist: hand-picked zippers, gorgeous hand-finishing. My mother, who still sews occasionally, is a bit less patient. I'm more like my mother: I love to sew and I want to get it done. *But*, I do think the inside of a garment should look as good as the outside, so I think that's from my Nana.

Tell me about your creative community. You can define "community" as broadly or as specifically as you'd like.

After decades of sewing and quilting in white spaces, I crafted Black Women Stitch in 2018 as a space that centers Black women sewists and quilters. In 2019, I hosted our first Black Women Stitch Beach Week, a week of sewing solidarity in an oceanfront beach house. It was a restorative, healing, and amazing time. For the first time ever, I feel like I'd found an actual sewing community where I truly belonged. We didn't all agree on all things, but we valued what it meant to be Black in a creative space. We all had experiences where we had been sidelined, side-eyed, exposed, or shut out because of our race. This was a space to exhale.

In the beginning, this retreat was a tough sell. I built it from Instagram, and trust had to be established. In the end, there were ten of us who got to experience this fantastic week. Many sewing/fabric/notions businesses ignored or denied my requests for donations—I thought because I said it was for "Black women," though it may have been for lots of other reasons. In the end, I found a few strong industry supporters such as Lisa Shepard Stewart from Cultured Expressions and Heather Givans from Crimson Tate, and we had amazing goody bags and swag. I also made a daily gift—usually personalized, since I am a long-term expert Silhouette Cameo cutting machine user—to commemorate our time.

After the sewing retreat, I wanted to continue the stitching sisterhood that was generated during that amazing event. So, I started a podcast. *Stitch Please*, the official podcast of Black Women Stitch, launched in September 2019. Today, the podcast continues to thrive as a place to center Black women, girls, and femmes in sewing.

When have you felt like an "other" within the context of your craft?

I have a long history within predominantly white spaces and institutions: college, graduate school, and my current job as a professor. This naturalizes the idea of being in the minority. For about twenty years of participating in guilds or retreats, I was the only Black face in the crowd. I overlooked the biased comments, the microaggressions. I simply tolerated the disdain these quilters and sewists seemed to have for Black people other than myself (this peaked during Obama's presidency). I held my tongue as they glibly wondered why Black people didn't just listen to the police, even as they shared personal stories of telling officers who had pulled *them* over to "just give me the damn ticket."

I was no longer able to remain silent in the summer of 2017. I live in Charlottesville, Virginia. That summer, there were white supremacist rallies in our town every month. The August rally was the largest white supremacist rally in modern US history. I was a founding member of our local Black Lives Matter group. We resisted all summer: protesting, teach-ins, presentations, media work, and more. I was locked in a church as white supremacists marched with torches on my campus on Friday, August 11, 2017. The next day, when a neo-Nazi drove his car through a crowd, killing one counterprotester and injuring more than twenty other people, I was there, about one hundred feet from the crash site. It was horrible.

Yet, the sewing and quilting group who I had worked with for years, who saw me on TV or read my quotes in national media, did not reach out to see how I was. That was hurtful. We have a tradition of reaching out to members when grief strikes. We send cards or make phone calls. My pain was invisible to them. But it wasn't the worst of it.

In September 2017, I went to a quilt retreat that I had attended for fifteen years. I had paid for this event and a future event for the following year. People there asked how I was, and I told them, with no weeping or gnashing of teeth. Just simple, short answers. Unbeknownst to me, the quilt retreat organizer had banned any talk of the "Charlottesville incident." I didn't know. I felt erased and unwelcome. When I got home after the retreat, I found that my check for her future retreat had been returned to me without a note. I had been barred from that event.

I apologize for the length of this response, but I wanted to share a small part of why Black Women Stitch, the digital space, and in-person events are so important to me. It is a way to intervene in the passive (though not always) naivety of a white industry. To create a space of welcome and solace. I'm deliberately Black, not coincidentally so. I want to center Blackness in this space because there are so many ways in which we are marginalized.

When do you feel recognized in your craft? Who recognizes you and how does that feel for you?
I feel recognized in my sewing quite often. I sew most of my clothes, so when someone compliments my wardrobe, I can say, "Thank you, I made it." This feels pretty great. Even my husband, for whom I sew dress shirts, gets a version of this. When he wears a shirt I made for him, a coworker will say, "Oh, that's a great shirt. I bet Lisa made that one." And just recently, when I asked my teenager (!) what he liked about me being his mom (who *knows* how that came up?) he replied, "Free clothes. I like the clothes you make me." I sew for family and some friends who appreciate what I do. That feels awesome.

Are there aspects of your work that you feel are misunderstood?
Not especially. I mostly feel misunderstood within the context of the larger crafting and sewing communities. There is something to be said for spending precious sewing time with people who believe that Colin Kaepernick should have been fired for kneeling to protest police brutality. That's where I feel erased and misunderstood. This is why I created Black Women Stitch: I would never again sew with anyone who did not believe that Black lives matter.

What adjectives do you use to describe your work?
Bright, colorful, retro, vintage silhouettes with modern, African, bold fabrics.

When you were younger, were you exposed to other people who looked like you, or who were from similar backgrounds as you, and who engaged in this craft?
Yes. I grew up in an all-Black community in South Florida. My mother and grandmothers all sewed.

Where did you get inspiration growing up? Who were your idols?
I was inspired by some of the Black teachers I had in high school. They were so poised and polished—old-school.

Who do you look to for inspiration today?
There are women scholar-activists that I admire: Angela Davis, Audre Lorde, bell hooks, Instagram accounts/podcasters like *The Free Black Women's Library*, *Tea with Queen and J.*, and *Therapy for Black Girls*. I love the sewing styles of Malacia Anderson of Li Li's Creations, Aaronica Cole of The Needle & The Belle. Celebrities like Beyoncé and Michelle Obama are smart, savvy, icons that have significantly changed culture.

What colors are you drawn to and why?
Purple! I love purple. There is something comforting and warm about it.

Where do you get your materials?
I buy fabric from the Garment District in NYC once or twice a year. I also visit the local JoAnn's and local independent quilt shop in town.

How do you choose your materials?
I choose materials based on texture, color, feel, and price.

Is there anything else you'd like to add?
Thank you for focusing your attention on sewists, quilters, crafters of color. I think it is important to talk about crafters of color who are finding ways not to erase or minimize or ignore who they are to better fit within a predominantly white landscape. Thank you for embarking on this work.

FINDING THE ANSWERS
IN EMBROIDERY

Interview with Raven Dock

JEN HEWETT: I have been doing research on everybody before I interview them. I looked you up and I did a little bit of research, and I realized that there's not that much about you out there. Is that intentional or is that just the way things have happened so far?

RAVEN DOCK: It's a little intentional. As an artist, I've been dealing with a lot of impatience. I feel jealousy toward painters and people who can get almost that instant gratification with their work. I feel because I couldn't share as many finished pieces, the opportunity to share more about me was glossed over.

With fibers being so slow, it seems like no matter what you're doing, it's a very slow process. I can't push myself to work past six hours a day because my arm and my eyes take a hit. Even at twenty-three, my body takes a hit. My body just can't take that strenuous amount of work every day. And, I get impatient with myself, I get frustrated. I want to see the piece finished and completed in two days, but I'm possibly going to be working on it for weeks and months. I think embroidery forced me to be patient. I started doing this three years ago, and I've been stitching every single day for three years. I don't think I've taken more than a week break. When I finish pieces, I can't go more than a few days without starting up something new. I get just so eager to see a piece finished. I can have six pieces lined up and it's probably going to take me a full year before I even finish them.

It's hard as an artist, as a person who's trying to do art full-time, to grow my portfolio, to build an extensive portfolio to do more shows, to work with more people when you're creating pieces so slowly. In reality, I am kind of doing a lot. I've been doing portraits for less than a year. I've already had three exhibitions solely off my portrait work and I think that's pretty good.

JH: You're twenty-three! There are artists my age who would kill for that kind of thing. You're doing fine, but I completely get what it's like to want more. Because that's what keeps you going, right?

RD: I don't share a lot and I also don't look for a lot, so I don't really know what anyone else is going through. I kind of get in a bubble. I don't see a lot of what other people are doing so I get tunnel vision. I don't share what I should be sharing on Instagram because I'm so focused on the piece. That's something I want to change. I do want to open up more to people and explain a little bit more about my pieces. I don't feel like I give them enough substance. A lot of my portraits stem from answers that I want or just things I'm feeling.

JH: I'm curious to know how you even started with the needlework. It's not an obvious choice for a twenty-year-old. What got you into it in the first place?

RD: A lot of it stems from my last two months of high school, in 2014. My guidance counselor talked me into dropping out of high school two months before graduation. My teachers got so mad because they were like, "You didn't even take your final exam. If you pass all your final exams, you can graduate." I'm like, "No. My guidance counselor said I can't do it." The following week, I dropped out of school. I remember my teachers were so angry because it wasn't just me that was convinced to leave. The school's administrators didn't want the school's A+ rating to be affected, so the counselors either kicked underperforming students out or talked us into leaving school.

I felt down. During that time, I decided to pursue something creative, even if I was never good at art. I used to be so fearful of art class. Art was a scary thing for me. I couldn't draw. I felt like I didn't have the capability or imagination to draw. I just felt horrible. I watched a video from these two girls called The Sorry Girls, and they were sewing on clothes. They put Drake's 6 God logo on a shirt. I was just like, "I love that. I want to try that." The following day, I went to Michael's and picked up a tiny three-inch embroidery hoop and white, red, and black thread.

I stitched to that. I practiced and I played around for a few months. A few months in, I started realizing that this is not the easy route to art because I still don't know what to do with these three colors. It was the equivalent of having paint—I still didn't know what to do with it. I like to equate the three years it took me to finally get to portraiture akin to changing the radio station for three years straight. I could not find my channel. And I was extremely frustrated. During my first three years of embroidery, I went from doing home decor to doing custom things with jackets and stuff like that. My early days of embroidery were not that happy, but they were still fun. I think not knowing my voice as an artist and not knowing exactly what I wanted to do with this medium added to my frustration.

JH: But you stuck with it. What was it about embroidery that made you stick with it? Because it sounds like you had a love-hate relationship with it for those first three years.

RD: I think because I let someone get in my ear and talk me into dropping out of school, I decided at that moment nobody was talking me out of doing anything anymore, even myself. I got aggressively passionate about embroidery. I got intense about it and I fell head over heels in love with it the moment I found it, but it was almost like I didn't know how to carve my own way.

I looked at work from Cayce Zavaglia and a bunch of other artists, and they look like they're not doing what everyone else on Instagram is doing. They have a voice. I was like, "Why can't I have one?" One day, I started what became my first portrait, *Bending of Wills*.

I didn't know what I was doing. I didn't like the patterns that were available to me to use to learn. And, I was seeing so many people doing amazing things. It was a lot of trial and error. I was still turning those radio stations to find my station until I started *Bending of Wills*. I just stared at it when I was done, and I was like, "This is it. I feel like I'm finally home." I've been rolling out portraits ever since then.

I love the color palette of the kids' cartoon show *Over the Garden Wall*. I'm starting to notice a lot of my color palettes are starting to reflect this show. The show is about the unknown and it's akin to *Dante's Inferno*. The characters are going through these levels and this forest—that's what I almost feel with my pieces. I never intend my pieces to come off creepy—and I'm pretty sure they didn't intend for this show to come off creepy, but it is. I'm not a horror movie person. I don't like anything scary. I get disturbed very easily, but my pieces come off very creepy and I'm not sure how. I don't do it on purpose.

I think that a lot of my work reflects things that I'm not ready to really talk about or even confirm with myself. I'm not sure what they are, but they come out of my art and a lot of people take up on it and I don't. I was talking to this guy. He was just like, "Your art is scary." No. "What is scary? Why?" He was like, "They don't have eyes." I'm like, "Why does a lack of eyes scare you?" He's just like, "You don't know what that person's thinking." But that's the beauty of it; you don't know. The mouth can tell a thousand stories. The eyes can tell a million more. Your eyes say what you're not saying.

I think stripping that back from some of my portraits, like *Bending of Wills* and *Unrequited Love*. Is *Unrequited Love* about the person, the portrait, the subject—not feeling the same love back from the person that they love, or is it a different story? I don't like to tell people "This is what it means and you can't change it." I want you to write a story for yourself. I want you to determine if in *Unrequited Love*—is she smiling or is she frowning? I want people to see themselves within the pieces and to really use the name of the piece as a foundation and then go on this adventure of figuring it out for themselves. The lack of eyes is off-putting to a lot of people like my family. My family is just like, "Where're the eyes?"

Some people find my work very off-putting and some people will connect with it. I had no intentions for either. It's almost like I use these two groups of people to almost map out what I was feeling when I started it because a lot of the time, I may not know my true intentions for a piece until I'm done. I don't know if other artists do that. I don't know if you do that. But I'm a very "jump in, hit the ground running" person. I just do it, and we're going to see how it's gonna turn out. I'll let the emotions follow as I'm doing it because I do feel a lot of emotions while I'm working.

JH: Tell me about that.

RD: 'Cause I'm staring at a piece for hours every day. It's so hard to explain, but when I'm working on a portrait, let's say the face is somewhat complete, I'm staring in someone's face for hours, even though they're not reciprocating anything. I'm still staring at this person and I almost use it as a therapy session. I just let it all go.

Every piece has a feeling attached to it. Even more so based on what music I'm listening to or the book I'm listening to while I'm working because

I don't watch TV at all while working. My work requires a lot of concentration. So, concentration, on top of listening to a book or music, on top of feeling whatever I'm feeling while I'm stitching. I'm never angry at my subjects because I cannot stitch someone I'm mad at, because it would be horrible to stare at them that long.

JH: I was reading through your descriptions of your work. You do the work of someone who's been to art school. You're twenty-three years old. You have a portfolio, practice, and a way of talking about and thinking about your work that people who've gone through four years of art school and have done a number of years of professional practice would be so jealous of. How did you learn how to talk about your process? Was that just something that came naturally to you or is that something that you watched other people do, or did you take a class?

RD: It became natural. I had to figure out a way to state things in a way that's efficient. I couldn't find anyone who was doing anything close to what I was doing in cross-stitch form. It came more natural to just phrase out my words.

I have notebooks of the hours I worked and I know exactly what day, down to the minute, how long I worked on a piece. I record all my hours because that's one way I price my things. I don't include material prices. A lot of people say that I need to change my pricing. I get so afraid that people are going to say that my work is too expensive. I try to price in a way that I think it's fair. But some people think I charge too little. Pricing scares me.

I feel like I need to lower my prices a little bit more. I need to make this more accessible to people. The gallery told me my pricing is low. I'm like, "The piece was $950" and she was like, "You need to double or triple that." I think yes, I mean I need to bring somebody in to sit me down because if I keep doing it myself, I'm just going to keep pricing everything under $1,000 for the rest of my life. I need someone to almost shake me.

I've never had anyone tell me my prices are too high. I've never had anyone tell me that, period. I think that fear ballooned in myself and I went and I followed it. No one has ever told me that embroidery shouldn't be priced that high because it's not taken as seriously as an art form. I just keep on with the bad habit of pricing low in the hopes that people will want it, and that's a very bad way of being an artist. I know that I need to change that and I need to be more confident with myself and more encouraged to charge what I know I deserve or what I think I deserve. I'm going to do a better job at that.

JH: Did you get your GED? Are you still working through high school stuff?

RD: I have not gotten my GED. I don't want to have that shame, but I'm going to get my GED. I'm going to do it.

JH: School failed you. It was not you failing school because you're clearly incredibly smart and very talented. If your high school was not able to help you get through high school, then that was their fault and not yours because you were a child, and they were not doing their job. Especially that guidance counselor . . .

RD: I talked to other people that went to different schools, and no other school has done that. There was actually an article about my high school and I had no idea it existed. I think it was back in 2008. The school does it every single year. They get students who are right at the brink and they kick them all out. I had no idea this was happening the entire time I was in school. They've done this for going on ten years

I read the article and heard other high school seniors' experiences with the alternative school the guidance counselors recommended—it took them two years to graduate after dropping out and enrolling at the alternative

---

> I don't want to use art as a vessel to carry
> me further away from people. I want to use
> it to bring me back. It definitely has.

---

school. My guidance counselor was trying to put me into that situation. She was trying to put me into a vicious cycle of going into a school she knew I wasn't going to graduate from. It's almost like they had a quota of the number of students they needed to leave.

I'm not gonna keep that experience in the back seat anymore. I am going to bring that to the forefront, and that's something I am going to mention in my art more. I want people to know more about me. These are things that we need to talk about as artists because a lot of the time, we don't mention anything, and I think that's where a lot of disconnect happens. There's a lot of times that we were going through something alone when there's other people going through it, too. So, that's why I want to be more connected. I feel like people are more connected to my art when I'm a little bit more personal. I want to be closer to my collectors, new friends, and artists. I think because of my school situation, I isolated myself from people and I became an introvert. I don't want to use art as a vessel to carry me further away from people. I want to use it to bring me back. It definitely has.

WHAT ARE YOU MAKING NOW?

Sewing a tunic from fabric I shibori dyed.—TARA HARRISON

Quilts: I have about twenty-two quilts in progress from "merely cut out" to "Seriously, just attach the front side of the binding. It'll take like thirty minutes tops—*just do it!*" Machine knitting: two sweaters waiting to be seamed, one waiting for the body (I hand-knit the yoke). Knitting: at least seven sweater works-in-progress. Most are stalled out at the shoulders because I get bored before sleeve island; I may frog a few as they're too big now. Plus, two shawls. Spinning: working on some Corriedale, likely a worsted once plied. Crochet: a shawl. Sewing: a *Game of Thrones*-inspired cosplay gown, plus some kids' clothes. No weaving works-in-progress currently.—KRISTINA KOO

A denim skirt with hand-printed fabrics showcased.—MARGO COFFEY BALDWIN

YARDS AND YARNS OF HAPPINESS

Personal Narrative of Dana Williams-Johnson, as told to Jen Hewett

I'M THE youngest of three girls. My parents would always say, "We don't know where this artist came from." I come from a family where education was key. My dad was the first Black man to graduate from Notre Dame Law. That was in 1969. My dad went to Notre Dame for his JD and went to Duke for his MBA and he was a college professor. My mom always taught adult literacy. She's very into reading and literacy at any age, so my two sisters and I were very well-read kids.

I'm getting a PhD in communications, culture, and media studies. But I have always focused on art and creating. I was very obsessed with paper crafting, painting, and drawing. I remember as a kid, making clothes out of paper for myself. My grandmother was a seamstress and my father sewed. In middle school, I learned how to sew. I'm not the best sewer. I have friends who sew stuff that looks like someone bought it in a store. That's how I am with knitting. I am a really great knitter. I didn't learn to knit until my thirties, so less than ten years ago.

As a kid, I was always painting, always drawing. I had eight billion journals. My parents fostered my creativity in different ways. At one point, my father owned a carpet and flooring store, so we always changed the carpet in our house. Once, my mom went away for a conference, and she asked my dad to replace the carpet in all the girls' rooms while she was gone. My dad let us also paint our rooms and pick whatever colors we wanted. I, of course, picked this wild wallpaper with stars and a rainbow. The wall color was the same as one of the stars, which was this crazy green. I painted the trim gray and then had another shade of the green on the carpet.

When my mom saw this, she was so mad. She asked my dad, "Why would you let her do this?" My dad said, "'Cause it's her room. I want her to be happy. I want her to express herself and feel like it's her space." From early on, my parents have always said, "You do you." I've always felt different. Even in how

I dress or in what I do, I always express myself differently than everybody else. My parents didn't want me to feel bad about that, which I'm grateful for.

I've always been bold, always spoken up for myself, always done my own thing. I think part of it is when you're the youngest (my siblings are six and nine years older), you kind of have to figure out how to be heard. So, I always made sure that I was heard.

I went to elementary school in Durham, North Carolina. I went to middle school in Andover, Massachusetts. I went to high school in Williamsburg, Virginia. And then I went to Howard University for undergrad in DC. When I graduated, I moved just outside of Baltimore for my first job and never left Maryland.

I think the first time you do it, moving sucks. But I learned how to make friends. I mean, I'm loud. I'm the kind of person who can walk into a room and talk to anybody. It doesn't matter if you're an adult or if you're a kid. I always went to things with my parents when I was a child and people would be like, "Dana is just a delight." My parents would say, "Oh, she'll talk to anybody." My family traveled all over the United States and exposed us to things. My parents always made us a priority, which I think is great. They took us everywhere. They exposed us to everything. And, they told us we could be whatever we wanted to be.

For me, family is wherever home is. Over our bed is a sign that says, "Home is wherever I am with you." My husband's a structural engineer; he's always known what he wanted to be. I didn't. I didn't figure out that I wanted to be a college professor until several years ago. I told him, "We can move wherever because it was based on your job." I can get a job. And I told him, I said, "Home is wherever you are. That's all that matters to me. As long as you're there, I'll turn whatever we have into a home."

He likes the State Department. And since I'm going to get my PhD, I'll probably teach at one of the schools here. I had worked in the private sector, I'd worked in higher ed for a while as an administrator, and I worked for a trade association. I have a master's degree in publishing. I did a lot of emphasis on the digital side of publishing, built up my web skills, and started a blog, *The Art of Accessories*. A lot of people know me from that blog.

PROFESSOR WILLIAMS-JOHNSON

I started that blog in grad school. I got jobs that were web based and social media based because of my grad school work. I started working as an adjunct professor at Howard University four or five years ago. I used to guest lecture for one of my girlfriends who would bring me in every semester to teach a course on design and InDesign for their advertising class. Every year, she would tell me, "You need students. You belong in a classroom."

One day at work she messaged me, "Hey, the social media person quit. I need to know if you're willing to adjunct next semester." My boss at my full-time job knew that I was miserable, but really wanted me to stay. My boss said I could do whatever I wanted to do. I started adjuncting part-time while working my other job, and I realized very quickly that when I walked into a classroom, I came alive in a way that I never had with any other job. When the semester ended, I was sad 'cause I thrived with students. I started crafting a plan. When you teach, you get scored by students and the dean's office looks at that, so I made sure I always had good scores. I had a meeting with the dean of the school of business, and it was just me and him because no one else showed up to the meeting. He started asking me about my class. We ended up having an hour-long meeting about what I taught, how I taught, and he said, "We need to get you on full-time." They brought me in this year as a full-time instructor.

The undergrads in my social media marketing class each have to create their own blogs, create content, content strategy plans, and social media campaigns. They come in like, "I know Twitter." My response is, "No, you don't. You don't know it on a level that I do." I did a lot of political campaigns and things for the trade association that I worked for. Y'all have no clue. What you think is popular on Twitter because it's funny isn't what's going to make money or get you noticed.

They all blog every fall semester. They have to run analytics. My graduate-level class this year helped me build a website for our department. We did some email marketing campaigns to our student body, within the school of business. They got to understand WordPress. We use HubSpot. I'm very about hands-on, practical certifications that they can get when they come into class. I want them to be able to put a domain name and a certification on their resumes that can point people to something of value. Some of them come back saying, "I got a job because of my blog." I'm like, there you go.

YARDS OF HAPPINESS

One of the reasons I started my blog *Yards of Happiness* was because I was making my students blog, but I had stopped blogging. I said, "I gotta blog and be back in it," so that when they ask me questions—I can't be the social media person and let my presence go down. You know, now they're like, "Oh, she has over ten thousand Instagram followers. Our professor's legit." I'm like, "Calm down. It's more than just how many Instagram followers you have." But to them, I have credibility because I have a presence.

The other reason I started *Yards of Happiness* was my dad's death in 2015. He had pancreatic cancer, but he had gotten diagnosed really early, so he survived about five years with it. My father was the kind of person who said, "I can't wallow in this." Instead of saying, "Why me?" he actually said, "Why not me? I wouldn't wish this on my worst enemy. It's my time." My dad was a bear hugger of a person: a big, tall guy who loved hugs, who was very demonstrative about his love and affection. He loved his daughters to pieces. He loved my husband like he was his son. I got heavily into knitting when he was ill. I would be in the hospital and I would knit. I knit him a blanket for chemo, and he had specific hats that he liked to sleep in because he was always cold. Knitting became this expression of love.

When we put him in hospice, I went online and bought expensive Madelinetosh yarn that I had been lusting over 'cause I needed something good in my hands while I coped with his illness. Then he passed away. When someone passes away, people fill your house. But they don't know how to respond to someone when someone dies, so instead of people asking me, "Well, how are you doing?" people asked me, "What are you making?" And they would focus on that. I could talk to them about that, but I couldn't talk to them about my dad. I was a daddy's girl. I was his girl. I was a mess.

Yarn and knitting bring me this level of comfort and joy and a solace at times when I'm stressed. I knit twenty-seven sweaters one year because my job at the National Association of Home Builders was killing me. It was slowly killing me. And so, I knit. I knit to cope. It helps me center and refocus.

When I started *Yards of Happiness*, I felt like there was no one else out there that looked like me with a knitting blog. I felt like a lot of the knitting blogs were white women who all looked the same and knit neutral gray sweaters again and again. And, I knew that I had a voice and that I wanted instead to focus on the aspects of knitting that I really love—the joy of it and the happiness that it's brought to my life.

I don't have children. I had a miscarriage years ago. That's how we ended up getting my dog Cher. I love kids; we just don't have kids. I have a picture of my girlfriend handing me her newborn baby swaddled in a blanket I'd made her. I infused so much love into that blanket. I give to the people that I'm super close to. And that girl, that specific girlfriend, her mom had died. This was her second child, but the first child after her mom had died. At her baby shower, my gift happened to be the last thing that she opened and she just bawled, "I know how much love is in this."

I talk openly about things because I don't want people to feel stigma. I don't want people to feel like they're alone. Yes, I've had a miscarriage. What got me through it was knowing girlfriends who had been through that, so now they send other people to me. I want to then share the good things. I want people to know, "Hey, don't feel bad because you like acrylic yarn." I did stuff with acrylic yarn all the time. There's so much shaming and snobbery in the knitting community—I got shamed by a teacher once 'cause I knit one of her patterns with acrylic yarn. I will never buy another pattern from this person ever again because she judged me because I used acrylic yarn.

I want people to feel like whatever they want to do is okay. You don't have to have a billion dollars to knit. I buy cheap stuff. I buy expensive stuff too. It's okay to like what you want to like. People tell me that they like that I'll talk about high-end yarn but that I'll also talk about low-end yarn to give them options. At one point, I was in a job making well into six figures. So yeah, I will splurge on some Madelinetosh at full price, and then sometimes, I'll go to JoAnn's with a coupon and call it a day.

CHOOSING JOY

I felt like nobody else was talking in that way to people, being genuine. I'm a fairly happy person. My mom and I both live with the philosophy that sometimes in life you have to choose joy. It's not always easy. You still have to find that reason or that thing that makes life good, especially after losing a parent. But I'm still here. My dad would be thrilled right now to know that I'm going into my doctoral program. That was one of the last things that we talked about. I have a life of . . . I choose joy. I randomly will text my husband, "I really love my life and I really love you, and I just needed to say that." The other day he called me. "I'm on my way home and picking up pizza and I'm so excited just to come home and watch a movie with you and snuggle with the dogs on the couch. And I really love this life that we've built." I was like, "Well,

I'm happy 'cause I love it, too, and I love you." I think when you are that way with other people, it's infectious and you can't help but think, "Oh, she loves me. I want to spread that joy, that happiness that she gives me to somebody else." That's what I try and do in blog form. I found that when bad things happen or when I am concerned or worried, my readers now give that back to me.

One of the reasons why I went back to Howard was that in previous jobs, I felt very ignored. I've been in meetings where I knew I was the only person in that meeting that had all the information that they needed, and no one would ask me a single thing. Or, if I said something, I wasn't heard, and then the man next to me would repeat exactly what I said and be told, "Oh, that's a great idea." I was tired of being ignored in that way or being told, "You're really smart." I shocked the hell out of one of my VPs who told me that. I said, "Then why do you continue to give me menial tasks if you think I'm so smart?"

Or always being the only woman of color at the table, even at the director level. So, part of when I was adjuncting and at Howard in the beginning, it was one of the reasons why I was there. What I'd loved about being an undergrad at Howard was walking into a room and seeing all these brown faces that probably went through something similar that you did or understood that level of struggle. For me, I make a choice to enrich the lives of students of color. And give them opportunities and expose them to things that I wasn't exposed to maybe or that I think would be more beneficial to them and to push them to excel in different ways because we don't get those opportunities as often.

We watched Beyoncé's *Homecoming* the other day. My husband and I kept saying, "This is Howard." That's like a football game for us. She encapsulated my four years at Howard University in a two-hour concert and it's this amazingly mind-blowing thing that makes Black culture, it makes us look so beautiful. It's one of the reasons why I tell people, "Well, I don't see myself out there, so I put myself out there." When my friend Andrea Pippins' book came out and I went to one of her book signings with our other good friend Jessica, they were interviewing people about why it mattered. I said, "'Cause we aren't represented in the world." People love to post those photos of themselves on Instagram where they crop their heads out of the photo. But, I made this and I'm proud of it, and you're going to see my face. Of course, I'm smiling. 'Cause I made this. Yes, I'm tooting my own horn, but I have a reason to. If I don't, who else will? Yeah, I made this. It's awesome. I don't feel like it's bragging. I don't feel bad saying "I made this."

I knit dolls that look like the little girls in my life. My parents never let me have a white doll because my mother said that when you play with dolls, you are envisioning yourself that way and she wants me to see myself in the dolls that I played with. I make dolls for the little girls in my life in their like-nesses, down to the skin tone. My girlfriend is Asian, and I made her little girl a doll that looked like her. As soon as she saw it, she said, "That's a little Leia. That's me." I had seen her with a white baby doll and had to do something about that. To be able to see yourself in any environment makes you feel seen, heard, and validated. To be able to make a doll for someone that looks just like them—I like to make a dress for the doll that matches the dress for the girl—that matters. I don't think people realize that.

I knit for people who I feel appreciate what I make and the time that went into it. And will take care of what I make for them. So, that's my close circle. Everybody always wants me to make them a sweater. Not gonna happen, but

---

That's the stuff that I love. That's why I do it.
Knitting's a love language for me. It's really
how I let people know they matter.

---

if you have a child, I will knit your child the sweater 'cause baby sweaters take me like a weekend. A friend realized there's a formula: if I knit you a blanket, I love you, because I hate knitting blankets. They take a long time. If I knit you a blanket, that's a lot of love. If I knit you a blanket, I probably knit you a sweater and a hat, too. I know sometimes people invite me to baby showers 'cause they want me to knit them something. I can't make everything for everybody, but I will typically keep my friends' children looking adorable for several years.

A man who's like my little brother, Travis, who was my grad assistant at one point, now does cause marketing and speaks to my class every year. I knit Travis this one hat style that he loves in probably every color. I love it because I'll see him post on Instagram and as soon as it gets cold, one of those hats is always on his head. And, he thinks of me whenever he puts that on, and I know that it's being worn and that it's loved.

That's the stuff that I love. That's why I do it. Knitting's a love language for me. It's really how I let people know they matter.

Perception and
Representation

< gather here's *You Belong Here* campaign

OTHERING AND BELONGING

Survey Question: When Have You Felt Like an "Other" within the Context of Your Craft?

The fact that I am not a part of any of my crafts communities in Tampa is a testament to being an "other." I never see women of color in bead or yarn shops, and I don't feel comfortable shopping at these places. I discovered a bead shop in my new neighborhood. The owner followed me around that tiny shop my entire visit. I felt compelled to buy something because she made me feel like I was a potential thief.—TRACEY RICKS FOSTER

I felt out of place at the one public stitching group I attended. I felt like the group was extremely cliquey, and I felt out of place as the youngest person and the only person of color. I did not feel welcomed. I never went back due to the rude and disinterested organizers. They assumed I was in the wrong place the entire time.—MJ BARAJAS

I have felt this way at some knit nights. Everyone would talk around me or smile an awkward smile and nod slowly when I would chip in. At fiber festivals, I've seen vendors actively engage with white customers and wait until I'm the only one left before engaging. The most surprising time was while working at a yarn store: A customer came in asking for help. I cleared a space for them and said I could help them. They walked around to the other side of the table and asked my white coworker if she worked there. My coworker obliged and helped the customer, and then the customer left. My coworker was very weirded out by the situation and said that I probably could have helped the customer better.—NORIKO HO

There have been times when I've felt very out of place at my local yarn show. There are a few staff members who work there part-time who have condescended me or flat out ignored me when I walked in (the door is directly in front of the cash register, so it's not like they could reasonably play the "I didn't see you there" card). After a few encounters like that, I committed to memory which days those people were working so that I knew not to go to the yarn store when they'd be there.—ARIA VELASQUEZ

JEN HEWETT: I was taking a pattern drafting class in New York's Hudson Valley with a handful of other people—all-white women—when the subject of this book, which I'd already been working on for a few months, came up. One of the other participants told me about her quilt guild and said that one of her big disappointments was that only one woman of color belonged to it, despite that it was based in an area with a fairly diverse population.

"Why is that?" she asked me. "Do women of color just not like joining these groups? Is it not part of their culture?"

I took a deep breath and explained that, no, it's not that joining craft groups is not part of "our" cultures. It's more that these groups are often not comfortable or particularly welcoming spaces for people of color. Often choosing to be the "other" in a space means making yourself open to reactions varying from comments that assume that you're not as skilled as others in the group, to outright hostility—or somewhere in between. Or, you're putting yourself in a position where you're asked to be the spokesperson for all people of color, as, I thought but didn't say, I was being asked to do at that moment.

I explained that I'm used to being if not the only, then one of a handful of people of color in most craft spaces I'm in. I choose this because it benefits me professionally. With few exceptions, when I attend retreats, craft conferences, and trade shows, I find myself sticking out because of my race. If someone were to judge the composition of people who engage in fiber arts and crafts based on these events, or (until very recently) on the niche magazines devoted to these crafts, one would think that this group is almost exclusively white, affluent, able-bodied, and thin. Tullika Garg, a knitter from Danville, Pennsylvania, writes, "On Instagram and Ravelry, it seems like the photos of finished (knitted) objects are all aspiring to a particular type of aesthetic that is geared toward white women of means." If you do not meet these criteria, the message you receive is that there is no place in the larger craft community for you.

But, personal experience outside these events and groups tells me otherwise. My granny came from a long line of women who sewed because they had to. She also had a floor loom set up in her garage. I grew up watching my auntie Ming, whose grandchild Ava interviewed her on page 186 for this book, knit sweaters while watching her favorite soap opera and sew dresses without a pattern. The first thing I remember her making was my First Communion dress when I was six. I learned to sew from a Black teacher at summer camp. Most of the people I know in real life who sew and knit and crochet and weave are women of color. The majority of the people I follow on social media who engage in these crafts are people of color.

But, the questioner interrupted, she connects with people in her group based on their skill and projects. I could already predict the next thing she was going to say because it's a statement I hear all too often: "I don't really see race. I mean, obviously I do, but also, I don't . . . " she stammered at me, the only person of color in the room.

I explained that I do see race and that I can't escape it (nor would I want to, because my Blackness and Asian-ness are important parts of who I am and how I move through the world). My everyday experiences are based on my race. I have to constantly think about how I act when I go into certain stores. I have to be extra careful walking around unfamiliar neighborhoods. Going to a craft conference or trade show means bracing myself for constant microaggressions, such as regularly being confused for another Black woman. By claiming that she does not see race, she is implicitly questioning the validity of my very real experiences and fears. And, at the end of the day, I don't want to spend time engaging in hobbies that are meant to bring me comfort around people whose questions and treatment of me may be uncomfortable at best and outright hostile at worst.

So, when I asked survey respondents when they've felt like an "other" within the context of their craft, I wasn't surprised that the vast majority of respondents had had similar experiences as mine. Many find themselves the only person of color in craft spaces. Sahara Briscoe, a textile designer from the Bronx, wrote, "Honestly? I don't feel like an 'other' (I belong wherever I am); more like an 'only.'" This sentiment is echoed by Tracey Rivers, a knitter and crocheter from New Jersey, who wrote, "If I'm in a place where I'm the only person of color, I always try to get in the mindset that I belong where I am, just like everyone else who is there."

But, believing that you have every right to be in a space or at an event does not stop the underlying feelings of exclusion, especially when you have experienced hostile encounters in stores or public craft groups. Most respondents wrote about their very real experiences of being—and not just feeling—

othered. Bri Woods from Boynton Beach, Florida, wrote about being "closely monitored and not addressed" in a yarn store. Anita Ansari was told, "I didn't know your people knitted." Vanessa Foo from Fremont, California, was asked soon after the 2016 US presidential election, "So, are you going to be deported now?" Lisa Woolfork, a quilter, sewist, and professor in Virginia, found herself barred from a largely white quilting retreat that she had attended for fifteen years because, during the 2017 retreat, she had spoken about her experiences living through and being targeted during the white supremacist rallies in Charlottesville, Virginia, that summer. In these settings, the comfort of white participants is valued so much that people of color can find themselves banned simply for mentioning their own discomfort, for talking about their own lived experiences. When we are "allowed" to participate, we're often accepted as long as we don't upset the white status quo.

Back in the pattern drafting class, I became tired of answering the question, of, once again, being the proxy for other people of color and their experiences. Repeatedly having to have these same discussions and talk about these experiences is draining. I'd already completed my class projects, so I excused myself from the class and left for the day. I bought an ice cream cone and went for a long walk. I tried to shake off the disappointment of having what I'd hoped would be an enjoyable morning sewing turn into yet another experience of being othered while engaging in a craft I love, simply because I'm not white.

I heard later that that exchange led to an uncomfortable discussion among the remaining participants that lasted the rest of the day. The person who had originally asked the question realized that she'd done all the things I'd listed. Learning that didn't take away the resentment I'd felt at having my morning upended in that way. But, I was glad that a handful of white women had, for a few hours, started to understand the discomfort that so many of us feel when we attempt to practice our craft in white-dominated spaces.

I continue to go to those classes, conferences, and trade shows. They're good for my career and, after a decade in the industry, I've figured out how to navigate them. At the end of the day, though, I'm glad that I'm able to retreat to my own, smaller, more diverse community, where I can have unfiltered, nuanced discussions about race, craft, and life. I'm grateful for a community where belonging and discomfort aren't mutually exclusive but a way for us to connect on a meaningful level. I might be othered in white-dominated spaces, but in my own communities, I am seen and heard.

RACE, GENDER, AND CRAFT: PLYING MY EXPERIENCES

Essay by Shanel Wu

MY NAME IS Shanel. I am a nonbinary Taiwanese American craftsperson and my pronouns are they/them. I knit, crochet, spin, weave, and design—I will try anything else that looks shiny. To be clear: I am not a woman. I am nonbinary, which for me, means that I am neither a man nor a woman. This is *my* definition of a term that fits *my* gender; other nonbinary people may define themselves differently. For most of my life, people called me a girl, then a woman. I bought into it, too. Then later in life, I realized that I didn't have to stick to my assigned gender.

I went back and forth on whether or not to submit my experiences to this project. Would I be interjecting myself in a women's space as a non-woman? Did I want to seem flaky on my rejection of being assigned womanhood and femininity? I decided that I would fill out the survey because I wanted a space to parse out my experiences in craftwork as a queer person of color. As I typed out my answers, I realized that I was spinning a yarn of my self-discovery, where my own racial and gender identities plied with the running thread of making things with my hands. Craft has been a constant thread in my life since childhood, and I would say that without my crafting, I would not be here proudly declaring my various identities to the world.

I was always a creative and tactile child. I drew (fairly well), sang (badly), and always did something with my hands. Sometimes, I just made messes or fidgeted with a scrap of paper until it was shredded from folding so much. But my hands were constantly moving and seeking out materials to touch and manipulate. I learned how to knit, crochet, and hand-sew several times before I was in high school. However, it never stuck for more than an afternoon. My attention span was much too short to focus on multi-hour projects (which I later would realize was due to undiagnosed ADHD), and any chance I had of developing that practice was squashed by school. Once I showed a talent for math and science, my parents probably sighed with relief: "Great, we can put Shanel in STEM programs and there won't be a starving artist in the family." From sixth grade to the end of college, I was on a strict academic track to a stable, well-paying tech job. Like a strange cave fungus hidden away from polite society, my inner crafting urges were free to grow amorphously and emerge sporadically when building robots or decorating for school events.

College was the right environment for something to shift. I had a bit of income from work-study jobs, and I was an extremely stressed physics major. I went on Amazon to order decent-but-affordable yarn and needles online (shoutout to Lion Brand and Clover Takumi), pulled up YouTube tutorials (shoutout to Very Pink Knits), and stumbled upon Ravelry and its free patterns (shoutout to Tin Can Knits). I cranked out a hat for my first real project, then a pair of fingerless gloves, then another hat but with cables—all during Thanksgiving weekend. There was no going back to empty finger-tapping and pencil-chewing during homework. Whether reading, listening to lectures, or thinking about problem sets or code, I was never without a knitting project to stimulate the long-ignored parts of my brain.

I don't think it was a coincidence that within a year of learning how to knit, I also began questioning my gender identity and dealing with my chronic mental health problems. In the summer of 2015, I was in Houston for a research internship. I felt like I had barely survived the previous semester. I had been taking an unhealthy course load, then just one stumble from a dating mishap sent me into a weeklong depression spiral. I would have withdrawn from school if my professors didn't extend my final grades. A bright spot during that spring was that I met a friend of a friend. Our mutual friend introduced them, "This is [Person], and they went to high school with me." They were very vocally out (as in "out of the closet") about their gender and publicly used they/them pronouns in their artistic work. My brain short-circuited for a moment. "People can do that? That'd be nice if people used they/them instead of she/her for *me*."

I continued to sit with that thought throughout the summer. As I learned how to knit lace shawls and stranded colorwork from various websites, other online resources taught me terms like "nonbinary," "gender dysphoria," and that trans identities were so much more than "switching to the opposite sex." I accepted that femininity, female-ness, or everything about the word "woman" and all it entailed didn't resonate with me. Never had. I didn't want to be a woman anymore. I also didn't want to be a man. Did I have to be either? Both just seemed like arbitrary boxes that were placed in front of my parents (and the doctor birthing me). They had to put me down in one box or the other. Why did there only have to be two boxes for a baby? Why were there any boxes at all? I felt like I finally had the words to understand who I truly was, but the vast majority of the world wouldn't even see me. I was far away from my hometown of Las Vegas and had no family members nearby. I felt completely alone.

I only had my knitting. Shortly thereafter, I added medication for my depression and anxiety. In my senior year of college, I added spinning to my self-soothing regimen. While I was still mentally unwell, I could limp past the end of my teens and finish college. I saw a few different therapists, but we never talked about my queer identities. In fact, they wanted to focus on my Asian racial identity and family background. My earliest memories are of Las Vegas, specifically the city's Chinatown. My parents had moved us there from California when I was a few months old, and they still live there today. Many people, especially tourists, don't know that Las Vegas has a lively Chinatown community. My parents enrolled me and my two younger brothers in Chinese school. I danced in a Chinese folk-dance school starting at age five and continued until I graduated high school. Every year, we performed in and volunteered at the Lunar New Year festival held in Chinatown Plaza's parking lot. As part of our family's Autumn Moon Festival celebrations, I would give my non-Chinese teachers mooncakes as presents. Growing up as an American-born Chinese/Taiwanese child in Vegas, there were so many activities to instill cultural pride within me and my friends.

There are no perfect childhoods, but I believe that my parents tried their best. My family was working class, maybe lower-middle class growing up, so we couldn't afford piano and tennis lessons or yearly trips back to Taiwan like wealthier families in our community. But, my parents worked overtime to get all three of us into violin lessons and the occasional summer camp. I inherited their attitude of "shut up, put your nose to the grindstone, and work until you get what you want" to an unhealthy degree. At home, we would rarely talk about anything besides how much homework we had left to do and whether or not we had eaten. I never explained how I sometimes had trouble concentrating on my work, or how I would have anxiety attacks in class, or how much I hated myself when I made mistakes. Most therapists I saw concluded:

these mental and emotional problems, left to fester without adequate coping tools, combined with the pressures of race and class, explode into anxiety and depression in young adulthood. The better therapists would also note the pressures of being an "Asian girl/woman." I'll give them props for considering intersections of race and gender, but it's just the wrong intersection.

Again, my crafting was my private space to process my experiences without anyone misinterpreting them. After college, I thought that the way to resolve my angst with growing up and going to school in a working-class, urban community of color was to teach kids going through similar situations. I accepted a teaching fellowship in New Jersey and moved across the country to start fresh. Long story short, launching myself into toxic environments that were very similar to the environments that traumatized me (albeit in a more powerful position), moving thousands of miles away from loved ones, and trying to learn the ropes of adult life—it was a bad combination to juggle. During this time, I began to write my own knitting patterns to temporarily escape from my abusive workplace and financial stress. After I left the teaching program, I was more broken than I had ever been. I kept myself afloat (both emotionally and monetarily) with knitting and crochet commissions for those first few weeks. Craft was no longer just a medium for self-soothing; it was a tool for survival.

As I rebuilt my confidence in my skills, I did more and more types of work to make ends meet. I kept designing patterns and taking on commissions. I went to a knitting/needlecraft group every week, where I fell naturally into helping the other members with their projects. That led to people asking me to teach knitting classes, and I rediscovered my love of teaching. Seeing my own voice as a designer and educator develop, I finally felt confident enough to come out as nonbinary to my friends and use they/them pronouns around people. But, even though I was working enough to cover rent and regularly went to social gatherings, I still felt that I was on the margins, that there was no place for me anywhere. Most members of the knitting group were straight, white, middle-to-upper-class women who were twenty to thirty years older than me. I felt like a novelty in the group, or at best a surrogate "daughter" (I tried to explain the nonbinary thing, and it didn't seem to land). While my crafting and teaching skills got me work that I enjoyed, that work forced me into a subservient role and didn't guarantee financial or social stability. When I tried to find community in queer spaces, they were also overwhelmingly white. And yes, even in these spaces, people would misgender me as female. I didn't fit the stereotype of a nonbinary person; I wasn't a stick-thin, white AFAB* individual with a funky haircut wearing men's button-down shirts. I was short, East Asian (historically, Eurocentrism and Orientalism hyperfeminize both men and women), and did stereotypically feminine crafts. Maybe craft was healing me in my private life and helping my identities make sense inside of myself. However, in public, people weren't able to see how my crafting and the other parts of me fit together.

My race. My gender. My craft. All of these parts fit in my body and continue to tangle like three unruly yarn strands. Today, the strands are in a different arrangement: I'm living in Colorado and working on a PhD. I knew that my time in New Jersey wouldn't last once I left my teaching program, but I wasn't really sure what my next step was. I wanted to find a position where I could do all the kinds of work that I loved: learning, making, and teaching. Academic research in an exciting, interdisciplinary field fit the bill. But if I'm being honest, I wasn't thinking rationally about going back to school. Again, the impulse that drove me to apply for grad school was the same impulse that drove me to take a teaching fellowship and move to New Jersey. I was suffocating in an environment that wasn't right for me, so my best idea was to catapult myself to a new place and hope for good things. I found a research lab with a strange webpage that confused me at first. I reached out to the professor and we clicked on how we wanted to blend engineering with art and design. I got accepted to her department's PhD program. She sent me to learn how to weave in North Carolina. A month later, I rented a car, shoved everything I owned inside, buckled my new spinning wheel into the passenger seat, and drove from New Jersey to Colorado.

Fortunately, Colorado seems to be turning out better than my past locations. In my lab, we handweave circuits into fabrics to create smart textiles, combining ancient technology with modern digital systems. I get to combine my physics and engineering background with my self-taught textile skills. I'm also out as nonbinary in my workplace and recently came out to my brothers. Several of my colleagues will even educate others on my pronouns.

The state of my weaving practice reflects the current relationship between my craft, other identities, and my trauma. It's been almost five years since I

* Assigned Female at Birth

started knitting in college. Besides crochet, spinning, and weaving, I've also added sewing, welding, and basketry into the mix. Rather than distracting from my development as a weaver, these other crafts help me see weaving from new angles and push me to grow even more. While I am still working on

I'm crafting and realizing bits of a dream, a collective dream of a decolonized, sustainable, and *liberated* world.

a lot of accumulated trauma, craft isn't just a coping mechanism for the past anymore. Craft has not only shaped my past but it is also fueling my present and building my hopes for the future. Through connecting with fellow crafts-people online, I'm pushing my practice even further and expanding my empathy for experiences beyond my own. When I design and weave a fabric in my research, I'm not just making a garment or a gadget. More importantly, I'm questioning the fundamental categories of what gets to be called "high-tech," shining a light on the invisible labor of women of color in both textiles and electronics, and holding up the contributions of Indigenous innovation to our computers. I'm crafting and realizing bits of a dream, a collective dream of a decolonized, sustainable, and *liberated* world.

SURVEY PROFILE

Aliya Jiwani

Age: 46
Location: Toronto, Canada
Profession: Visual artist.

What types of fiber crafts do you engage in, and how many years have you been engaged in each?
Crochet (40+ years), knitting (30 years), sewing (35–40 years, intermittently), embroidery (30+ years, intermittently), weaving (approximately 10 years), hand spinning (6–7 years).

How do you self-describe/identify yourself?
Knitter, spinner. South Asian. Disabled, cis woman, raised in a Muslim household, Canadian settler. Artist, activist, intersectional feminist.

What's the first thing you remember making?
A small (lopsided) crochet blanket for one of my dolls, using leftovers from one of my mum's crochet projects. I was about five years old, maybe?

What are you making now?
Socks (a gift for a family member), crochet shawl, several handspinning projects in progress, scarf using embroidery on upcycled clothing scraps, crochet . . .

What's your favorite thing you've made?
Hard to pick one . . . love my hand-knit socks, and also hand-knit lace shawls.

How and why did you learn your crafts?
I was taught the basics of crochet, sewing, and hand-knitting by mum, who sewed and crocheted a lot when I was young. I'm a self-taught handspinner

and weaver and have always loved creating things, especially working with yarn/fiber and textiles (and also painting). My maternal grandmother was also very creative and did a lot of sewing, knitting, embroidery, etc. Though I didn't know her very well until my late teens, I definitely take after her!

Does anyone in your family practice this craft, too? Are your pieces similar or different aesthetically?
Yes, mum, niece, and a couple of cousins. I think I'm by far the most committed and prolific, and my skills are more advanced simply because I've spent a lot more time doing these crafts (especially knitting). My pieces are definitely different and reflect my love of color, pattern, and detail. I think I'm the least product-driven crafter in my family, as for me, it's about the process rather than the finished object (until it's done, or unless it's a gift for someone else). I prefer finer yarns and can more easily manage lace (or colorwork) than cables, which also gives my work a different aesthetic than, say, my cousin's large crocheted baby blankets.

Tell me about your creative community.
Other knitters and spinners, many of whom I initially met at a local yarn store, or through the art college I now attend, and through Ravelry and more recently, Instagram. Other artists, primarily but not exclusively visual artists. Friends who enjoy discussions on a broad range of topics. They are mostly (90 percent) non-male, of diverse cultural/ethnic backgrounds (though probably at least 60 percent non-BIPOC) of nearly every age from preteen to 80+ years old, and include online, local, and nonlocal persons.

When have you felt like an "other" within the context of your craft?
Definitely at most local yarn stores, craft stores, and in-person events like fiber festivals, where I am often the only/one of very, very few POC, also when knitting in public. The "otherness" I feel is/was definitely due in part to skin color/perceived race, though in the past, it was also because I looked "too young" to knit. I get the "Where did you learn to knit?" question very often, usually from a certain type of person, quite early in the conversation. The surprised reaction when I say my mum taught me and my gran used to knit is a telltale sign that the underlying assumption is that brown people don't knit, or crochet, or whatever. It definitely feels like the "Where are you

really from?" question, which is usually racially motivated, in my experience, because my first answer never satisfies as it exposes certain assumptions. All of this is very wearing, especially since I live in a very culturally diverse and supposedly progressive, inclusive city and region where BIPOC are not a small minority of the population.

I'm also disabled, very obviously so, as I now use mobility devices, which also definitely makes me feel "othered." Accessibility issues often mean I'm less a part of things, I get a lot of looks, and it tends to be the first thing people want to talk to me about. This is all newer to me as I hid my disabilities for years, and the difference in people's behavior, especially when I'm using a wheelchair versus crutches, is startling. I haven't actually participated in any local fiber events or gone to a local yarn store since getting my wheelchair, in part because of concerns about accessibility and also worry about being, once again, visibly different, excluded, or on the margins. I've only really felt comfortable in one local yarn store over the years—all the others have been overtly or subtly discriminatory. I've had several negative experiences at a local yarn store I frequented close to work over the years.

When do you feel recognized in your craft? Who recognizes you and how does that feel for you?

I feel most recognized when people, primarily other knitters/fiber crafters, notice and/or compliment my work—on Ravelry, at one local yarn store, with my creative friends (fiber crafters and artists), and, to a lesser extent, with non-crafting family.

Getting recognition and positive feedback from other crafters is, to me, a sign of acceptance and inclusion, and it gives me confidence and makes me feel like I belong. Praise from non-crafters is less satisfying, as most can't appreciate the work, except on a very superficial level.

Are there aspects of your work that you feel are misunderstood?

Non-knitters don't generally "get" my love of knitting and wearing shawls. It used to make me self-conscious when wearing them, but I'm less invested in what others think of me. Non-fiber people don't understand the draw (heh) of spinning; it's very bizarre to them. "So, you . . . make yarn . . . and then what?" I'd never seen someone spinning in real life until a year after I learned, so I do appreciate that it's unusual.

I also believe that fiber crafts are accorded much less respect because they are so-called domestic crafts and are erroneously seen as women's work, and therefore of less value than other crafts like cabinetmaking, for example. The skill and time involved are very undervalued—I would argue that if I were to charge for my knitting, I deserve to be paid hourly *at least* as much as a highly qualified lawyer; I have decades of experience and informal, but no less valid, training. And, it's probably more difficult to find another knitter of similar skill than it would be to find another lawyer. This is an argument I often make to silence those well-intentioned but very patronizing family members who tell me I should sell my knitting—apparently doing something just because you enjoy it rather than to make money is somehow inferior. Obviously, I have huge frustrations with the capitalist assumption that value = productivity, a belief that is embraced by most of my family, which undermined my self-worth and, subsequently, my health for years.

Do you engage in these crafts for income or as a hobby?
Hobby. First, because I feel it would take away much of the rewarding aspects of the process to do it to generate income. Second, because I can't see myself being fairly compensated (especially as regards skill and time). And third, because the nature of my disabilities makes it impossible for me to be reliably productive.

If this is a hobby, how much of your time and money do you estimate you spend per year on it?
Currently, I spend about forty hours a month and less than $100/year on it, due to both physical limitations and financial circumstances; however, I've accumulated a large yarn, fiber, fabric, and bead stash. When I had the disposable income, I would spend over $1,000/year. For about ten to twelve years, when housebound and unable to work due to disability, I estimate I spent thirty to sixty hours per week or more, as fiber crafts (knitting, and later, supported spinning) were one of the few things I was able to do.

Do you exhibit your work? If so, where? Tell me about those experiences.
No, I have wanted to apply for a few textile art shows (locally, at galleries and through a craft association), but always feel intimidated as I'm self-taught and also doubtful that my work is good/creative enough.

When you were younger, were you exposed to other people who looked like you, or who were from similar backgrounds as you, and who engaged in this craft?

Only my mum. I didn't really know anyone else (anywhere near my age *or* of similar background) who did any fiber crafts. I learned to knit from books from the library as a teen, as mum only knew very basic cast on, knit, and purl. My grandmother lived very far away and I don't think I knew that she was a knitter until I was much older.

Where did you get inspiration growing up? Who were your idols?

I always loved fashion/clothes, drawing, painting, and making things, especially from yarn, fabric, or paper. Growing up well before the Internet, my only sources of direct inspiration for fiber crafts were from craft books, which were often boring and too old-fashioned for my taste, and fashion magazines, which only seemed to show highly impractical knit/crochet works. I didn't have any fiber craft–related idols.

Who do you look to for inspiration today?

I don't look to others for inspiration as much as I did, say, ten years ago, as I've developed much more confidence in my own style and taste, and also find myself leaning more toward experimenting with artistic expression in my fiber crafts. I'm also always on the lookout for inspiration when I go out, and draw from the colors, patterns, and textures I see, especially from the built and natural environment. I would say I look at certain designers and knitters on Ravelry, Ravelry friends, textile artists, and more recently, many BIPOC crafters on Instagram, though not usually for direct inspiration. I also get inspired by other crafters in my community.

What colors are you drawn to and why?

All of them. Love complex colors, rather than flat, solid, single shades. I'm always drawn to blues (any shade from pale sky-blue to cobalt to deep navy), grays, and other sky/sea colors (blue-gray, blue-green, aqua, turquoise), and also cool red-purples (all the edible colors, from cherry wine to grape and eggplant), bright yellow-greens, rich browns, and leafy greens. My least favorites are probably warm, bright red, and red-orange, though I've warmed up (excuse the pun) to certain shades of orange in the past few years. The why is partly because of the range of colors I thought looked flattering on me, partly because I love and am inspired by nature—trees, plants, flowers, birds, and color are also very evocative of mood and memory for me. Color is almost tactile or lyrical to me—kind of the opposite of synesthesia, I suppose.

Where do you get your materials?

Much of my most prized yarn/fiber was purchased online over the years from small, indie dyers, online from nonlocal yarn shops from Canada, the United States, the United Kingdom, and the European Union (back when the exchange rate was better), but I also have a small amount from local yarn shops, some from the handful of knitting/fiber-related fairs I've attended locally within southern Ontario over the past four to five years, and a few gifts from friends and swaps.

How do you choose your materials?

Based on fiber—I prefer natural, mostly animal, fibers, partly due to chemical and skin sensitivities—color, source; ethical, fair trade, and sustainable sources. I also look at customer reviews, feedback, and reputation, and have become more aware of the need to support marginalized craft suppliers like BIPOC-owned businesses and designers. At this time, I'm deliberately buying less and trying to use what I already have.

MISUNDERSTOOD: THE REAL VALUE OF CRAFT

Survey Question: Are There Aspects of Your Work That You Feel Are Misunderstood?

I hate when people call it a hobby. It is a craft, a skill that I've worked years to hone (I'll never say "perfect").—ATIYA JONES

When people find out that I made a garment, a question that arises is "Can you make one for me? I'll take one in gray, please." If I could, I would make clothes for everyone. Time is precious, and I give all my spare time (in fact, I have to create spare time) to sew. It seems presumptive that because I made this top for me, I can, or will, make one for someone else. Often, people will also comment: "You could sell that on Etsy. Why don't you start selling those?" I love to sew, and again, if there was space for me to do it for income, I would love that opportunity.—CARMEN ALI

I have a hard time separating my making from my daily life. I don't use words like "hobby," and I don't think of my making as separate from the work of living. I'm home all day with children, and moving from baking bread to knitting a sweater or weeding a garden all feels like part of one continuous thread to me. This type of lifestyle seems to be more common in traditional and Indigenous settings, but is not common for people of my background, and I sometimes struggle to explain the interconnectedness of making.—LIA ROSE

The time and effort that goes into bringing a design from idea to release are absolutely underestimated.—LISA SANTONI CROMAR

Fast fashion and consumerism as a whole have ruined the average person's conception of clothing. People don't know what quality is, the time it takes to produce quality, and the time and effort it takes to master sewing skills.

In return, no one knows or understands the cost behind a custom well-made garment. It can feel like a chasm between a maker and their potential clients. Also, it seems that most people don't see sewing as a practical hobby anymore. There was once a time when most poorer people made their own clothes. Even with the disposable clothing available today, sewing is a worthwhile thing to learn. It helps develop patience and mechanical ability, and you can look like a million dollars for a fraction of the cost. —MARGO COFFEY BALDWIN

People have said to me that lesbians don't knit, or that I am too social to be a knitter, or that knitting is for lonely people who have no friends, or that knitting is a hobby for white women, or that I am too young to knit. (I started knitting when I was in my twenties.)—PETRINA HICKS

Some people will never understand why I spend hours and hours knitting when I could just purchase my clothes in a store.—VANESSA FOO

I feel as if people who don't knit don't realize what the appeal is or don't think you can participate in a conversation actively since they've never knitted themselves. Some people label me as "domestic," which I find insulting. Some people think that knitting fights the progress that women have made, while I find it empowering to know that I can create a piece of clothing or accessory, loop by loop.—SOPHIA A. CHANG

My insistence that even making/crafting is not devoid of politics.—YAMIL ANGLADA

JEN HEWETT: I sorted survey responses alphabetically by first name, so Amanda Scott's response to the question "Are there aspects of your work that you feel are misunderstood?" was one of the first I read. It was also the response that summed up the sentiments behind the majority of the remaining responses:

> People misunderstand the time and investment that go into crafting.
> If people see my knitting and want to buy it, they only think I craft to

sell things and that it should be done/sold for a small price. People also don't understand that Black women knit and that young, professional women engage in crafts for the love of the craft and the therapeutic benefit of it. I constantly have to educate people about who knitters, spinners, crafters are and where they come from.

What Amanda, and many of the other respondents, said is that a lot of the misunderstanding around these crafts has to do with three things. The first is the undervaluing of the labor and skill that go into these crafts because of a disconnect between consumer and producer as well as the undervaluing of women's work. The second is the idea that everything, including hobbies, has to be monetized. The third is the lack of visibility of makers of color. These misperceptions come from the market forces of capitalism as well as from pervasive racism that both undervalues the work of people of color while erasing them from the more mainstream narrative of who practices these crafts.

At the turn of the twentieth century, the majority of women in the United States made their own clothes. Or, if they were wealthy enough, had them made by seamstresses who would customize a dress through fabric and fit. This continued through the middle of the century when home sewing peaked.* The 1960s through the 1990s saw a dramatic increase in American women's participation in the workforce.† With increased incomes and less leisure time, working women replaced home sewing with shopping as a hobby. By the 1980s, most commercial sewing had moved to developing countries with lower labor costs. It then became cheaper for a woman to purchase her clothes rather than make them herself. With this shift, most women in developed countries have become the consumers, rather than the producers, of much of what they wear.

But, home sewing and other garment-making crafts such as knitting and crochet persist, often for leisure rather than necessity. Carmen Ali writes that she makes things "to fulfill a greater creativity in myself, to have clothes

---

* National Women's History Museum, "Fashioning Yourself: A Story of Home Sewing," October 2016, https://www.womenshistory.org/exhibits/fashioning-yourself.

† US Bureau of Labor Statistics, "Women in the Labor Force: A Databook," December 2018, https://www.bls.gov/opub/reports/womens-databook/2018/home.htm.

that fit my body, and to create a space for self-care." And, with these hobbies comes a greater sense of the skill, time, and resources required to create garments. Jocelyn Murray writes that "most people have no idea where their clothing comes from, what it's made of, and how it's made." Likewise, Luz Sotomayor, a knitter from Washington, responded that "some people don't realize the amount of work and time involved in a project. Or the amount of yarn, and its cost."

Because people are so disconnected from the production of their clothing, they don't—according to Melissa Gonzalez, a knitter and sewist from Illinois—understand the time and cost associated with making a piece. She continues, saying that people are "usually surprised when I tell them that the yarn alone for a sweater could cost up to $300, not to mention the hours that go into making it. Their expectations are based on what they can buy in a chain store, where a sweater might only cost $30." Jocelyn Murray seconds this, writing that people who don't craft "do not understand or value the objects we make. A guy I dated suggested that I sell my handmade socks for $20 a pair . . . Maybe that's why he's an ex." For me, every time my mom admires a piece of clothing I sewed for myself, she suggests I start a business sewing and selling clothing, not recognizing that I often spend more on the fabric for a garment than I'd pay for something comparable in a retail store.

For those who practice these crafts professionally rather than as a hobby, this undervaluing of the time and skill that go into the production of their work can be demoralizing. Adriana Hernandez Bergstrom, a multidisciplinary crafter from Florida, writes, "I think in general, creatives are frequently exploited, and add to that being a minority . . . Knitting design started to feel very underpaid for all the work that went into it, and so I left it." Ainur Berkimbayeva, a knitting pattern designer in New York, adds to this, saying,

A lot of knitters undervalue knitting patterns and the amount of work knitwear designers put into publishing patterns. This undervaluing shows up in knitting forums, where knitters openly discuss how they prefer free patterns instead of paid ones and that they'd rather spend that money on yarn. This also shows up in how local yarn shops make illegal copies of patterns or when knitters share the patterns they bought with many others. This also shows up in the tight deadlines/low pay for design commissions even by well-recognized and established publications and yarn companies.

This was my own experience, as well. In the early days of my career as a print-maker, I printed on fabric and sewed the fabric into bags, which I then sold. I quickly realized that I was pricing my items far beneath what it cost me, labor-wise, to produce them in small batches. Yet, when I participated in craft fairs, potential customers balked at the prices I was charging. When it became clear to me that it was incredibly difficult to make a living selling only handmade work, I scaled back production work. Instead, I've focused on teaching others the craft and licensing my designs so they could be accessible to a larger audience. Sewing has become a hobby for me, rather than my livelihood.

The majority of the survey respondents (61 percent), however, are strictly hobbyists, rather than professionals in their crafts. Which brings me to the second misconception: hobbies must somehow be monetized, even if the compensation is low compared to the skill and effort involved, as Adriana and Ainur both noted earlier. The proliferation of local craft fairs and online handmade marketplaces such as Etsy has made it easier for small producers to sell their products to audiences beyond their friends and families. Indie knitting, crochet pattern designers, and small-batch dyers can now sell their wares directly to customers worldwide on Ravelry, described as a "social network for knitters."[*]

Late-stage capitalism has forced a productivity mindset onto us and has created a culture of busyness. This culture of busyness has pushed us to the point where David Scott, a professor of leisure studies at Texas A & M University, writes, "For many Americans, leisure time is frenetic. . . . A preoccupation with consumer goods, status, and busyness undermines Americans' ability to live simply and enjoy the peace and quiet that many leisure scholars associate with leisure."[†] In addition, the gig economy has promoted the

---

[*] Farhad Manjoo, "A Tight-Knit Community," *Slate*, July 2011, https://slate.com/technology/2011/07/ravelry-and-knitting-why-facebook-can-t-match-the-social-network-for-knitters.html.

[†] David Scott, "Leisure, Consumption, and the Speed Up of Time in the United States," in *Leisure from International Voices*, ed. Karla A. Henderson and Atara Sivan. (Urbana, IL: Sagamore, 2017), 240.

idea that free time and leisure must be commodified. Hobbies—in particular, those traditionally practiced by women—are only viewed as valid if they're tied to revenue, or at the very least, save the person some money. Aliya Jiwani, a knitter, crocheter, and visual artist from Ontario who is profiled on page 256, responded that she's regularly told that she should sell her knitting, adding, "Apparently, doing something just because you enjoy it, rather than to make money, is somehow inferior." Nique Etienne, a sewist from Florida, says that "Most people think it [sewing] saves money (as compared to ready-to-wear), and don't understand why I do it when they find out that it doesn't." What 'Nique's detractors don't understand is that hobbies have value in and of themselves as forms of rest and as vehicles to express creativity and skill. Tenille Foreman, a multidisciplinary crafter and dyer from Arizona, writes that she believes the slower skills involved in craft "are needed today to allow those caught up in the rat race an opportunity to breathe and slow down." If technology, as Scott suggests, has "accelerated Americans' standards regarding timeliness" to the point that they "expect speedy results in virtually everything," the slower speed of craft forces us to slow down. What hobbies offer are an antidote to the culture of productivity, where every hour and activity must somehow be revenue-generating. Craft hobbies provide us rest and pleasure for their own sake rather than as a means to serve a grueling economic system whose aim is to extract the highest level of productivity from us.

Tenille Foreman adds, "I think that most people my age (and younger) see quilting (and knitting, weaving, etc.) as something for old people. It's looked at as something from long ago, which it is, but it's also from the here and now, and it has relevance." This leads to the third misunderstanding respondents reported: who engages in these crafts. Charnita Belcher, a knitter from California, writes, "People seem surprised to see a (relatively) young, Black woman knitting." Jessie Maimone seconds this, saying that she's been made to feel that "these crafts are for old, white grandmas." There is definitely a perception that these crafts are, as Tullika Garg responded, for older "white women of means." This is a demographic that is, in theory, allowed to have more leisure time for and disposable income to spend on their hobbies. (I write more in-depth about how respondents feel excluded from the dominant narrative in the chapter "Othering and Belonging.")

Statistics, however, do not support the notion that white women have substantially more leisure time than women of color. A 2019 time use study by the

US Bureau of Labor Statistics found that white women averaged 4.91 hours of leisure activities* per day, while Black women reported 5.02 hours, Asian women 3.63 hours, and Latina† women 4.25 hours.‡ And, survey respondents for this book reported spending eighteen to sixteen hundred hours per year on their crafts. The age ranges and spending ability of survey respondents also show that the perceived profile of the standard crafter as an "older white

---

> Thus, the art of making as a person of color is
> slyly revolutionary, an assertion of our right
> to creative self-expression, rest, and joy.

---

woman of means" isn't accurate. A 2012 study done by the Craft & Hobby Association found that "ethnically, crafters are representative of the US population."§ Respondents to my survey range in age from twenty-one to seventy-four, with the median age of forty-two. Respondents who are hobbyists reported spending anywhere from $100 to $10,000 per year on their crafts.

Yet, the racist belief held by the dominant culture that people of color do not participate in these crafts shows up in the ways that we are erased from historical craft narratives and have been excluded, until very recently, from

---

* The leisure and sports category includes time spent in sports, exercise, and recreation; socializing and communicating; and other leisure activities. Sports, exercise, and recreation activities include participating in—as well as attending or watching—sports, exercise, and recreational activities. Recreational activities include yard games like croquet or horseshoes as well as activities like billiards and dancing. Socializing and communicating includes face-to-face social communication and hosting or attending social functions. Leisure activities include watching television; reading; relaxing or thinking; playing computer, board, or card games; using a computer or the internet for personal interest; playing or listening to music; and other activities, such as attending arts, cultural, and entertainment events.

† Persons of Hispanic or Latino ethnicity may be of any race.

‡ US Bureau of Labor Statistics, "Table 3. Time Spent in Primary Activities for the Civilian Population by Age, Sex, Race, Hispanic or Latino Ethnicity, Marital Status, and Educational Attainment, 2019 Annual Averages," accessed March 1, 2020, https://www.bls.gov/news .release/atus.to3.htm.

§ Craft & Hobby Association, "2012 State of the Craft Industry: Key Insights," accessed March 1, 2020, https://www.craftandhobby.org/eweb/docs/2012.State.of.the.Craft.Industy .Public.pdf.

industry publications. It shows up in the ways that we are ignored or given poor service in shops. And, it's the underlying belief when others express surprise at our skill. Of course, the pervasive racism in the craft world is a reflection of the racism in the larger society. In essence, the biggest misunderstandings survey respondents reported around craft have to do with who practices these crafts, why we do, and why craft is valuable. We live within a culture that places a premium on productivity and consumption, and that values the contributions of one group over those of others. Thus, the art of making as a person of color is slyly revolutionary, an assertion of our right to creative self-expression, rest, and joy.

WHAT ARE YOU MAKING NOW?

I'm working on the Interpretive Commons for Embodied Textiles (ICET, pronounced I See E.T.) which is a speculative performance and installation of my sculptural textiles and garments. The work will show at the International Fiber Art Fair (FAF) in Seoul and then at the Oak Spring Garden Foundation (OSGF) in Virginia.—JEANNE MEDINA

A doll for a world champion boxer.—LA-SHONDA "LALA" RICE

My mother passed away in 2014, so I am making throw quilts for myself and my three sisters using her clothes.—DEBBRA MURPHY

I'm venturing into bra making, and I'm also making a suit coat for my son to wear to his prom.—SIENNA MCMILLAN

BETWEEN TWO CULTURES

Interview with Jessica So Ren Tang

JEN HEWETT: I like to start all my interviews by asking everybody about their childhoods.

JESSICA TANG: I'm a San Francisco native, and other than my uncle, I'm pretty much the only "creative" person in the family. Coming from a Chinese family, it was typically frowned upon for us to go into the creative arts. I'm the middle child, so thankfully, my parents' attitude was, "Let her do what she wants. Do what you want, middle child."

I've been pretty much doing art since probably before I could remember. Pretty much since I could talk, I guess. I've been told this story by my aunt, who likes to bring it up every now and then. My aunt and my mom both worked for a baby diaper factory. They would babysit me at their job—free child care, just let the kids run outside free—and their coworkers would also watch over us. They'd ask me questions like, "Oh, how's your family? Where do you stay in your house? How do you like living with your sisters?" Rather than talking, because I was shy, I drew a map of the room and explained, "I sleep here, my sister goes here." I, obviously, don't remember any of this, but it's a super cute story.

Throughout elementary school, I always took art classes. I tried private art classes, but it was expensive. I took an afterschool program in middle school while I waited for my mom to pick me up when she got off work—free childcare! I didn't want to walk home, so I'd take after-school classes. I'd just be there, doing art. I didn't have much interest in other subjects.

JH: Where did you go to high school?

JT: I went to a charter school, City Arts and Tech. Then for college, I went to Mills College, where I got a BA in studio art.

JH: You were studying studio arts, but you had family that wasn't all that excited about arts as a career.

JT: I mean, they weren't saying no, but they weren't saying, "Here are some resources for you." It was more like, "You want to do this? Okay."

JH: At some point, you pick up embroidery.

JT: By fluke.

JH: By fluke? How'd that happen?

JT: It was an assignment in my senior year to experiment with materials and record it. After a few tries with different materials, I ended up finding something nearby. It was a Cup Noodle container. I was like, "Huh, it would be interesting if I sewed into it, see how it works." It sucked, but I liked seeing the thread on it. I thought, "Why don't I just make the cup out of fabric instead?" From there, my *Object* series started. I started thinking about what else I could make. After college, I made the Chinese bowl. I was also exploring different ways I could use embroidery. I made a few pieces when I was unemployed after graduating. What else could I do in my spare time while I was looking for a job other than embroider? I was like, "I'll just make work I like," and went on from there.

At City Arts and Tech, juniors and seniors are required to do an internship in whatever field they're interested in. I knew what I wanted to do already, so I was an assistant for an artist. He suggested I create an Instagram account and said, "People would be really interested in seeing this sort of studio work." That propelled my work. That's how I pretty much got "discovered." It was a lot of self-promotion, PR. I'm sharing my process because my work takes forever, so why not just share while I'm working? Maybe people will like it. Maybe people will give me suggestions.

JH: So, after college, you graduate, you have a BA in studio art, and you're unemployed. Is that when you started the *Girls* series?

JT: Yeah.

JH: For the benefit of people who will not have seen the *Girls* series, please describe it.

JT: I've taken specifically Asian female figures in suggestive poses, and rather than show their ethnicity via features beyond their black hair, I replace their skin with what started with Asian textile patterns, Asian florals, and Asian motifs. It's all embroidery.

JH: Why did you choose women in suggestive poses?

JT: One of my main inspirations for the series was the painter Yasunari Ikenaga. He does these really beautiful, classical, but more contemporary, definitely wood-block-style paintings of women, and the fabrics of their clothing have really interesting patterns on them. I thought, "What if they were switched—the pattern is on the skin, and the clothing is the plain background?"

It's not something I've explained a lot, but with the suggestive poses . . . it's mainly to explore my identity as an Asian American woman. I'm not good at explaining myself.

JH: That's okay. Take your time.

JT: Another thing that kind of drives the series is how people say, "Oh, Asians all look alike." Which is another reason why I remove the facial features and replace them with another Asian signifier. At this point, they all look the same, but why does it matter? I'm taking away that identity. With the suggestive poses, I'm trying to take away the "male gaze." But I'm still using the suggestive pose, which I've gotten to not really like at this point. Part of me knows that the pose is attractive as hell, but by putting the pattern in the skin, I feel it negates the male gaze. It feels a bit more intimate. You don't see where the eye is.

JH: The eye of the subject?

JT: Yeah, the subject. I don't know. Maybe I'm just trying to make it more intimate, not for the viewer but for the subject. Part of me is also like, "Oh, because it's pretty." It's aesthetically pleasing. That's also how I decide which patterns to use.

JH: If you're using traditional motifs, those are also geared to be aesthetically pleasing. So, in a way, if you want to make them aesthetically unappealing, you'd have to create your own motifs or turn existing motifs on their head.

JT: Yeah. I'm focusing on how, with Asian identity—Asian American identity, specifically—we're often caught between two different cultures. With my work, I'm trying to address that by creating what looks to be an Asian person, but created by an American.

JH: The American is you?

JT: Yeah. When you look at an Asian person, you're not going to know, "Oh, that person's from America," or from another country, or that something about how they present indicates what country they're from, which doesn't necessarily mean it's correct. With my work, I'm addressing the Asian American identity both ways, but I only have Asian imagery in my work. I haven't done much to explore this area by using an American motif versus an Asian motif in the skin. I feel like, if I did something like that, it would be a more obvious play on the idea of an Asian image, a questionable American subject.

JH: I think that's interesting because you would still use essentially the same base image, but you would change up the pattern so there would still be signifiers of Asian-ness, but then you'd have to overlay it with signifiers of American-ness.

JT: I think this intention of playing with the duality of the identity is more obvious in my *Object* series. There, I'm physically recreating the "Asian" or "Asian American" object by not necessarily using anything of Asian mainland but recreating something that looks Asian but is actually not.

JH: Describe your *Object* series for people who won't be familiar with it.

JT: It's me recreating mostly Asian American objects out of embroidery. Objects like the Chinese takeout box, or the Chinese bowl, or White Rabbit Candy. Items that are pretty common in Asian America, but not necessarily in, say for example, China. The takeout box was, I believe, invented in the

United States, but it's culturally significant to the Asian community. The *Object* series was my exploration of the identity of being two things at once. Then, I'm trying to explore that identity in my *Girls* series. The *Girls* series was born out of, I want to say boredom, but it was just like I had the time, I saw this image, why not deal with it? This would look interesting, I'm going to make it. It's not like I'm finished with the *Object* series—what do I do next? Because I like figurative work, I think I wanted to branch into that. So, by keeping it with, obviously, embroidery, keeping with the Asian motifs, female Asian figure, that's the logical fact that I made subconsciously.

JH: You had classes in painting and drawing, and then you made the leap to embroidery. Why have you chosen to stick with embroidery, which is maybe the most painstaking, slow process?

JT: When I was trying to figure out what I wanted to do for the senior show, I was tired of painting, to be honest. I felt like the window of exploration of what you could do with painting had already been discovered. It's a flat surface. You can paint whatever image. That's fine. Then with sculpting, I was just kind of bored with that. Before I started embroidering, I had seen the work of an artist who folded clothing into towers. They stacked them by color, and it was very pleasing to the eye. I'm like, "Huh. Fabric. That would be interesting." I tried playing with the sewing machine and that didn't work because I don't like sewing machines. They're too complicated. I was like, "Okay. I'm going to have to do this by hand." Hence, Cup Noodle embroidery.

I just really enjoy how versatile and tactile it is. It has this nostalgic feel to it. It's clothing. It's intimate. It's readily accessible. You can find fabric way more easily than canvas. I just really liked how it felt. I didn't know then how long it would take to create future series. Because the Chinese bowl only took me a week. I thought, "That's not bad." But now it takes a month, on average, to make one thing.

I enjoy it. I feel like it can go beyond a flat surface, which is what the first series was like. It felt like there were more possibilities with embroidery. I love the history of embroidery, too.

JH: You have these incredibly elaborate pieces now that are much larger than the Chinese bowl. They're, what, 8 x 10 inches?

JT: On average. Now they're getting to be a little bit bigger. A lot of the shows that I get invited to are geared toward painters, so they usually have a minimum size. That minimum size is a little too much for me. It's generally like 11 x 14 inches.

JH: It's also just really intensely physical work.

JT: Last year, I had a lot of shows that took their toll on me. Toward the end of last year, I started getting serious pains from it, mainly because I'm craning my neck down a lot. I get wrist pains if I'm going too hard at it. I'm sitting for a few hours each night, at least, and I'm always looking down. So, my pain issue is mainly the neck and back at this point. If it's not one side, it's the other, and if it's not, it's both at the same time. I get a lot of migraines and headaches, so I take a lot of ibuprofen.

At this point, I'm like, "This is not healthy." I got to the point where I'm buying all these massage thingies, pressure point things. Eventually, I was like, "Okay. This is enough. I can't work because I'm in pain." I booked a massage out of desperation. Thankfully, I live across from a spa place. I got a massage. I've seen the chiropractor. I've tried acupuncture. I've tried cupping. So far, massage is doing pretty good. I was hoping I'd do one massage a month in between shows. It was working for a little bit. I am terrible about stretching. I bought this foam roller and I'm trying to get into the habit of rolling on it and stretching. I'm currently working on that. I had to buy a neck support–specific pillow, and then every night, I have to wear these wrist braces.

JH: You're too young. Don't let this happen. And you work a regular, full-time job, right?

JT: Yep. I first started at the company as part of the warehouse production team. Then I got promoted to accountant. I have no history of accounting. They just asked if I could do a few things. Then their accountant was leaving and they had me trained, and here I am.

JH: So, you're an accountant by day and an artist by night? Those are two very different skills.

JT: I feel like one of the reasons why they were keen on hiring me was because, as an artist especially with embroidery, I'm more focused on the detail. You kind of have to be.

JH: Who knew that that's what you were going to use with your BA in studio arts?

JT: It was worth it, I guess.

JH: My last question for you is: What's next? What are you working on now? What do you want to do in the future?

JT: I pretty much have the rest of this year booked with shows. It's like eight shows. A lot of them are invitations I received last year. I was like, "Oh, I'll have time. Sure, I'll do it." Then this year started, and I got a few more invites. I want to say yes because I've already said no to them before and I don't want them to shun me. Maybe I can do it. I just finished a piece that's going to be in a show in San Francisco next month. Then I have a pop-up in New York and then more shows following that in the city. Then one in Irvine. I have a lot of shows with Spoke Art and Modern Eden.

JH: How did you go about getting gallery shows? Did they approach you or have you been going to them?

JT: It's mostly them approaching me. After graduating, I did get invited to show at a small gallery in The Mission. A grad student or a teacher at Mills saw my work in college and he invited me to participate in a small show. The gallery director of Spoke Art followed my work because she's a really big fan of textiles, and she invited me to show there. Then I got attention for my *Girls* series. From that, I got interviews, features, magazines, and articles. That boosted me, made me appealing to galleries.

The same artist that I worked for in high school and every now and then is friends with the couple that owns Modern Eden Gallery. He was in the show and was like, "Hey, you want to be in this show? I think your work would fit. Let me know. I'll email my friends." I was like, "Yeah. Sure." That's how I got in. Little did I know, I'd eventually get a mini-solo show with them.

JH: I imagine it would be hard for you to have a solo show just because your work is so labor intensive and you're also working full-time.

JT: It takes me about a month to do one of the *Girls* pieces. That's not including wrapping the piece and framing it. That's just the stitch work because I have a day job. I use nights and weekends for stitch work.

JH: You probably also shouldn't be sitting, working on that eight hours a day, five days a week. Don't hurt yourself. Stretch, get up, drink water.

JT: Yeah. Working on it.

JH: I know. It's a process. Is there anything I didn't ask you, that we haven't talked about, that you want to talk about?

JT: Oh, I remember. You mentioned asking what I wanted to do next. Beyond what I already have scheduled for this year, I want to go back to my *Object* series, honestly. For Irvine, I do have an object piece that I'm planning on making, which is nice. I'm like, "Of course, I would like to participate in the show because I'll get to make a sculpture piece." I would like to go big and small. Bigger scale pieces, maybe like a full-size person piece. I'd like to integrate more texture than colors in my work. But, I also would like to go and replicate smaller objects as well.

JH: Well, you've got time. Hopefully, you have a long life ahead of you. I know the desire to do all the things.

Well, thank you so much for your time. Hopefully, you'll get some time to relax tonight and not have to work all-night long.

JT: A few hours, maybe. At least an hour.

JH: Get some sleep! Thank you, again.

Craft as Community

< Kenya Miles's dye garden (not to scale, clockwise from top left):
Hucatay Southern Cone Marigold, Indigo, Amaranth Hopi Red
Dye, Sunflower Hopi Black Dye, Yellow Dock, Madder Root

OUR CREATIVE COMMUNITIES

Survey Question: Tell Me about Your Creative Community

When I picked up knitting again four years ago, I would frequent a local yarn shop that held knit nights every week. Through that, I met three other wonderful women of color who knit, and we have since become close supportive friends. We've come to call ourselves "The Knitbabes." Though we all have alternate, somewhat high-stress careers outside of knitting, we make it a point to meet regularly to knit, create our own knit-a-thons and knitalongs, travel to knitting/fiber conferences/retreats each year, and have grown to be a tight-knit group of women (no pun intended). I consider these women to be my creative community. I am also a member of our knitting guild and will find community at knit-togethers at a new local yarn shop that recently opened.—MARTINE CUMBERMACK

Becoming part of my local chapter of the Modern Quilt Guild was life-changing for me. I met a community of people so passionate about their hobby (most are hobbyists). The whole subculture of quilting is so intriguing and binds strangers together. The broader Modern Quilt Guild is also a place with similar people—generally supportive and open. I really value these groups. Since then, I have found other creative communities to be a part of—my provincial craft association and arts organizations, SAQA (Studio Art Quilt Associates), and others. Most of these groups are largely made of white people because of how "white" quilting is, and because the population of Nova Scotia, especially those practicing in the arts, is predominantly white.—ANDREA TSANG JACKSON

I belong to a group called Women of Visions, Inc., and we have been together for thirty-seven years. We believe that we are one of the only groups like this that has been together for such a long period of time. We meet once a month to plan exhibits, do community outreach, and to support each other. —LAVERNE KEMP

JEN HEWETT: I started printing and sewing right around the same time that blogs, craft fairs, and social media were becoming popular places for people to share their crafts. I was working a corporate job at the time and didn't have a ready-made craft community—none of my friends or close family members were interested in these hobbies. In these early days, the Internet felt like a smaller, friendlier place. I'd find someone on Flickr, click over to their blog, maybe meet them in person at a craft fair or an art opening, and strike up a friendship. Those friendships led to other friendships as the circle widened. Instagram replaced Flickr and blogs; its functionality helped me find people all over the world who were doing similar work and who looked like me because my early, in-person communities were very white (at large craft fairs, I was often the only Black vendor and one of a handful of vendors of color).

My communities, both online and in person, grew. More people became interested in my work, and I realized I could teach people my craft. I started teaching at a wonderful school, Handcraft Studio School (which had to close permanently because of COVID-19), and became a part of the diverse community of teachers and students that Handcraft's owner, Marie, created. I landed a book deal because of that class's popularity and heard repeatedly from readers that they were excited to finally see a woman who looks like them practicing the crafts they love. Licensing opportunities came my way because I was sharing my work online. I've built my career largely through all these communities, both online and in person.

My own creative communities have always been a natural extension of my work and interests. Unlike the majority of survey respondents, I engage in my crafts for a living, so my craft communities are both professional and personal. As I've written, I often feel like an "other" within the larger craft community that I engage in professionally, and so I turn to my smaller, chosen community for a sense of belonging. I was curious to learn about other people's communities, to find out how they've developed them, and what they actually do when they're in community.

Many wrote enthusiastically about their small, in-person and online communities while also talking about how these communities grew because they felt excluded from or unwelcome in larger, more formal groups. Amanda Scott in White Plains, Maryland, writes she doesn't attend public events because "I always have to do extra to make myself feel like a part of the group." Many join groups or seek online communities that are welcoming and diverse. When asked to describe her creative community, Tracy Weyhenmeyer, a multidisciplinary crafter from Salt Lake City, answered with a description that neatly summarizes the range of answers I received: "I have occasional craft nights with trusted friends, where we chat and craft (heavy on the chat). I no longer attend public crafting groups. I have had bad experiences since I left Brooklyn and the very nice neighborhood knit group there that I found through Ravelry."

If, like Amanda and Tracy, women of color find themselves largely excluded from or out of place within the larger craft community, many have still found or created their own craft communities. These range from online groups of people who have never met in real life (or who, like Tracy's group, initially meet online before meeting in person), to ad hoc groups of family members and friends, to knitting groups facilitated by inclusive organizations and stores, to quilt guilds with formal membership requirements and bylaws.

Many of the people who participated in the survey initially learned their crafts from a family member or a close friend, so it's not a surprise that family and friends are a big part of a number of respondents' communities. Vanessa Foo, a knitter from Fremont, California, writes that her community is pretty much her and her mom. "We live in different states and I think a third of our phone calls are about knitting!" Olive Lefferson, a knitter and beader from Seattle, says, "I generally knit solo unless I'm with my daughter Maggi. She and I usually carry a little project around that we can pull out and work on while we talk." Katika Jones, a multidisciplinary crafter from the Bronx, writes, "My creative community begins from my home and extends from there."

Often, creative communities then extend from the home into groups of friends and coworkers. Vanessa Foo knits with her coworkers over videoconference every Monday, while Rochelle Smith in Moscow, Idaho, has been a part of a group of knitters, spinners, weavers, and dyers for twenty-five years, saying, "Some of my dearest friends in the world are part of it. We're all quite devoted to/serious about making and very willing to try things and to encourage each other and help each other problem-solve."

Informal drop-in groups and craft nights, often hosted by yarn stores and craft spaces, are also popular, especially for more portable crafts like knitting and crochet. Even though people regularly noted in their survey responses that they often feel discriminated against in smaller shops, a few shops such as gather here in Cambridge, Massachusetts; Looped Yarn Works in Washington, DC; and A Verb for Keeping Warm in Berkeley, California, were regularly named as welcoming places that have lively and thriving craft communities and inclusive events.

Jocelyn Murray, a knitter from Washington, DC, says that her community is the women she's met at Looped Yarn, that she's "met so many great women and men there, from all walks of life . . . Many are famous in their respective fields, but in the shop, we are all just women sharing an ancient art." In the past year, Rachel Rangel, a knitter from Boston, has been welcomed into a crafting group of women her age. "They all came together as customers at a local crafting store where I recently decided to get a part-time job! The employees and customers are so diverse and support each other's crafts. The community that has been created at this store is very special."

Guilds provide their members with a more formal place to showcase their work, take workshops with experts, and commune with other like-minded people who are passionate about their crafts. Probably one of the best-known national quilting guilds is the Modern Quilt Guild, cofounded in 2009 by Latifah Saafir (profiled on page 74) "strictly for the sake of building an in-person community from what was a thriving online community at the time," she said. Valerie Dionne Parker is a member of the Kuumba African American Quilt Guild in Richmond, Virginia, and credits this group with saving her life when she was a full-time caregiver for her parents and grieving the loss of multiple family members.

Online communities have also become an increasingly popular way for people to connect, both for those without access to in-person groups and for those who are already actively participating in in-person groups. In fact, most people, regardless of age or other group participation, reported having some aspect of an online community. Regina Gee, a multidisciplinary crafter from Vine Grove, Kentucky, says that she isn't sure how welcomed she is by the crafting community in her semirural Southern town, so her primary creative community has always been on social media. She writes, "In the early, early years of social media, I met many creatives of color through blogs. I continue to follow them today through their Instagram accounts or continuing blogs." Kristl Yuen, a sewist from Durham, feels that they have a "small, but mighty" online creative community, "primarily made up of fat and/or queer sewists . . . on Instagram," though they would like to see "more fat, queer, Asians in that space."

For folks with physical disabilities or chronic illnesses, social media provides a community that can be accessed from the comfort of their own home. Caroline Dick, a knitwear designer from Kamloops, British Columbia, who has fibromyalgia, says her illness means she sometimes doesn't leave her house much, so "my creative community are the people I've met in the fiber world who I mostly stay in contact with via social media. They're a wonderful group of people and I love how wonderfully supportive [they] have been."

Bretony McGee, a self-described creator from Brooklyn, whose creative community is almost entirely online, summarizes why community of any kind is so important, writing, "The people who follow me are so supportive, inquisitive, interested, and truly seem to appreciate everything I make. It's also cool because there are people literally all over the world doing this thing that I thought nobody my age or demographic does! I wondered why I hadn't been looking for others sooner!"

As diverse as respondents' communities are, the consistent thread linking all of them is a sense of belonging. It doesn't matter how or where our communities meet; what matters is that these spaces hold the communities where we feel we are nurtured and seen, where we belong.

THE FARMER'S DAUGHTER

Interview with Candice English

JEN HEWETT: Where did you grow up? What was your family like?

CANDICE ENGLISH: I grew up on a farm about forty-five minutes from Glacier Park in Montana. Right on the front of the mountains—as you come off the mountains onto the prairie—is where our ranch was. My dad was a second-generation rancher. His family originally had sheep on the ranch, and then they had cattle and also farmed wheat. I have three older brothers and sisters. They have a different dad, so I was a lot younger than they were. I spent a lot of time on the ranch by myself, making up imaginary games. My mom is Blackfeet. She grew up on the reservation, so we would go up there and visit family quite a bit. It was a good childhood. It was really quiet. I had a couple of friends from town that would come out and see me or I would go in and see them. Besides that, it was just a very quiet childhood.

JH: So, were you creative as a kid other than making up stories in your head?

CE: My mom and my sisters are amazing painters, and they can draw. My paternal grandma did tons of fiber arts and I cross-stitched with her. She lived on the ranch in a different house, so I was exposed to a lot of that, but I was not good at anything that my sisters and my mom did.

I would get so frustrated because I had all this pent-up creativity within me, and I didn't know where to put it. My grandma showed me how to cross-stitch. It was all very uniform: here's a pattern, sit down, do the pattern, use these colors. A lot of those patterns and colors didn't inspire me.

JH: I read somewhere that you said that your mom, your sisters, and your cousins could make something out of nothing.

CE: Yes, totally. I think that's a cultural, traditional way of being in Native American communities. You really have nothing. So, you're taking all of these things and making something. My mom was a woodworker. I grew up basically in her woodshop. She was always making things—that's how she supported herself for a long time, too. Do you remember the Precious Moments? She worked with that kind of motif—little girls in the bonnets, that kind of thing—in the eighties. She made little step stools, cradles, and all kinds of things, and then painted Precious Moment types of motifs on them. She sold them at craft shows. In a small community, there's not a lot of shopping to do. Somebody would buy one of her pieces and then she'd have ten orders from everybody else in town. It was word of mouth.

JH: When did you learn how to knit?

CE: I was pregnant with my daughter, who is my second child. I was using the Knifty Knitter. It's a loom with little spokes. You take the yarn and flip it over. I really loved yarn. I was using the Knifty Knitter and made probably twenty hats out of it. My husband knew that our neighbor, Brooke, knit, and suggested I ask Brooke to teach me to knit. I told him, "No, I don't want to bother her." But, one day we saw her, and he asked, "Hey Brooke, would you teach Candice how to knit?"

I always say that those were his famous last words because knitting became a complete obsession very quickly. I went to the yarn shop, bought all the things I needed. I was pregnant, so I was nesting. I also like to keep my hands busy.

JH: But, it took quite a number of years before you went from knitting to actually dyeing your own yarn.

CE: It was probably, gosh, seven years before I started dyeing. I first started dyeing with plants. My mom is an herbalist and makes plant medicine, so I was really interested in that. I also wanted to incorporate my craft and her craft together. That was probably five or six years ago, and there wasn't a lot of information out there on plant dyeing then. There were maybe two or three plant dyeing books, and that was about it. A lot of it was just me gathering the plants and coming home and experimenting.

JH: Why yarn dyeing? What led you to that path? Because you also had a "regular" job at that time.

CE: I was really unhappy in my regular job. I was in my early thirties; I had two kids. I just woke up one day and asked myself, "How did I get here?" I had never really imagined myself in a position of having this white picket fence, two kids—you know, this very normal life. I just felt like I was not fulfilling what I was supposed to fulfill in a spiritual sense, too. I felt like there was more out there for me.

My brother is a really successful tech entrepreneur, and he does a lot of creative stuff with tech. He was always telling me to just do whatever I wanted, that I didn't have to settle, that I didn't have to do this nine-to-five job. Life is too short. He had been encouraging me for a long time to go out and do something else. I racked my brain thinking about it. I knew that I wanted to do something in the fiber industry or the knitting industry because I was so passionate about it. I knew that I could be successful, but I didn't want to knit for a living. I knew I couldn't sustain that. I don't know who can, you know.

JH: I don't either. You'd have to charge $2,000 a sweater.

CE: Yeah. I did it when my kids were little and that was just my path, I was at home anyways, but to make a career out of it or to actually pay the bills? It just wasn't gonna work. I don't even know what clicked in my brain to decide to start dyeing yarn. I just went for it. I bought all the things and got all the dye. I didn't even know if I was going to be good at it. It was a gamble for me.

I did know the business's name was going to be The Farmer's Daughter Fibers. My cousin still sings me the song "The Farmer's Daughter." Once I had the name, everything else kind of clicked.

I never felt like I fit in anywhere. I think that anybody who's mixed-race goes through this. My dad's family is fairly racist. My mom's family are all lovely people, and they've never made me feel that I didn't belong. They never made me feel like I wasn't Indian enough for them, but there's still this sense that because I didn't grow up on the reservation, I don't quite fit in there. It took a toll on me. I couldn't for a long time figure out what was wrong with me or why I never felt like I belonged.

So, when I created The Farmer's Daughter, I allowed myself to become me and to not worry so much about those things. I let that go and let me meld together. It was just such a surprise that that was what it was created out of. I didn't expect it. It wasn't my intention at first.

When I started to dye yarn, I was experimenting. I was looking at the color wheel and looking at inspiration pictures. But, once I threw those constraints out the window and let dyeing yarn become more of a spiritual thing for me, it clicked. The colorways I developed were the ones I was excited about, and it was who I was—and it was The Farmer's Daughter. Some of it was intentional branding, but everything else kind of fell into place.

JH: It's congruence, right? Whatever is on your inside is somehow reflected on the outside. You wanted something that was about all of you. I love hearing stories like that because I think it's what keeps us in the game for a long time, much longer than someone who has a much more corporate attitude toward it. It is such an extension of you. But, it also makes things hard because the work that you're doing is that extension of you. You've got a whole bunch of things going on: you have a brick-and-mortar, you still dye the yarn, you do these trunk shows, you're online, and you have your annual knitting retreat. How do you manage all that?

CE: That's a good question. I think I get this drive to do everything from my mom. I've tried to grow enough, settle out, grow a little bit more, and then settle out. So, there have definitely been crazy times. At the beginning of last year, I realized that I could not sustain what I was doing. I was dyeing in my basement. I knew that I had the potential to grow more, but I wasn't going to be able to do that alone. I had people helping me skein and tag and those types of things, but either I needed to step back and just dye a little bit and be okay with being a little dye company, or grow, get into a new space, and hire more people.

My husband was in the Air National Guard, and he was unhappy. I think that he was going through the same thing that I was going through, whether he knew it or not. When I had first started the business, I joked around and said, "You should come in and help me dye yarn."

Last year, I asked him to come and help me. I knew that there wasn't gonna be anybody else out there who cared as much as I did about the business as him, because it's our livelihood. So, he left his job. We moved into this awesome space that has a retail space. Working in my basement drove me crazy because it was so unaesthetically pleasing. I knew that I would be able to do so much more if I created an aesthetically pleasing place for me.

Our retail shop is open for four or five hours a day. I'm not actively marketing the shop in my local community. If you know about us and you want to come in, awesome. But, I would say the shop is a very small fraction of where my focus is. Just having the space makes such a big difference for me. This is basically my home. I keep really organized to get all that stuff done. Right now, I have five employees. Everybody who works for me is just amazing. I could not be any luckier. They take care of a lot of the things I was doing in the beginning: skeining, tagging, dyeing, and rinsing the yarn.

I don't have to do much of that anymore. I dye new colorways when nobody else is here, I show them how I do my colors, and they replicate it. That's nice because that was also something that I was getting burned out on, doing the same thing over and over. That's why I always had these new projects and stuff going on. I like doing new, exciting things.

JH: You're a creative person, and we thrive on the new and the different. There are people who have the vision and then there are the people who implement. It's hard to be both. Do you want to be both?

CE: I just want to be the artist.

JH: How long have you had that many employees?

CE: I had one employee before we moved into the space and then I went to having two employees. We've just gradually added on. My employees are part-time. The schedule is very flexible. They can come and go as they want. Everybody knows what they're supposed to do, and they just get it done.

I'm really good at being a boss. I love it. Before I did this, I was a preschool teacher. I feel like I got a lot of my skills from managing children. Adults aren't always different than three-year-olds. I moved up in the company that I was working for and ended up being the director of the childcare center. I think everybody has things that they're really good at, and honing in on that is so important.

JH: Where in Montana are you located?

CE: I'm in Great Falls. We have a population of sixty thousand to seventy thousand people. There's an air force base here and that adds to a lot of the population. It's an interesting town. If you go to western Montana, it's a lot more artsy, it's very liberal, it's really fun. They have great community events, but once you get over the mountains, you're starting to get into more ranching communities. I love the west side of this state, but the central and east side of the state have such a simple way of living that, and I enjoy that. I think it's good for my kids too. I love Montana.

JH: I'm intrigued by the work that you're doing with the Empowering Native Women Initiative in Montana. What is the initiative about? How did you become interested in it?

CE: I think that domestic violence has always been a topic that's been really important to me. I want to empower women and to give them resources. When I was in high school, I volunteered for the YWCA and was the advocate all through high school.

On the reservation, there is so much domestic violence—and violence in general. A lot of that stems from drug abuse and alcohol abuse. So, that was probably why I originally became interested in domestic violence. As years have gone on, the number of murdered and missing Indigenous women has become something that people are talking about. There was a nineteen-year-old Native American girl who went missing two years ago in Browning. When she went missing, nobody did anything about it. The police looked for her a little bit and they kind of knew who did it, but then nothing came of it. That was so infuriating to me—if it had been a white girl from across the mountains in the resort town who went missing, you better believe that they would know what happened to her.

I think that a lot of times, if you're on the reservation, there are drugs or alcohol involved. Something happens, and a lot of time, it's kind of just brushed off. "Oh, she was just messed up. Oh, she was just with that guy, and she shouldn't have done that." That was really something that bothered me a lot, and continues to bother me. As more people were shedding light on the number of missing and murdered Indigenous women, I felt like I needed to do something.

I talked to my mom and she gave me a bunch of her tea to sell with a skein of yarn as a fundraiser. We sold out immediately, so I now do a different collaboration with a different maker every month. Every month, it has sold out. I really wanted the funds to stay local. I wanted the money to go to my reservation or other reservations within Montana.

Within the last six months, our senator has started working hard not only on bringing more resources to the reservation but also involving the sheriff, the police, the FBI—bringing everybody together on what works and what doesn't work.

JH: The girls and the women go missing and the police don't do anything about it? What happens is essentially they blame the woman for her fate?

CE: Yeah. I think on the reservation, it's just so prevalent, people—not only women but men too—going missing. My uncle was killed when I was just born. He was changing the tire on his truck and was shot by a white man. The only thing that happened to the white man was that he had to leave the reservation. He didn't get prosecuted, he didn't get any jail time, or anything like that. Stuff like that happens a lot. It's just such a prevalent thing that people get beat up, people go missing, and the authorities just don't take it that seriously.

I needed to do something, and I feel like the work is—you know, there's a lot to be done. I'm still trying to figure out as every month goes by where the money that we raise is going to be used the best. The YWCA here in town serves four reservations.

This is why I called it the Empowering Native Women Initiative: on the reservation, the women are going to be the ones who create the change. I would like to eventually focus on traditional craft and getting maybe a girls' group started. I'm putting it out to the universe—I know that something will come up that is exactly what we need to be focusing on.

JH: Tell me about the collaborations that you're doing to raise money. Your mom donated tea the first month, and that was sent out to people who bought the tea, and all the funds went to the YWCA?

CE: Yeah. People paid for the tea. I sold tea and a skein of yarn. All the funds, we donated directly to the YWCA here in town. Once the task force got started, we started donating to them. There are maybe five or six task forces in Montana. Originally, they were just human trafficking task forces. Then Jon Tester, who is our senator, put out there that we needed to include the missing and murdered Indigenous women in that group. The task force is Cascade County Human Trafficking, which is our county, but I think that they're also serving three reservations.

JH: What other projects have you done to raise money?

CE: I put out there, "Hey, if you're interested in collaborating, just let me know." I got a bazillion emails. So many people are so willing to help out. I've worked with Western Sky Knits. It's a yarn company and I thought that collaboration would be awesome because she's another Montanan.

JH: That must feel really good to be able to do this, to create, to meld your creative life, your work life, and your interests.

CE: It feels awesome. It feels good because for so long, like I said, I just needed to do something. Like I don't even care what it is. I feel like I need to be doing something to contribute to making a change, whether it was doing a walk

---

I would like to start some sort of traditional craft group because I know how much craft has helped me and helped so many others that I want to make sure that young girls are getting the opportunity to do that.

---

or marching. A lot of times, what it comes down to is money and finances. I knew that I could help with that, but I didn't realize how much I could help. I mean, people are excited and don't want to miss out on it.

It feels a little surreal, honestly, that we're, you know, able to do that. For me, being on the task force and helping in more of a tangible way also feels good. There are a couple of things I would like to do. Like I said, I would like to start some sort of traditional craft group because I know how much craft has helped me and helped so many others that I want to make sure that young girls are getting the opportunity to do that.

JH: Yesterday, I was listening to this podcast interview of you and you said something that struck me: "You have to persevere and keep going." What does that mean?

CE: Sounds like something I would say. I think that I have always had this attitude of you just gotta pick yourself up and keep going. I am one of the most optimistic people that I know. I just try to see the good in every situation. My mom grew up on the reservation and she lived in a house that was maybe a thousand square feet with fifteen brothers and sisters. I mean, extremely poor. She had a really tough upbringing. When we were little and had moved from the ranch over the mountains on the west side of the mountains to the resort town, she didn't have anything in a community that was pretty wealthy. But, she always made us feel like we had enough and that money didn't matter. We would go to Walmart with $5 and spend two hours looking around, joking, laughing, having such a great time.

That laughter and being together were the most important things. At the end of the day, you can spend a little bit of time being upset about things. But once you have taken the time to sit with it, I feel like it needs to go to the side and you need to keep doing what you need to do. Not necessarily shoving feelings down but moving on and keeping going. Whether it's something small that happens during the day—if I forget to send an invoice or forget to put the right amount of yarn in a box to, something that's much bigger—I really do try to just keep going.

MY BODY! MY WAY! MY SELF IN THIS WORLD. WHY I SEW AND SOME OTHER THINGS

Essay by Ebony Haight

MY SENSE OF self in the community has always been a little perplexed. I see myself floating in and out of other communities rather than gathering one around myself. I suppose I like my independence. But, it's also true that I don't feel like a "full member" of most communities. Communities seem to build themselves up around some sense of shared identity, around the ability to say "We are," and I've never much liked making proclamations about myself or my identity. (Like writing that, it doesn't feel great, even if it holds a truth. It seems like such an awkward little truth. A signpost, not a map.) To say "I am this" or "I am that" seems like trying to flatten something out and make it small enough to easily consume, to understand and accept. But being a human, being seen and accepted, it doesn't seem to work that way. If being understood were as simple as compiling the right combination of "I" statements well, couldn't we all be so lucky? I *do* want to be understood, of course. But understanding isn't easy. It's something that others have to want for you. Just like love, understanding is a gift you give to others, not something you can receive by request.

In my earliest memories, I see my desire to use the art of dress and storytelling to try and invite the type of understanding I desired. One reason for that might be that they're very available. Your words and body are always with you, irrevocably yours. It's also true that these simply spoke to me as good surfaces through which to express myself creatively. They still do. I was the kid who liked to hang out in my older sister's room, clomping around before the mirror in her too-big-for-me shoes. I was also very into lying, which is ironic because as an adult, I'm told I tend to communicate with an assertive sense of honesty.

Since I was a kid, I've always been very aware of being seen by others. From around the age of two, I lived and grew up in Palo Alto, California—a predominantly white community. I was raised by white parents, who adopted me when I was eight. Without getting into all the complexities of my family, I'll just say we were a sweet, if motley, crew. It was easy enough for me to see that I was different within my family, and outside in the world, it was easy enough to notice that other people saw my family differently. I enjoyed lying as a way to have fun with the questions people were always asking. And I suppose I played with how I was dressing because I could tell people were looking. There was then, as now, an uneasy relationship to the attention, but that's the art in my dressing. It's art if it draws you in aesthetically, but ultimately it seeks to hold you emotionally and intellectually.

I'm an artist who likes playing with pieces. Getting dressed is like making a quilt, a collage, or an essay: I collect disparate parts, then try to pull them together into something pleasing. Sure, clothes can be about looking good, but that's also an assertion of what "good" looks like to me. My clothes are just

---

As a Black woman, establishing a sense of truth, power, and beauty requires a lot of imagination and creativity. Growing up, I had to imagine the possibility that I was beautiful, because certainly the world I existed in wasn't trying to build that idea up for me.

---

as much about cool comfort as they are about power and control. It's a way of saying something, even if what's being said is just, "I don't give a fuck what you think about how I'm dressed." (Which, translation, may be that I just don't give a fuck what you think at all.)

As a Black woman, establishing a sense of truth, power, and beauty requires a lot of imagination and creativity. Growing up, I had to imagine the possibility that I was beautiful, because certainly the world I existed in wasn't trying to build that idea up for me. Nothing about me seemed to be as people expected or wanted it to be, from my taste in music (eighties pop) to my mom (Yes, that's her). In all my immediate communities I felt . . . weird. I'm sure I wasn't thinking about it this way at the time, but I used clothes to make a home for myself. I felt bolstered by a good outfit. And, if someone complimented me on it, I felt seen in a way that worked for me because I'd cultivated it.

This relationship with clothes definitely wasn't always healthy. I channeled a lot of need and longing into clothes and self-presentation. As if getting that right could somehow make it all right. In fact, it mostly just made for big credit card bills and strange, sad moments standing before a closet full of clothes, feeling empty and vaguely desperate. But that's why I sew. That full-closet-vacant-heart energy wants something, and it's not *just* a new outfit. Though that's undeniably, unabashedly, a part of it.

I sew to satisfy this thing in me that will never be fully satisfied by something off the rack. I sew to dress myself, yes, but now in a way that honors an ingenious, creative, feminine history. I sew to celebrate: My body! My way! Myself in this world. I sew to challenge, relax, and teach myself something along the way. I sew because it helps me be a better version of me. I sew almost exclusively for myself, and never think of that as sewing "selfishly." I sew to nourish my creativity. I sew because slowly sinking a sharp needle into fabric is just so satisfying.

I can't quite remember how old I was when I first started sewing. Let's say I was eleven. It took some arm-twisting, but after a few rounds of asking, I got my mom to show me the basics of using her Singer Featherweight. That machine was poorly maintained and, as a result, quite cranky. Much of my early sewing time was spent picking out thread nests and ripping back jumped stitches.

Still, using that machine I taught myself garment construction by copying pieces from my closet. I was immediately in love with the possibility. That I might take a lump of fabric, cut it up, and turn it into something. It seemed a little bit like magic. I remember making a vest (it was the nineties) out of abandoned upholstery fabric I'd found around the house. Somehow, I added a lining and buttons. The finished product was about as uncomfortable as it was ugly (because, upholstery fabric), but it was also pretty well done, even though I was just making it up as I went along. I had no fear of failure! That seemed natural back then, to dive in and see what I could make of something. But, experience has a way of curtailing bravery, and as I made my way into teenage-hood, my interest in wearing improvisational, handmade garments shriveled up and just about died.

A decade, or nearly two, went by. I was in graduate school studying fiction, and the Internet existed, so I was spending time on it when I might have been writing the next great American novel. But this is how I rediscovered sewing. Here were women making clothing that looked like ready-to-wear. Only better, because you couldn't actually buy it anywhere. Their clothes looked good, and they were uniquely, exclusively theirs. Within weeks of discovering this burgeoning online community, I had pulled out my old sewing machine and started making. Eight years later, sewing is an essential part of my life and identity.

Sewing certainly draws me in aesthetically. I love the process of choosing a pattern, matching it to fabric and notions, altering the design to suit my ideas, identifying construction methods, and working all this with my hands. But, what surprises me is how well sewing holds me emotionally and intellectually. Repeating this process over time has taught me so much about how I see, how I like to feel in my body, what I like, and why. And I'm happier wearing stuff I've made myself. It's a much richer and more satisfying feeling than wearing something I've purchased. It strikes me as funny sometimes how genuinely impressed people are when they find out you've made something you're wearing. But, I also forget how much time I've put in over the years, developing and refining my skills. My creativity and careful work are what's ultimately on display. It's useful to remind myself that people aren't just admiring my outfit, they're genuinely admiring me.

I sew because it helps me see myself in a world where feeling seen doesn't come easily. And no, I don't always feel seen by the online sewing community. But, at the risk of sounding like I'm willing to just lie down and take it from the status quo (which, certainly not), I'm not trying to let that bother me. Because I don't feel all-the-way seen by *any* community, and I'm not sure that's what I'm going for anyway. I long ago abandoned the idea of being offered somewhere to feel, "Naturally, yes. This is made for me." Maybe I like my independence, and maybe I don't. Independent is just what I am, any way you slice it. And I do like to slice it, to pull it apart, and put it back together again. To stitch it up into something pleasing. My way. Put that way, it seems my people might be those who are actively into self-creation. Those actively seeking to be drawn into understanding. That's my community. Through sewing and through life, I've been lucky to find a few.

SURVEY PROFILE

Kayla Fernandez

Age: 30
Location: Westminster, Maryland
Profession: Shipping management and customer service at a hand-dyed yarn business

What types of fiber crafts do you engage in, and how many years have you been engaged in each?
The craft that I'm most engaged in is knitting. I've been knitting for one and a half years now and thoroughly in love with it. Prior to knitting, I had crocheted for about five to six years, picking it up to make gifts for loved ones. Thanks to both of those crafts, I've also recently started to sew, seeing the slow-fashion movement, sewing, and knitting so interrelated.

How do you self-describe/identify yourself?
I identify as an Afro-Latina, a Latina that has primarily African features, cultural traditions, and background. Coming from Puerto Rico, there's a rich history of African and Taino traditions that I hope I'm representing well in the world.

What's the first thing you remember making?
I'm a former military wife, so I remember making baby blankets for other military wives who were far from their homes and families and wanting them to feel supported by their military family as well. They were pretty simple blankets, mostly double crochets for the entirety, but those women that received them did with so much joy and gratitude that it really fueled my fire to learn more techniques and simply get better at my craft.

What are you making now?
All the things! I'm working on a Nurtured Sweater by Andrea Mowry to layer over my ready-to-wear dresses, an Iskald pullover by Caitlin Hunter to wear

as my go-to comfy sweater in the house, and an As-If Tee by Shay Johnson as a dressed-up tee to wear for casual dressy or dressed-up events. I'm also knitting a mini self-drafted cardigan for my four-year-old daughter who asked for "a sweater I can snuggle in."

What's your favorite thing you've made?

I absolutely love my Tegna by Caitlin Hunter, which is a short-sleeved sweater with lace detailing along the body hem. My love for crafting and knitting in particular started with and was centered around gift knitting. I still get most of my joy by knitting for others. But with the Tegna, it was the first time that I allowed myself to knit something selfishly and not worry about deadlines or pressures. There was a beautiful shift happening at that time where I was first discovering that my crafting and knitting could be used as self-care. I was lucky enough that for a first sweater project, it came out beautifully and is my most worn knit to date.

How and why did you learn your crafts?

I learned to initially crochet because I wanted to make little garments and accessories for my son. While watching me crochet a hat for him, one of my friends suggested I could make items for other new mothers in our military community that might be missing handmade items for the babies from home. Once I began that journey, it was thanks to YouTube that I was able to learn new stitches and techniques and begin to experiment.

A couple of years ago, I really wanted to finally conquer knitting to help combat some loneliness for my husband's future military deployment, and when it finally clicked for me, I felt like I had that, "Ah-ha!" moment where I had found the right craft for me.

Does anyone in your family practice this craft, too? Are your pieces similar or different aesthetically?

I'm the only one in my family that practices any crafts, especially fiber crafts, but my mother grew up sewing and really identifies with seeing a garment in your mind or an inspiration in real life and discovering ways to tailor that garment to suit your body, your needs. Our pieces were drastically different aesthetically because, one, she was sewing for a tropical climate and was *never* in need of a sweater in Puerto Rico, and, two, she was in a different season of her life—a single woman in her teens and twenties. My journey began at the end of my twenties and into my thirties, and I'm currently married with four children, all of which makes for vastly different garment choices. But we do carry similarities in that we'll always gravitate toward shades of blue since it reminds us of our connection to the water and to the ocean that surrounds us in Puerto Rico, and that both of our styles have always pushed back against the belief that menswear is only for men. My mother sewed pantsuits for herself at a time when dresses were the only acceptable attire at events in her community. I personally love mixing traditional menswear silhouettes with feminine details.

Tell me about your creative community. You can define "community" as broadly or as specifically as you'd like.
I think I have two amazing communities to lean on. I have my work community at Magpie Fibers, where I work with a team of diverse, amazing women who are all crafting geniuses in their own right. Each of them brings a level of expertise to the table that leaves me feeling inspired and grateful each day that I clock in and out of work. I think our diverse opinions and experiences lead to amazing conversations that broaden each of our opinions about crafting and about the world. For me, it is truly a safe space where I feel heard, validated, and empowered.

Secondly, I have an amazing community on Instagram where I feel like I can choose to see more crafters that look like me or have different diverse experiences that I can identify with as well. Once I discovered how kind and gentle the majority of knitters are, it felt as if I had found the tribe I didn't know I was searching for. I've forged friendships with crafters from across the country and even some from around the world, and have learned much more than I imagined possible.

When you were younger, were you exposed to other people who looked like you, or who were from similar backgrounds as you, and who engaged in this craft?
I don't remember seeing anyone who looked like me or had a similar background to me doing the crafts I wanted to do. In addition to being a military wife, I am also a navy brat and so lived in many different places far from the majority of Puerto Rican communities.

I was very aware of the strong connection most Latina women have with sewing, handmade items, and artisanal expertise. It was something I sought out regularly off the island, but it wasn't until I was much older that as an adult I realized that I could be that link to the handmade items instead of seeking them out elsewhere.

When have you felt like an "other" within the context of your craft?
I think it is sometimes hard to walk into white-dominated spaces, speak your truth, and identify how your experience may differ from what they deem the norm. I remember my friends being shocked when I told them that when I walk into a local yarn shop, I make sure that my hands are out of my pockets and can be clearly seen so that I can't be accused of shoplifting, or that I won't place items on a stroller while shopping for the same fear that I'll be mistaken as a shoplifter, or that I feel better going to the local yarn store with white women because I feel the shop owners immediately assume I'm "different."

My friends were stunned when I told them these things, and sometimes that can be harder than the actual acts themselves because those are things that I have internalized and recognize as real. It's much harder when you realize that these are thoughts that someone else has never had.

EMBROIDERING COMMUNITY

Interview with Shahnaz Khan

JEN HEWETT: Tell me about your childhood and some of your early influences.

SHAHNAZ KHAN: I was born in London to a Greek mother and Pakistani father. He actually was born in India before the India-Pakistan Partition, so I consider that my ancestry is Indian and Pakistani. All of that is kind of relevant, depending on what the conversation is. My parents divorced when I was quite young. My dad moved to America, and then my mom and her second husband moved our family to Australia when I was eleven.

I grew up in England and Australia, and then after I graduated from college, I moved to America to spend time with my dad. He was quite ill. He had heart disease and he has subsequently passed away, but I did have a lot of time with him, and that was a big part of my journey geographically. More recently, when I started delving more into Indian embroidery, it was really as a way to connect with him. My mother's family all still live in Greece. They're from Katerini in the north of Greece. When we were children, we visited every summer because we were in England and we were close. That's where I learned embroidery. My mother has two sisters and a brother, and her brother owns an embroidery supply store that he runs with his wife, so that's always been the family business. Both of my aunts have made a living from embroidery. Doing work on the side, they supported their families. The way of life in Greece is still very traditional in a lot of places.

It's hard to wrap my head around it sometimes, but one of my aunts is in her seventies and she still grows her own vegetables in her garden to feed her family. When I'm there, I am reminded of how different their day-to-day life is. One of my aunts did hand tracings of embroidery onto cotton and linen, her brother sold that in his store, and my other aunt specialized in finishings, meaning she would decorate the edges of other people's embroideries. They all make samples for the store and my uncle and his wife do a lot of research around Europe, looking for different patterns and techniques that people might find interesting. Within my family, they practice a type of white work called Richelieu, which is a type of cutwork that is done using buttonhole stitch. But, there's also a lot of counted work that's traditional to Greece. My mother always had a plethora of embroideries that she made while growing up around the house. My grandma made beautiful embroideries and crochet bedspreads for my brother and me.

The tradition of handcrafts has always been really strong in my mother's family. My mother is a dressmaker, and she taught me how to sew when I was young. I've always had a needle and thread, a piece of fabric, a fashion magazine in my hands, or something that was related to textiles and crafts.

JH: To back up, you used a lot of terms that people might not be familiar with. So, embroidery tracing, that would be the actual design itself?

SK: Yeah. My uncle would import or otherwise source designs, and then they were traced onto cloth. In her house, my aunt had a glass-top table with a light underneath—a light box—and she would draw with a pen that washed out when the embroidery was complete.

JH: Then somebody would buy that?

SK: Yes, and they would purchase that from my uncle's shop along with all the necessary thread.

JH: You mentioned "counted work," which is something I'm not at all familiar with.

SK: That's any kind of embroidery that's done on an even weave fabric where you count the stitches, like a cross-stitch. That's a big part of the Greek tradition as well, and a lot of the island embroideries that you would see are counted work.

JH: So really, very meticulous work. White work is beautiful, but it's also one of the hardest things to do because you're using white thread on white fabric.

SK: Yes, and everything has to be perfect.

JH: Exactly. Which, in many ways, is very different from traditional Indian embroidery, which is not to say that it's not perfect and meticulous, but it often is very colorful—

SK: And irregular, and you can see that they follow a design sometimes, but it's definitely not coloring within the lines in the way that a lot of Greek embroidery is.

JH: Your mother is a dressmaker, and you grew up around fabric. Did you go on to study textiles or costume?

SK: I started out studying theater. I wanted to be a performer when I was very young, and because I could sew, I always ended up making costumes. I ended up doing my graduate degree in costume design in Las Vegas at UNLV, and then when I moved to New York, I took a detour into fashion for a few years. I missed theater and I wanted to get back to it. That's when I started working as a costume tailor. I started doing repairs and alterations at a long-running Broadway musical, and now I've been there for eleven years. I thought it was going to be the job that I took while I decided what I was going to do next, but I fell in love with being in the theater and working with the costumes. I feel so spoiled that I get to do that as my day job.

JH: What do you do specifically in your day job?

SK: A lot of alterations. I work on a long-running show, and we are at the point where we have a pretty high cast turnover. We do fittings and refit the clothes for the new actors, and then there's everyday maintenance. We patch and darn holes, replace trim and remake linings, anything to keep those clothes together in one piece and looking beautiful and brand-new, even after sixteen years.

JH: It's such an interesting career path because it's not what you think of as a traditional career. You have to be in it to understand that it is a possibility.

SK: Absolutely. I was interested in design, but I didn't want the lifestyle that went with it, the long days, the late nights, and working seven days a week. I wanted a job that could be more nine-to-five, could give me time to have a creative outlet, do things for myself, and travel a lot more. That's the direction that my life is taking now.

Three or four years ago I decided to take textile classes at the Fashion Institute of Technology (FIT). I took classes in textile design, in weaving, I did silk painting, screen printing—just any basic introductory textile things I could do.

I heard about this program in India. It was around the same time that I had decided to make a lot of changes in my life. I'd turned forty. I was trying to decide where I wanted to live, if I wanted to move back home to Australia, and it all tied in together in a strange way as I just wanted to learn about the world of textiles. I wanted to find a way to connect to people in other cultures, look at the ways that we're all similar, and celebrate the ways in which we're different. It was a moment when I was looking at myself and my own cultural heritage in a different way, and thinking about life and legacy. My mind opened up to these things at a point in my life when everything else was settled, and I could finally say, "What is it that I really want to do if I could do anything with my life?" And really, it was just to travel more and learn about textiles. That's what I started doing.

I started looking for study abroad programs, and I came across the FIT program in India. India has such a personal connection for me because of my dad. The program was in Rajasthan, the same area of India where my dad was born. I got to have that experience of going somewhere that's so different from where I was from, and knowing that this is how the earth smelled to him when he was growing up, and this is what he saw, and also understanding how environment is just so different. You can't explain it. You can't learn that from looking at a photograph or watching television. You have to be there to feel it. To have that in your bones and to understand how that connects to something handmade—that is a textile.

We were at a *dabu* (a form of mud resist) block printing workshop, watching the printers mixing the mud. Somebody in the class asked if there's a machine that can do it because the printers mix the mud with their feet and their hands. We were told that a machine couldn't do it because it would make the mud too thin. The only way they can know when it's ready is to feel it. I just love that about handmade things. There's something about needing a person to do the job, the way that when you have an embroidery or a block print, you can see the person in the work. You can see their handprint in a way.

I teach an Indian mirrorwork embroidery class and I love to share this story with my students. When I was a young child, my dad went to Pakistan, and when he came back, he brought me a shalwar kameez that was white and it had little tiny mirrors embroidered all over it, each one embroidered in a different color. I loved it. Jen, it was my favorite thing. I have such strong memories of it and how the cotton felt in my hand, how smooth the mirrors were. So, from that nostalgia, I knew that when I went to India, I wanted to learn that technique and find out about it. It always felt very mysterious to me. I learned a little bit about it. We didn't do a lot of embroidery in the India program in the way that I wanted, but it was a springboard for me to do a lot of research when I got back to the United States. I watched every single YouTube video I could find and looked for every book on the subject.

About six months later, I was in Greece with my mother. Every afternoon, my aunts get together, they bring their embroideries to work on, and they chat. I pulled out my embroideries and everyone was chatting. There was this story that I'd never heard before about my maternal great-grandmother, Katina. They referred to her as "the Bulgarian." I guess she must have been descended from Bulgarians, and she also cooked with Eastern spices. She was very different and she used that same mirrored embroidery technique on her husband's—my great-grandfather's—horse saddle. She embroidered these mirrors onto his saddle as a talisman.

There's this really sweet story about my grandmother. When she was a little girl, she'd watch her dad ride his horse up into the fields. They were farmers. In the afternoon, when the sun was going down and she knew he was about to come home, she would go and she would perch herself on the little rock in the garden and wait for him to come home. Before she saw him or the horse, she would see these little flashes of light. It was the mirrors reflecting on the sun—she knew that he was coming home.

JH: What a lovely story.

SK: I love the connection of just thinking of my grandmother as a young girl, thinking of my great-grandmother as this woman who had the same technique as was practiced in my father's tradition, but growing up, I never connected Greece and Pakistan. They were always these two very separate things in my mind. I came across something reflective of both sides of my culture and it just tied that in together. It added another layer.

I've been doing a lot of work with these mirrors, and since I've started teaching the class, I realized that it's something that people want to learn about. They want to have a connection to the technique. The people in my classes always want to know about the history. They always want to know about the women. They always want to know about where this came from. I mean, this technique has been going on for centuries.

JH: What do you know about its history?

SK: It's interesting because there is no official documentation of these techniques. Historians rely heavily on surviving textiles, of which there are few.

The technique is known as *Shisha*, which means "tiny mirror." It started out with anything reflective that they would embroider onto cloth to deflect evil spirits. It's another version of the evil eye that we see all over the East and parts of Europe. Originally, mica was used, along with tin, silver, beetle's wings, and coins. When they were eventually able to blow glass, they would hand blow these spheres of mirrored glass and then cut them by hand into tiny pieces. I believe they were originally embroidered onto textiles, animal trappings, wall hangings, and ceremonial textiles for weddings and births—anything where they wanted to have good luck. Mumtaz Mahal, the wife that Shah Jahan built the Taj Mahal for, is often credited with bringing the mirrored embroidery tradition to India during the Mughal reign in the seventeenth century. I believe it dates even farther back to Afghanistan; the oldest textiles they have found come from Afghanistan, not India.

It was tribal women who first started attaching the mirrors onto their clothing and accessories as protection. One of these tribes—Jen, I don't know if you've seen pictures—the Banjara tribe, they're just covered in mirrors, all over their heads, all over their clothes. They're amazing. They traveled the technique around India because they're a wandering tribe.

JH: It's probably spectacular to see.

SK: Yes. I mean, it's shiny. That's what everybody wants. That's what all the gold and the silver was about.

JH: My mom is from the Philippines, and there is also very much a tradition there of wearing shiny, bright, gold, plus platinum, and lots of diamonds.

We crave the shine—I think that's visceral and built into our DNA. Light was probably very important. I find that fascination with gold and with shine so interesting.

At the same time, it's something that as we become more "modern" and "Western," that love of bling almost gets beaten out of us. If we look at minimalism, it's all about being matte and being dull. Shine is seen as something tacky.

SK: I've never thought about it that way, but it's true. I noticed it in India, the way they layer their jewelry, all the way up their arms, all over their hands, all over their faces, all over their heads—it's everywhere. We have lost so much of that.

I remember my mom saying that my grandma often didn't have enough candles at night to provide enough light to do her embroidery, so the women in the village would all get together and bring all their candles together, and then they had enough light. I just think that is so fabulous because, out of

---

Community is about connecting culture and history and people.

---

necessity, maybe you have to do a repair on your husband's shirt, or maybe you really want to finish the embroidery—that's what community is. That's how community grows. I think there are so many layers. There are so many levels of textiles, and we've talked about a few. I think it really is about community. Community is about connecting culture and history and people.

JH: Tell me about teaching. When did you start teaching?

SK: I have always been interested in teaching and have taught various things on and off over the years. I'm a part of a union, the International Alliance of Theatrical Stage Employees (IATSE), for the work I do in theater. IATSE has an education program, and I've been teaching for a few years as part of that, doing specialty sewing classes.

More recently, I have been interested in taking classes and learning new things. Six or seven years ago, my mom and I went to the Royal School of

Needlework (RSN) in London. I remember during that class thinking, "Could I do this? Could I make money from it? Could I teach?" I think the seed was planted, and things all came together, the dots connected. I started teaching introductory embroidery classes at the union, and then I went to India. When I got back, I started teaching my Indian embroidery class in Brooklyn at Tatter and on the West Coast at the San Francisco School of Needlework and Design.

I've always loved teaching, and I am so interested in cultural preservation. It's really important to me that these techniques continue. It's important that there's a way to share these techniques, and I love that we're in a maker culture right now, that people want to slow down and work with their hands.

When we took that class at the RSN, my mom and I had all these discussions about what we do in our lives for decompression. Perhaps embroidery was what women did as decompression, even though anything that my grandmother made, like during the war in Greece, was used. Everything my grandma knit was worn, then it was taken apart and re-knit into something else, taken apart and re-knit into something else, and eventually when the yarn couldn't be used for clothes anymore, she wove it into rugs. She hand-dyed things. My mother has these rugs in her kitchen—one of them is made from old yarn and one of them is made from old clothes that were cut into strips and made into fabric. Everything was out of necessity. There's also an element of doing it for pleasure, during a time and a place where there weren't all the things we have now to provide us with pleasure. I think that's where women took pleasure.

JH: I agree. Because none of those things need to be as beautiful as they are. And yet, they are.

SK: And they are. That same grandmother, my YaYa on the Greek side, grew up on a farm. She knew the odd places where the chickens would lay their eggs, and she would collect the eggs and sell them. With the money, she would buy crochet thread. She'd climb into the trees and she'd crochet secretly. I can't even imagine what the punishment would have been for that kind of idle behavior then, but just the idea that she risked punishment because of a need within her to express herself.

I think that is very human, and it's so easy to connect to that. I think we all want to connect to each other. I want to connect to her. But, I also want to connect to other cultures outside of my own. I have many things to say. First of all, I was really touched and moved when you contacted me because thinking of myself as a woman of color is something that is very new to me. I've always felt very different. In London, I was brown-skinned, so I was never English in the way that an English person is, and in Australia, I was brown-skinned, but obviously, I wasn't Native. People called me black in Australia because there weren't many black people living there at the time. It's just this blanket thing. It was always this idea that I came from somewhere else, whether it was a racist "Go back to where you come from" or an innocent "Where are you from?" Then I would say, "England," and then they'd be confused because that's not what they're asking. They're really asking, "Why is your skin brown?" It's like we don't have the language.

Moving to America was interesting because of my accent. Americans ask, "Where is your accent from?" They don't say, "Where are you from?" so it's an easier question to answer. My identity was very wrapped up in being Australian, but I always felt like I was from somewhere else. Wherever I was in the world, I was always from somewhere else.

Going to India was just this amazing experience of looking like other people, recognizing myself in other people, and feeling like I have never had that. I didn't necessarily think of myself within the community of people of color until recently, when the conversation changed.

The idea of people of color coming together politically and hearing other people's stories . . . Now, there are authors and comedians who are Indian Americans and Pakistani Americans. Reading those stories, watching those television programs, and seeing those characters and going, "Oh that's me." Sort of identifying in a way that I never have, and thinking it's so strange that I'm a forty-year-old woman and my identity is something that feels new to me. That has been a beautiful, new experience for me.

When you contacted me, I felt so touched that I'm part of not just the craft community, which is an amazing and inclusive community, but also within that, part of a community that's made up of so many different cultures. That's just awesome, and within that, the embroidery that I am particularly interested in are things that connect us to culture, so it's sort of come full circle.

JH: You say in your artist statement that you're particularly interested in the way that textiles connect us to our cultures. You've talked so much about the craft that your maternal side of the family engages in. Was there also a tradition on your paternal side of the family?

SK: It's not something that my dad and I talked about. What I do know is that his family was in the cotton trade, so there is definitely a connection to textiles there. I know that the textile community in India, in terms of caste, are Muslims, so that all sort of ties in that side of it, but I wish I had more information about that.

What I'm finding interesting is that my journey is just very organic. Things are unfolding and I feel like I'm following a path and I'm being led. It's like that story with my grandmother and the mirrors. I didn't know that story. I'd already started researching this technique, and then all of a sudden, it's opening up another way of connecting to my own culture but also of continuing to travel around the world. It's like I want to go everywhere, Jen, and see everything, and I'm impatient for it. But, I feel like I'm on a path even though I might not know what it is. When you asked about teaching, that is such a big part of what I want to contribute because I am a people person. I love being around people. I love hearing their stories, and I love having an opportunity to share a little bit about myself, to share a little bit about a technique that was done by women partially out of necessity, partially just out of wanting decoration.

In India, there's professional embroidery that's done by men in factories, but what's interesting to me is the work women did for themselves in their homes—the wedding canopies, the tablecloths, and the clothing. I love these cultures that have parades of traditional dress. That's big in the Greek culture. Just this idea that it was something that women were doing for themselves. Like you said, none of it had to be pretty, in a sense, but it doesn't matter.

JH: I don't know what specifically it is about textiles that makes it a thing that binds us. Even if we go to cultures where people don't wear clothing, there's still some type of thread.

What's next for you? I know you just said you're not sure, but you've got a path. What do you want to do next?

SK: So many things. I feel like I'm just beginning. I mean, I am just beginning. I feel like I have been spending a lot of time on the Indian side of things, and I want to delve a little deeper into the Greek traditions. I'm dying to find time to delve into the Greek side, and there is a lot of research that I want to do in Greece. I'd love to go back to India, but also there are so many techniques I haven't even . . . I've just hit the mirrors, and I've sort of been going

---

So many of these traditions come from our ethnic cultures. We look to how our ancestors lived. We look at how other people lived. I like connecting.

---

on that. The short version is I definitely want to work more on developing an artistic body of work based around these techniques. Part of what I want from teaching is to inspire other people to use these techniques in their own work and create modern interpretations. That's how you keep things alive. I want to have time to do that for myself. I want to find ways to combine things.

So many of these traditions come from our ethnic cultures. We look to how our ancestors lived. We look at how other people lived. I like connecting. I don't like this idea that we all have to be the same and that we're doing everything right. I like this idea that there are other people in the world who do things differently. I think there's something in all of this that excites me and makes me curious about life. It makes me want to understand that more because, to me, I think that's the secret of life. I think that's hidden in all these little things we want to know.

The path that I would like to follow is to travel around the world and create site-specific embroidery tributes to areas. So, learn a new technique from a specific area and then embroider a portrait of some kind. I'm still working on the format, but I think that will happen organically. I'm applying to do some artistic residencies, and I'm hoping that through that I can travel to different places. I can learn new things. I can teach new things. And then, I can sort of build that into what I'm teaching as well. So yeah, that's the dream.

JH: Now that you've said it out loud, it will happen.

SK: It will happen.

WHAT ARE YOU MAKING NOW?

I am making clutch handbags that combine embroidery with local, hand-spun wool and fabrics from El Salvador. The original prototype included LED lights to show a proof of concept of wearable technology to Latina youth learning about circuits and LEDs in a sample project.—HELEN TREJO

A dog sweater!—DINA ALI

I currently have three sweaters on the needles, I'm knitting socks for my husband, and I'm about to start on an experiment with embroidering a pair of TOMS!—VANESSA FOO

So many things! I am finishing up a stylized embroidery of a brownstone made up of the letters BRKLYN. I'm also knitting up a dress on size six needles using fingering weight yarn.—DENNIQUE GRAHAM

Teaching Craft

< Some of Ellie Lum's bag-making tools

SURVEY PROFILE

Ellie Lum

Age: 39
Location: Portland, Oregon
Profession: Bag designer, maker, and teacher. Founder of Klum House Workshop

What types of fiber crafts do you engage in, and how many years have you been engaged in each?
I've dabbled in all kinds of fiber crafts over the years—cross stitching, knitting, crocheting—but the one that stuck is sewing. I started sewing when I was a little kid and never looked back! At this point, I've been a professional stitcher in one form or another for over twenty years, specializing in rugged, industrial sewing and bag making.

When I was eighteen and working as a bag messenger in Philly, a friend and I cofounded a custom messenger bag company called RE Load Bags, which is still in operation today. We went on to open shops in Philly, Seattle, and San Francisco, all of which had in-house production, so the bags were manufactured right there in the shop. In the beginning, I was the only stitcher, but to keep up with demand, I quickly needed to train my business partner to do production as well. Over the fifteen years that I ran RE Load, I trained dozens of stitchers on how to produce rugged, heavy-duty bags on industrial sewing machines. In the process, I discovered that I had a real passion for teaching, and I saw the way these skills opened creative and professional doors for those I taught.

These days, I run a workshop space, bag pattern, and kit line called Klum House, with education and hands-on skill-building at its core. My love of making has naturally evolved into helping others discover their own love of making. I want everyone to know that these skills are accessible to them, that they can do things they never thought possible, and find as much fulfillment from working with their hands as I have.

How do you self-describe/identify yourself?

I identify as a teacher, a bag maker, a community-builder, and a surfer.

My mom's side of the family is Indigenous Mexican. My maternal grand-mother was born in northern Mexico and my mom was born in Santa Barbara. My dad is Portuguese Chinese and grew up in Honolulu. Being Portuguese Chinese is basically synonymous with being from Hawaii. It's kind of the only place in the world where these two cultures have integrated for so many generations. My parents met when they were both living in San Francisco. My background is a blend of Mexican, Chinese, Portuguese, and Hawaiian cultures coming together against the backdrop of San Francisco in the eighties and nineties.

What's the first thing you remember making?

The first thing I remember sewing was a cotton napkin. I was four years old, and my mom taught me how to hand-sew the hem. I remember concentrating really hard to try to make the stitches straight. Making things by hand was common in my family growing up, and I was invited to participate in that.

What are you making now?

These days, I manage a business and a team of people, so making for me is rarely just sitting down to sew a thing and then call it finished. It's all tied into a larger vision and a whole, intricate web of operations, which includes branding, marketing, pattern writing and design, packaging and shipping, processing large quantities of fabric and leather, product photography, and on and on! In a way, Klum House itself is a big project that I am constantly working on. But whether I am working on a new bag sample, designing a new workshop, or creating a new pattern, the end goal is always about supporting others in their making journeys.

What's your favorite thing you've made?

One of my favorite things I've ever made was a radio holder for a messenger bag strap. As bike messengers, we always had to carry around these two-way radios close to our bodies so we could push the button and talk while riding. I got that design right on the very first try. That had never happened before and it hasn't happened again since. I made one sample and it was perfect. It solved a problem in a really satisfying way. That design went straight into production at RE Load on one of the first bags we sold back in 1998.

How and why did you learn your crafts?

I learned hand-sewing from my mom when I was really young. She found machine sewing frustrating because she could never figure out what all the knobs did, but she sewed all kinds of amazing things by hand. She used to make fancy fiesta dresses for me and my sister when we were kids and she sewed awesome, hippy-style embroidery on all of her friends' jackets in the seventies.

Thanks to my mom, sewing was always a part of my life. I hand-stitched my sixth-grade graduation dress, and at that point, my mom started bringing me to her friend's house for machine sewing lessons. I began making a lot of my own clothes after that, most of which didn't fit well or turn out the way I hoped. Actually, that's still true today—probably why I didn't become a garment stitcher!

A few years later, when I was living in Philly and working as a bike messenger, all of my bike messenger friends would bring their damaged bags to me to repair because they knew I could sew. One thing led to another and I ended up cofounding RE Load Bags, a custom messenger bag company, and started making and selling bags full-time.

Does anyone in your family practice this craft, too? Are your pieces similar or different aesthetically?

Growing up, both my mom and my sister sewed. My mom did a lot of embroidery and she hand-stitched little pouches, which is probably the closest she came to bag making. My own sewing style has departed quite a bit from what I observed at home. I like making bags with rugged materials like waxed canvas, leather, and metal, and I like working with tools and industrial machinery. Culturally and historically, sewing has always been women's domain, but I was never interested in the overly feminine version of sewing. I've always wanted to make things that are durable, highly functional, and stylish in a way that is gender-neutral.

Tell me about your creative community. You can define "community" as broadly or as specifically as you'd like.

Today, I live and run my business in Portland, Oregon. Portland is a rad place to be a maker. The design community is thriving, and there are lots of resources to support small, creative businesses. We have garment sewing and bag sewing factories here in Portland, as well as raw good sources for fabric and leather, which makes it that much easier to build a life as a professional maker. I feel called to contribute to the creative community by creating spaces, both physical and digital, for people to gather, learn, and make. I believe that, as makers, we aren't just making things with our hands. We are making the world we want to live in, shifting cultural understanding about the value of handcrafted

---

> We are making the world we want to live in,
> shifting cultural understanding about the value of
> handcrafted goods, creating alternative economies,
> and awakening folks to their creative potential.

---

goods, creating alternative economies, and awakening folks to their creative potential. That's the kind of community I want to live in, and Portland is a great place to make it happen.

When have you felt like an "other" within the context of your craft?
As a first-generation Mexican American, my mom was proud of her culture (she studied ethnic and Latina studies in college), but she was also concerned with making sure that my siblings and I were as Americanized as possible—so much so that she made the decision not to teach us Spanish, her first language. She wanted us to have every possible opportunity and not be limited in the ways that she was. While I'm sad that I didn't have a deeper connection with my parents' cultures as a kid, I'm grateful to have grown up with a big sense of ambition and possibility.

As a teen and young adult developing my own sense of identity as a maker, I found myself drawn into subculture, first in San Francisco and then in Philly, where I worked as a bike messenger beginning at age seventeen. Bike messengers, skateboarders, graffiti artists, and activists became my people. Subculture swooped in to fill the gap where my own family history and cultural identities felt lacking. As it often does for kids trying to escape chaotic home environments, DIY punk culture became like a second family to me. It gave me a strong sense of identity within a community, and it made it possible for me to be independent at a young age.

My first sewing studios were in punk houses in abandoned warehouses. Sometimes, I'd roll a mat out on top of my cutting table and it would double as my bed! During that time, my community was made up of folks for whom life was really hard. There was a lot of addiction, homelessness, and incarceration.

Everyone was just trying to hang on and survive another day. For me, sewing was my lifeline. Unlike the majority of my peers, I had an anchor. Especially once I founded my first business and became responsible for other people's livelihoods, falling off the deep end simply wasn't an option. I had to show up and work my ass off every day. I'm not sure where all that focus and ambition came from, or why I had it and others didn't, but I do know that sewing was my saving grace. Through my business, it allowed me to keep others afloat as well.

Who recognizes you and how does that feel for you?
As a teacher, I feel recognized every time a maker trusts me and my expertise enough to sign up for a workshop or make a bag using one of my sewing patterns. I sometimes have students travel great distances to come to Klum House for bag making workshops, and I always feel so honored when they do. It validates all my hard work and fuels me to keep going. When students leave the studio a few hours later with an awesome finished bag, totally lit up and blown away by what they just created with their own two hands, that makes it all worth it. The same goes for makers who are using my sewing patterns to make bags on their own. Witnessing their excitement and their creative triumphs is just the coolest thing.

Are there aspects of your work that you feel are misunderstood?
I'd say one of the biggest misunderstandings folks have when they see my bag designs and patterns is that they must be really difficult to make. Makers can sometimes be intimidated by working with heavy-duty materials like waxed canvas, leather, and metal hardware. Because the finished bag looks so impressive, they assume they can't do it. They take one look and say "Nope, too hard," or "I could never do that." But the truth is, they can! Anyone who is willing to show up and invest some time in learning new skills will be successful. I've seen it thousands of times. At the end, everyone says, "That was easy! I can't believe I made that!" But I can believe it. I believed in them the whole time.

If you sell your pieces, who are your customers? How long have you been selling your work? Do you employ other people to help you create your work? What challenges have you faced in building your creative business?
I do sell my work, but rarely in the form of finished goods. I sell patterns, maker kits, and workshops (online and in person) that support others in

making bags themselves. At its core, my offering is about high-quality educational experiences and high-quality materials. So, makers not only end up with a gorgeous finished bag but they also build skills and confidence along the way. To me, that's way more satisfying than selling a finished bag.

Currently, the Klum House team consists of five people, in addition to myself. Five strong, smart, talented women who help keep all the gears turning on a day-to-day basis (and are also just really fun to hang out with).

In a society that is accustomed to cheap, mass-produced goods, it's always an uphill battle to communicate the value of ethically produced, high-quality materials, and all the hours of human labor that go into every leather strap or carefully cut and marked piece of fabric.

From packaging up maker kits, shipping orders, processing leather straps, writing marketing strategy, designing new sewing patterns, photographing products—there's no way I could do it all without them.

One of the biggest ongoing challenges we face as a business is communicating the value of our products. In a society that is accustomed to cheap, mass-produced goods, it's always an uphill battle to communicate the value of ethically produced, high-quality materials, and all the hours of human labor that go into every leather strap or carefully cut and marked piece of fabric. This is a challenge for anyone producing goods in the United States and paying their production staff a living wage. It's a systematic, economic problem that is more complicated than any one small business can solve, but I do feel a responsibility to help educate and shift consumer culture wherever I can. That's another reason why I love teaching folks to make things. When you personally have sat at a sewing machine for an entire day to make one bag, you can't help but see a bag in a store, look at the price tag, and realize how little someone, somewhere, got paid to make it. Demystifying the making process automatically creates more conscious consumers.

Do you have an artist statement or any principles that guide your work?
For me, education is really at the core of everything I do. Before founding Klum House, I spent two years studying adult education and at the University of California, Berkeley, where I researched the way people learn in

an embodied way, gaining confidence through working with their hands. I already knew this from personal experience, but delving into educational theory and getting to test out some of my hypotheses took my commitment

---

Demystifying the making process automatically creates more conscious consumers.

---

to teaching to a whole new level. Making, for me, is entirely wrapped up in teaching. I can't separate the two. Everything I create is in the service of helping others discover what they are capable of creating. That's what guides me and gives me the greatest satisfaction.

What adjectives do you use to describe your work?
Approachable, encouraging, fun, laid back, quality, rugged, heavy-duty, classic, functional.

Where did you get inspiration growing up? Who were your idols?
Besides Madonna and Michael Jackson? As a teenager growing up in San Francisco in the nineties, I looked up to the professional artists in my community. I used to have sewing studios in artist collective warehouse spaces and thought it was so cool that these "real" artists were traveling around the world for art shows. Watching their success was inspirational and made me feel like anything was possible.

Who do you look to for inspiration today?
I have always been inspired by the work of the poet and Jungian psychoanalyst Clarissa Pinkola Estés. I've read her book *Women Who Run with the Wolves* many times throughout my life, and it's helped shape my identity as a strong, "wild" woman; a feminist; and a creative being. I'm also inspired by the radical philosophy and critical pedagogy of writers and activists like Audre Lorde, Myles Horton, and Paulo Freire.

What colors are you drawn to and why?
In terms of my wardrobe, I tend to be drawn to mostly neutral colors. I wear a lot of black, gray, and navy blue. Colors that feel classic, gender-neutral,

and don't easily show dirt, because I'm making stuff all day every day! At Klum House, we take color cues from the natural materials we work with and from the seasons. These days, as the weather gets warmer, we're feeling warm browns, rust tones, and pops of sunny marigold.

Where do you get your materials?

All over. Our waxed canvas comes from mills in Scotland and New York, but all canvas originally comes from India and Pakistan because that's where the cotton mills are. There just aren't any in the United States anymore. Our leather is sourced locally from Oregon Leather and die-cut by a local contractor. Up until fairly recently, we strapped all our leather in-house, but now we don't have the space or time to keep up! When it comes to our specialty bag making tools and hardware, we spend a lot of time researching and ordering samples from all over to find exactly what we're looking for. My favorite recent discovery is this amazing Japanese tool that makes removing rivets super easy. Having removed a lot of rivets with pliers and angle cutters, this tool is pure magic. We now carry that in our supplies shop!

How do you choose your materials?

I like to work with materials that are natural, durable, and high-quality. Rather than working with synthetic fabrics and plastics, I prefer organic materials like waxed canvas, leather, and metal. I like materials that wear and change over time, telling the story of their use. Our tan leather, for example, begins quite light, but with use, it softens and darkens into a beautiful caramel brown. Similarly, waxed canvas develops a weathered patina over time, proudly displaying its wrinkles and creases. There's a lot of beauty to be found in a material's story and imperfections.

GLORIFYING MY REST

Interview with Brandi Cheyenne Harper

JEN HEWETT: We can start where you want to start. I've been asking everybody to start with their childhoods, but you can decide where we'll begin.

BRANDI HARPER: I like the idea of starting with my childhood because it lays the foundation of where I am right now. I'm revisiting it and realizing that it's so connected. I am thirty-three.

I was born in Miami, but I grew up in New York. I was raised in New York, Harlem, and then Brooklyn. I've been in Brooklyn since I was four. I grew up in inner-city projects; we lived on welfare. I lived with both my mother and my father, and my father was kind of in and out. He was always around, but emotionally, he was in and out. Together, they had six children. So, it was a total of eight of us living in this three-bedroom apartment in inner-city projects.

As I've gotten older, I've realized that I had my hands in all the pots. I was writing on the walls. I was always rearranging the room, which terrorized my sisters. When I was fourteen, I taught myself to crochet. I was deeply inspired by my grandmother's afghans. She lived in Florida, and I've only met her once because we didn't have a lot of money to travel back and forth to see family in Florida.

But she did send us all these huge, crocheted afghans. They were fancy and made of acrylic, the Lion Brand acrylic that you get from the dollar store, and they were huge. We all got to choose our own colors, and over the year, she would send them to us. They were these beautiful afghans with flowers at the center of them, and I wanted to know how to make those flowers. So, I taught myself to crochet using *Scholastic News* and books from the library. At the time, the Internet was just becoming a thing, and there were a lot of You-Tubers at that point who were showing how to do basic crochet. A year later, I taught myself to knit. That was pretty much the beginning.

I started teaching at a yarn shop when I was sixteen. I was teaching knitting classes throughout high school, throughout college, while working for two different yarn shops. And I taught knitting to staff and students for the multi-cultural department at Pace University here and there throughout college.

Basically, we grew up under the poverty line on welfare. When I taught myself to crochet, I told my mom, "Mommy, I want to buy some yarn from the yarn shop." She was like, "How much is it?" I'm like, "$10," and she's like, "$10 for a ball a yarn? You need to go get yourself a job. That could put food on someone's table for a week!" I think I was fifteen. A year later, I started working at a yarn shop. I was walking down Atlantic Avenue in Brooklyn and I saw a yarn shop called Knitting Hands. They were hiring. I went in and I said, "Oh, I know how to knit—can you hire me?" At the time, it was owned by a Black man. A yarn shop in the middle of an affluent Brooklyn neighborhood, a yarn shop run by a Black man, was really novel and interesting. The shop's manager, I think she was Bangladeshi. So, I was in the knitting community working with, from the very beginning, people of color. Most of the yarn shops I've attended in New York City and even around the world have been run by white people or white-passing people.

Quickly, I realized, "Oh this is a place for me. I feel safe here. I feel welcomed." They gave me a dollar raise to $8.15 within the first couple of weeks; it was nothing, but at sixteen, it was fantastic.

JH: Especially if you've grown up not having a lot of money—to have your own pocket money and to be able to help your mom out, that's a big deal.

BH: Exactly. There's a lot more to my childhood, but I think that's the foundation of my craft: teaching myself and having to work to be able to do it.

JH: You go off to college. Did you say in New York or did you leave town?

BH: I stayed in New York. I went to SUNY New Paltz. It's an hour and a half outside of New York City; it's so cute and I loved it. I studied international politics with a minor in French and a focus on gender development. It had nothing actually to do with knitting or fashion or design, but I ended up connecting gender development within international politics to this idea of entrepreneurship and the global economy. I got interested in the ways women in the developing world used their talent and craft to lift themselves out of intergenerational poverty.

When I applied for the Peace Corps, I was excited to explore this in a real way. I was selected to be a community economic development advisor on another continent. I left during my tour because of the things happening in the country at the time and the way our government was handling it. I did not feel safe there. But, I ended up connecting my craft with economic development.

JH: How long were you in the country?

BH: I was there for six weeks. The program is twenty-seven months, but the first six weeks is your training. You get to begin learning the language, you live with a host family, and you get to meet your community partners.

But at the time, this was when our country was having all those Senate hearings around Peace Corps volunteers being raped by the people within their programs. And, things were happening in my host country that weren't communicated to us before we got there. A volunteer had been killed a year before. A lot of changes happened within the program and they didn't tell us until we got there, which was really unsettling. There was a volunteer within our program who had already been there for a year and was raped by someone within the community. She was medically evacuated. The Peace Corps, the US government, told the existing volunteers that were left not to tell us (the incoming volunteers).

At that time, I had just met my partner. We've been in a relationship now for ten years, but back then I had just met her and I just was like, "You know what? I think I'm just going to go home."

The Peace Corps application process was a year and a half. I learned a lot about myself. I had a lot of different trainings, HIV/AIDS testing and counseling, and I took a rape crisis counseling training with the Anti-Violence Project to prepare for my tour there. During the time I did spend there, I learned so much. I taught people how to crochet while there, which was awesome. I did find a way to connect my craft to what I was studying in college.

JH: How did your craft become your living? I know that you have a regular job now, but there must've been some kind of transition coming back. What did you do when you came back to the United States?

BH: When I came back to the United States, that's when I launched my Etsy shop. I was like, "What do I want to do?" My partner said, "Do what you want to do."

For five years, I was just a full-time entrepreneur, an independent contractor. When I got back, I started working at the café I'd worked at while I was applying for the Peace Corps. I was a barista, just slinging espresso, but it was nice and familiar. While I was there, I started actively launching my Etsy shop.

I designed twenty-seven pieces. I learned how to use Etsy, and about a year into my process of launching my shop, Etsy had become this incredible partner. They were just so supportive of my work, and they started featuring my knits on the front page. They featured me on their blog. I think that took my Etsy shop to a whole other level.

I think it's really hard to launch an Etsy shop in a saturated market, but I think once you're consistently posting and sharing your work, Etsy can really take your business off the ground. They helped me sell most of my work during the first year. Their promotion was just incredible.

About a year after, I joined Etsy New York, which was a street team of Etsy sellers within the Tri-State area where there were conditions to apply and qualify for the team. Through this team came a job opportunity to teach a course called Craft Entrepreneurship, which was fantastic, Jen. It was funded by City Development in collaboration with Etsy and Small Business Services of New York. It provided a five-part course for low-income creatives to launch their own Etsy shops. The students were mostly women of color.

I applied, I got the job, and I taught while I was running my own business for about two and a half to three years before I left the program. It was wonderful. I would teach three or four or five classes throughout the year, with about twenty to twenty-five students per class, on how to use craft to generate secondary income.

It wasn't just about full-time income. How do you pair this with the job? How do you pair this with also raising your children? How do you go to school and run a small business? That's how we marketed the course, and it just kind of all came together. I was running my Etsy shop, which was doing really well. And I just started doing all kinds of design work. I was literally picking up anything I could get to piece together an income.

JH: What were you selling in your Etsy shop? Were you selling finished products?

BH: I was selling finished products. I was so tired.

JH: Were you pricing them fairly for you in those early days?

BH: No. Because I put my best foot forward, I was making my most intricate work, and I would do it all in natural fibers. A lot of the fibers were already a part of my personal collection, so I was using materials I already had. I didn't really incorporate the price of the materials. While I was teaching that course, Craft Entrepreneurship, I was also learning how to be a better seller. I was learning how to price my items better. And I started selling work made with a chunky acrylic blend. When I started doing that, my prices changed drastically. I started selling for more and spending less time making a product. But it took that initial year of putting my best foot forward, and my prices were high, relatively. I've had people tell me they're too low and I've had other people tell me that they were nicely priced, but by then, I knew better. I knew that I was seriously undercharging because of how much time I was spending on some of these pieces. Some of them took twelve hours and I was charging $120, which was like nothing.

I was a full-time freelancer for about five years. When I got into my thirtieth year, I realized that I wanted so much more; growing up in poverty and living in New York, I wouldn't be able to afford to buy a home or save up for a storefront. That's not something I wanted until recently. I would love to have a storefront or a space that housed my studio independent of where I live. Then I started working full-time.

JH: Yeah. You work for a cooperative, is that right?

BH: I work for an organic food cooperative, the Park Slope Food Coop. It's a decent job. I am paid relatively well for someone who works in retail and I have a generous benefits package, paid vacation, and I feel really good about it. I've been able to save and build my credit and do all the things that I want to do as a young person trying to acquire more in my future.

When I joined the co-op, before I started working there, I was twenty-three. We didn't eat well as children. We ate out of cans, we ate out of boxes, and we ate a lot of sweets. My mother made it fun. We would have hot dog nights where we ate hot dogs on Wonder Bread and we had our choice of toppings: sauerkraut, pinto beans, onions, or just ketchup and mustard. It wasn't the healthiest food. It was quick. It was accessible—we loved it.

When I joined the co-op, it made organic, quality food accessible to me in a way that it is normally not accessible to poor people, or even to Black and brown neighborhoods. We have KFCs, we have McDonald's, and we have corner stores. For me, joining the co-op made it possible for me to eat better and to be healthier, and to take more control over my life.

JH: You said that you did a whole bunch of different things when you were freelancing full-time, and you were taking whatever work came your way. What were you doing?

BH: I feel like I worked way too much for free. But, it built this reputation around my name and my work, being connected to these really large companies like Better Homes and Gardens. I did corporate events, sometimes with Etsy, and they were covering the materials, but I wasn't being paid for my time.

It boosted my Instagram numbers, connected me to these other artists, and built my relationship with Etsy, and that was nice. I was saying yes a lot to build my reputation, and these opportunities always felt like the big thing that would break my name and make me blow up. I realized that was just a lie. It's not true at all. What has made me money is actually working.

JH: And getting paid for it.

BH: Creating content for some random company with half a million followers on Instagram, that never made me money. But I was teaching. I was teaching with Small Business Services of New York. I was selling my knitwear. I started writing patterns, which is something I should've done sooner. Sooner!

When I started selling my knitting patterns, that really boosted my monthly sales. I spent some time writing patterns. Patterns can be complicated, but once I wrote them out, they ended up being eight-page PDFs. I started selling those, and that was wonderful passive income. It was flowing in.

Almost three years into my business, I finally created an Instagram page and it completely transformed my business model. All of a sudden, Instagram was generating income for my business. Opportunities started flowing in.

Getting paid to write an article was something that I had never considered—I could write a blog post and get paid $250 for it. So, I started contributing. I contributed to Design*Sponge, I contributed to my friend Marlee Grace's book, *How to Not Always Be Working*.

So, I started writing and making money. I'm selling my patterns and making money. Selling finished work, doing craft markets, is incredibly profitable. I only have time to do one market now, and that market will make me like $2,500. I realized that my business had become like a lifestyle business and empowered me to save money and to travel. It empowered me to keep on doing the work that I was doing.

Whereas my full-time job makes it possible for me to save for the future and find stability day to day. With my full-time income and my business income combined, I actually have enough funds that could take me into some stable ground now and in the future.

My mother worked a lot. She'd spent her whole life—and still does it—taking care of other people. This is something that informs who I am as a woman, as a Black woman: this need to take care of everyone before I take care of myself. This is something that's constantly coming up for me, being of service to others and always putting myself last. My mother was that person for all of us. She was a nurse. She took care of her patients all day and then she would come home and she would cook two separate meals, one for us and one for my father because he was a pescatarian. She would make a meat dish for us and then she would make a vegetarian dish for my father, and then she would start all over again the next day. This is my mother.

I think the reason me and my sisters are all in these stable places in our lives financially and emotionally, becoming the people we want to be, is because we saw our mother working constantly. So, we are always constantly working. I never really stop. There was stability in that my mother had a job. My father was bringing in income illegally at the time, and I felt like financially, we felt settled. In 1995, when the welfare requirements shifted, it changed. You needed to be dirt poor. I mean you needed to have absolutely no funds, working at McDonald's, making $5.50 an hour to qualify for welfare. There was a shift in how much food we had access to and how much money we had. As a nurse, she made a decent income, but with so many kids living in New York City, even in inner-city projects, it was expensive. But she no longer qualified for welfare. I remember there being a noticeable shift in our quality of life. I didn't feel unstable in the process, but I did notice it. The food that we ate and didn't eat anymore. It was years later that I started noticing how creative I was and that I needed creativity in my life. But I think I found stability in this kind of aloneness. I was always a crab, tucked away, twiddling and tickling with something, always cutting construction paper and coloring. I felt like I found a safe place within myself. I kind of protected myself from the toxicity of my father and the sadness that poverty brings to a large family.

JH: You just turned thirty-three and you've been talking online about how this is the year you just decided you were setting boundaries for yourself. What does that mean?

BH: I'm telling you, Jen. There's this meme that I really resonate with. There's this big dress and basically, this big dress is a reflection of all the times you were way too nice and didn't win because of it. I feel like I wear this huge dress all the times I said yes when I should have said no. I'm covered in this big dress and I've decided that this year I'm taking that dress off. I want to be free, I want to feel energized, and I'm not working for free—

JH: Don't work for free.

BH: I'm telling them, "I don't work for free."

JH: That's my number one rule: don't work for free.

BH: Not only that, telling people that it's not okay to ask me to work for free. Not only saying no, but not being nice about it while still being respectful about it. That, for me, was the number one boundary that I've been working on for the last three years. When I turned thirty, I just didn't have enough time. I was working a forty-hour-per-week job and I also had my own personal goals with my knitting business. So, I just couldn't say yes to things anymore. Every time something comes into my inbox, I ask myself, "Does this feel good? Does this feel reciprocal? Will this help bolster the voice that I want to have in the world?" Being paid cash money is not necessarily the only exchange of energy I'll accept for a job, if that makes sense.

JH: It does.

BH: I no longer work for large companies for free. It doesn't feel good to work with white people for free. There are reasons when and where I will—when there's a reciprocal exchange of energy and resources.

I'll tell you this because I think it's relevant. There's a program called We Grow or Women NYC, a New York City–funded organization that helps women entrepreneurs in the city of New York. They've reached out. They were having a huge gala at the Brooklyn Central Library. I was a speaker at a similar event and I had worked it for free in the past because someone I trusted contacted me and said, "Hey, we would love to hear your perspective as a female entrepreneur and the impact Etsy has had on your business." They were honoring Etsy at that gala.

I went with my partner; I had a really good time and it was fun. We had a nice dinner and it was beautiful, but I didn't get a dime for it. That was stupid because I looked around and I said "Wow." It was a four-course meal. There were these elaborate centerpieces. Everyone was dressed in black silks, with hairdos and makeup done. And I'm one of the speakers on stage and I'm not getting paid anything. That for me was incredibly alarming, and I felt cheated. I did feel duped. I felt stupid.

When they came back around and said, "Oh, would you create a Power-Point deck and lead a talk about your experiences as a female entrepreneur in the community?" I was like, "What is the pay? What's the budget for speakers?" They said, "Oh, it's not in our budget to pay speakers." I am done. Don't come and ask me again. You can ask me, but please don't because it's just insulting. It's frustrating. You're getting paid to write me this email. So, money is being shelled out. It's just not to the people it should be going to. I said, "Thank you, but I can't create a PowerPoint deck for free. I think it's also important to recognize the irony that this whole conference is about empowering female entrepreneurs and you're asking a female entrepreneur of color living in the city this program is funded by, to work for free."

This was pitched as an opportunity for me. But, what it ends up being is an opportunity to lose money because instead of generating income for myself doing the work that I love, I'm using that same time to work for free for this event. I said, "You're not going to have any trouble finding women to do this now that I've said no, but we need to think about why that is, and how we can change that paradigm a little bit. I only say this to you because I've worked with this organization before, I care about you all, and I hope this feedback helps you all the next time you create a budget." Something like that. The response was "Oh, of course, I completely understand. Thank you for your feedback."

A company reached out, they create knitting supplies that are beautiful, and I was really excited. They said, "We want you to create three photos. We want you to create three staged photographs using these products that we'll send you and include copy, talking about how you use these products. We also want a couple of mentions in your stories on Instagram, and what we're going to give you is a tote bag." For three static Instagram posts, story mentions, and marketing captions. In exchange for a tote bag.

JH: It's so much work, right? That's a day's worth of work, all of that. You've got to style it. You've got to photograph it.

BH: It's terrible. I'm telling you, Jen. I try not to take it personally, but the audacity! The audacity, especially when it's coming from white people who I know are getting paid. Asking me to work for free. It's just so demoralizing. I try not to take it personally and suck it up as a business where people are always going to try to get things for free. But, I know that it's so deeply rooted in misogyny, anti-Blackness, racism, and not paying people adequately for their time. Continuously, our history of literally working for free and even doing the work that we love, we're expected to do it for free.

So, I said, when they asked me to create free content for them for a tote bag, that I couldn't possibly do this kind of work for free. This is my work: content creation, photography, photo editing, and copy creation. It takes a lot of time and a tote bag isn't adequate compensation. That's all I said, and I didn't get an answer back. I had a lot of fear when I was creating boundaries, worried about ruining my reputation or my chances of working with these companies in the future. I realized that the company that I really want to be working with is my own. If people don't respect that, then they're not the partners that I want. I want to work with people who actually want to see me buy that house, who want to see me buy products that help clear up my skin. And people who want to see me flourish. Companies that want to exhaust me for their benefit, they aren't my people.

So, it got really easy to say no when I stopped looking at it as a missed opportunity or an insult but more like something that isn't for me. This isn't for me. It got really, really easy. I used to pain myself over these emails, and now I'm like, "Okay, dah dah dah dah." Send. Which feels really good.

But boundaries for me, the biggest I've had to set for myself is around how much I work. It's crazy, Jen, how much I work—and to the point of being sick. I have eczema and I will literally work myself to the point where my skin will just go berserk. The last couple of months, I've had difficulty even knitting. There was a time I couldn't knit because my hands were so cracked and dry because of my eczema. So, I've had to be very self-determined in setting boundaries around the food that I'm eating, making sure I'm getting enough rest. The things that seem so basic like eating fruits and vegetables, drinking enough water and tea, getting enough sleep, not taking on more than I can chew even when it is paid work—I'm in the process right now of setting those boundaries for myself.

Saying no to others has been really, really easy. Saying no to myself has been very difficult. That's where I'm at right now in my life: saying no to simple sugar, and seeing the connection between my health and my ability to do my craft. I've recently finished a collection of Audre Lorde's essays, which has been so transformative. The book is entitled *A Burst of Light: and Other Essays*, and it's one of the most beautiful books I have ever read. She talks about how her health and her struggles with cancer is so connected to the other parts of her being as a Black feminist lesbian writer and poet, and how that is also connected to her activism.

She just draws a line through it all, her health, her activism, her art, in such an incredible way. I connected with it as I'm seeing connections between my health and my diet and the things that I love to do, and also how I grew up. I think this does not necessarily have to do with color. I know this is about crafters of color. This is not color specific, but—

JH: It doesn't matter. It's about you.

BH: Seeing how my health connects to my ability to make things, it's interesting. It's something that I've been exploring. Being like, "No, Brandi, sleep. No, Brandi, eat vegetables." I eat a lot of vegetables, but I also eat an abundance of sugar to the point where it affects my ability to knit. I'm actively dealing with this right now in terms of my health and creating healthy self-care habits, not diving into diet culture but long-lasting changes around my lifestyle so that I have more energy and I'm better able to do this work.

JH: You have your mom as a role model for overwork. It is really, really hard to let go of those role models. And, I think a lot of it too is so cultural in that again, we didn't traditionally have access to, and still don't traditionally have access to, lots of capital and wealth-building in a way that white folks do. We were always paid less. My dad who managed factories when I was a kid also had a side job, which is that he was a photographer. I'll do these podcast interviews and people will say, "Oh, so you always just had that work ethic." I'm like, "It's not even a work ethic. It's a mere fact of survival." I grew up seeing that everybody in my community, even really well-educated people in my community, had something on the side because you were already getting paid like 70 cents, 68 cents, whatever on the dollar to what white folks were having.

As a child, I had stuff on the side. I made cookies and I sold them and my parents were proud of me. I'd pay them back for the groceries. One day, I came home from track practice and my mom was already home and she was making Rice Krispies Treats and I thought those Rice Krispies Treats were for me. She said, "No, you're going to sell these."

BH: I love that. But this is what we learned though. This ingenuity that we learned at a very young age to generate income because we know that's something that we need.

JH: Among the people that I've interviewed, there isn't this sitting on your ass trying to figure out your next move, because we've never had the time to sit on our ass and figure our next move.

When people ask me where my motivation comes from, how am I able to just do it? I'm like "Well, I've always had to just do it," right? There's been no "Oh, I'm scared to." I mean I am scared to do things all the time, but there's no running around in circles not knowing where to start because I've never had the luxury of just not getting started.

God forbid my parents see me idle at the house. I at least had to be reading. If I was just dilly-dallying, my mom's like, "What are you doing?" Okay, must always be busy, and it's hard to let go of that.

BH: It is because it's deeply connected, I'm realizing, to my self-worth. Which again, I'm writing through this idea that when I take a moment to rest or I neglect my social media or my email—even that word, "neglect." Language. Even the language that something is wrong if I am not working is something I'm noticing and working to unlearn.

I'm also thinking about this word, "decolonization," this idea of decolonizing the way I work that's vaguely connected to capitalism and racism that constantly keeps me working and busying myself. And for a long time, it was working for all these other people in a way that wasn't equitable.

So, actively changing the language that I use around work and rest helped me to have stronger self-worth. My work isn't who I am, which a lot of ways— given our history, a lot of our history is our work. The work we were doing to

---

For me, it's really about having deep, personal reflection around my work. Not only looking at what generates income for me but also the work that I feel like I need to be doing in the world to feel like I'm the person I want to be.

---

build this country. That's a lot of what our history is: our connection to our ancestors is their work, or their inability to work on their own and build their own. It was constantly working for other people.

I'm trying to disconnect from this destructive way of looking at rest so that I can take better care of myself, so I can keep on doing the work. Because if I continue working the way that I have the last five years, constantly having something going on to the detriment of my body, I can't even see myself continuing to do this. For me, it's really about having deep, personal reflection around my work. Not only looking at what generates income for me but also the work that I feel like I need to be doing in the world to feel like I'm the person I want to be.

They're connected in a lot of ways. Knitting generates income for me, but it's also the work I feel like I need to be doing. I'm inclined to do it whether I'm paid to do it or not. It has been really powerful to think about how I define my work and how I glorify my rest.

JH: I like that. "Glorify my rest."

BH: The emails are going to get answered. The comments are going to get responded to. I never want to feel like I'm leaving people hanging. It's getting harder and harder to manage. So, yeah. Glorify my rest, yeah. Celebrate it.

WHAT ARE YOU MAKING NOW?

Right now, I am making the Branches and Buds Pullover by Carrie Bostick Hoge. It's a really pretty sweater with some easy colorwork on the yoke.—MARIA PARKER

I'm knitting a gray, tweed, oversized grandpa sweater for puttering around in the garden, something I love to do first thing in the morning. I'm in the middle of knitting Christmas stockings for my twin nieces and I've also started a maxi dress made from a vintage silk sari.—JENNIFER KEE

I'm making home decor items and clothes for myself. I also do some light furniture building (I built my massive craft table, our coffee table, and our dinner table).—YETUNDE RODRIGUEZ

WEAVING HAND

Interview with Cynthia Alberto

JEN HEWETT: You grew up in the Philippines and didn't come to the United States until you were thirteen? Is that right?

CYNTHIA ALBERTO: Yeah, in 1977, when I was thirteen years old.

JH: Tell me about that.

CA: My family immigrated in 1977 because martial law in the Philippines was at its height. My mother came first and left my three-month-old baby brother with my grandparents. And then my father followed in '73 or '74, and then we followed in '77, and landed in Jersey City where a big Filipino community had gathered. It was a very tight-knit community where we were all supporting each other. People took care of one another during that time.

We definitely followed Filipino traditions at home, but there was also a push from my parents to blend in, to assimilate. And I still speak the language. But during that time, I mean, it was a different time. There was no such thing as political correctness then. You got called "chink." You got called "flip." Walking down the street, people would yell at you, say, "You chink, go back to where you come from."

My father died when I was sixteen, when I had only been in America for four years. So, I took care of my four siblings. I helped my mother raise them; that's the way it's always been in Filipino families. I took them to PTA meetings, to the doctor, to the dentist. When I turned twenty-one, I said to my mom, "It's time for me to move to Manhattan."

JH: Was she okay with that?

CA: No. It wasn't okay. I mean, my siblings were okay, but my mom had a hard time. I moved to Chinatown in 1981, or '82. So, that was the beginning of the eye-opening of the whole world, and that was the beginning of me being exotified because I was an Asian woman. I would wear my best dress and go to the club, all these white men flocking over me. Back then, I was coming from a colonized mentality, so it was like, "Oh wow, we made it."

JH: You'd left home at twenty-one. You were living in Chinatown. Had you finished school at this point too?

CA: Yeah, I had. I studied computer science at Saint Peter's College, where I did night school. My parents said, "You need to study something so you can make a living." After that, I worked on Wall Street, this is like '83, '84.

JH: Primetime.

CA: I was there, I was programming. I was working for a nice man, but I'm not loving the culture. And dating all the stockbrokers. I felt like a trophy. You know what I mean?

JH: Mm-hmm.

CA: There was an ad in *The Village Voice* for an advertising coordinator, so I went to *The Village Voice*, and I got it. Then I'm like, "I'm going to the East Village." I loved it so much. It was a whole different time, a whole different reality, a whole different mentality of people. There was a whole vibe happening downtown. When the market crashed and I was not doing well economy-wise, I decided to move to California. I also started making art in California. Started painting, started trying to see what this is about. But I always felt like because I didn't have a degree in art that my skills were not credible. I think that's been my insecurity—that you're not good if you don't have a degree. I always felt like an outsider.

JH: So much of it, too, is cultural. You go to school to get your credentials and your credentials are what you become. And, maybe our parents didn't want us to go to art school to become artists.

CA: No. "What are you going to do with that?"

JH: I think it's very much ingrained into us that it doesn't matter the work you do, or who you hang out with, or who accepts you—if you don't have that degree, that paper that says, "artist," you're not an artist.

CA: It's like they shut you down, even before you can try. And, there's always that belief that you have to make money, you have to buy a house, you have to marry somebody rich, marry a doctor. The doctor, the lawyer, is the prize, the trophy. Right?

JH: But you made the huge leap from those beliefs to being an artist.

CA: After I came back from California, I met the father of my children, I got pregnant, and moved to Brooklyn. He was a lawyer. He was a prize. I thought, "Okay, I'm going to be taken care of. It's time to start a family and to be a housewife."

I went back to school in 1999 because I had an intuition. I thought, "I need some kind of career, so just in case something happens, I can take care of myself." That's what I did—I went to the Fashion Institute of Technology, got a degree in textile surface design, and specialized in weaving. And sure enough, in 2006, my marriage was falling apart. I was like, "Okay, let's move on with our lives." We're all very good friends. Everybody's good.

In 2007, I opened Weaving Hand with the money that I got from the divorce settlement. Not knowing what to do, I just knew that I needed to move forward with the next journey of my life.

JH: Tell me about Weaving Hand.

CA: I started working with the healing arts, with adults with disabilities. That door opened, and then I realized, "Okay, here is my next journey, the reason why I opened this studio." And just kind of went through the day to day, year to year, adding more programs, doing more classes, making commissioned work, anything to do with weaving. Working with museums, doing sustainable zero-waste weaving, which is taking off right now.

I needed to do this for myself. This is my journey and I'm going to fully embrace it. When the healing arts component came in, that gave me the foundation and the funds to pay my operating costs. I just took it day by day, year by year, and it's been thirteen years and we're still here. We are expanding. My kids are learning the business; they're somewhat taking over. I mean, this Weaving Hand is what has fed us for the last thirteen, going on fourteen, years. There's no other way but to keep it going. Because we love it, I love it. I'm very thankful every day that I can do this, weave, help people, do commissioned work. We have a pretty incredible reputation. People like to work with us.

JH: What are the different things that Weaving Hand offers?

CA: We have classes. We have healing arts, where we work with a pretty good amount of government agencies and programs, for senior citizens, for homeless shelters. We do healing and weaving with participants.

JH: What is it about weaving that you think makes it suited to providing healing?

CA: I'm going to talk about my journey, where it all started. When I left my marriage, I remember that weaving kept me sane. It kept me grounded. And it kept me relaxed because my mind was racing a mile a minute. "What am I going to do? How am I going to survive? How am I going to make this work?" I remember I would weave and it was just like, "Okay, I'm making cloth now." It made me feel like the world is not just an angry, bad place. This is the way I relax and get back to someplace safe.

During World War I, veterans used weaving as occupational therapy to develop hand motor skills. Weaving does quiet the mind, and the repetitive motion is very relaxing. Weaving is great, but you also have to dress the loom. That's just part of the whole process. I used to hate it when I started it, but now I'm not so impatient anymore. You have to learn how to be patient. You have to make sure that you are doing it correctly. You don't do the foundation right, then the project is not going to be the way you want it to be.

JH: I teach printmaking and there are parts that people want to rush through because they just want the glamorous fun part of it. Especially when I teach screen printing, people don't want to set up their screens properly. They don't want to mix their ink. They just want to go straight to printing. I think that we forget, especially now that everything's so instant, that there actually is so much preparation and so much skill and patience in the preparation. That the reward, yes, is the activity, but to get to that, you actually have to do 95 percent of the work, which is setting things up properly.

CA: Yeah. It's like there's an immediate gratification, but then it's also good to learn the whole process. Because we are in this place where everything is immediate, you order it from Amazon Prime, it's, "Get here."

JH: We don't think about what it takes for that to get here in four hours or three hours, or whatever. That there's actually a very real human and environmental cost to be able to get everything right away.

CA: I think technology is making us more and more impatient and disconnected from the process.

JH: Now, we have these iPhones that you can't even open up, so you have no clue what is in them. Our electronics are so inaccessible to us on such a very basic level that we have no clue how things work anymore.

CA: Or how to repair them. How do we repair something when it breaks? What if things break down, and who are we going to go to repair them? I saw

---

Craft connects us to human beings and to the tools. The tools are so important because if you don't know how to use them, they're no use. You need people to show you how to use the tools.

---

a watch repair shop in my neighborhood, and I was just like, "Oh my gosh, I wish I had all the time. I'd learn how to do watch repair. Or umbrella repair."

JH: In San Francisco, we have fewer and fewer cobblers to repair shoes. Shoes now are designed to be worn out and thrown away and never fixed, anyway. It's a feature, not a bug. Manufacturers don't want us to repair our shoes anymore. When I do have shoes that need to be repaired, it makes me happy. I have boots that I've had since 2013 that I paid a lot of money for and I get new soles put on them every year. But, that's the exception rather than the rule.

CA: I think that's why craft is having a revival right now because it's the one connection we have with making things with our hands. Craft connects us to human beings and to the tools. The tools are so important because if you don't know how to use them, they're no use. You need people to show you how to use the tools. Like with screen printing, somebody has to show you how to do that.

JH: Exactly.

CA: I mean, it's a process, that's why we can't lose mending, sewing.

JH: You also have a program in which you're taking . . . is it offcuts?

CA: Zero-waste.

JH: Tell me about that.

CA: That practice started about five years ago, and it's taking off right now. Among fashion designers, I think there's been a realization that the fashion industry, that textile waste, is really a problem. How do you keep the waste from going into the landfill? There's a spotlight right now on all these big designers—couture—who are shredding their collections, throwing them away so nobody can copy them and to keep the prices from coming down. It's sick.

Anyhow, Weaving Hand works with a lot of designers that are saving their fabric scraps from their previous collections. We reweave them to create new fabric. I tell the designers it has to be a commitment, instead of this being a one-time deal, just to show that they're doing sustainability. I tell them that they have to be committed to the cause. I don't want sustainability to become just a marketing ploy.

We're very thankful that we have a couple of designers that we work with. Jonathan Cohen Studio is one of them. We're doing yardage for them. Not a lot, because it depends on the fabric scraps. We get a handful of designers who do zero-waste weaving. We also take zero-waste weaving to different museums, school programs, and companies that want to learn more about textile industry waste. We go to, say, a showroom, bring the looms, do a workshop, where they weave with the fabric scraps. For example, the Kate Spade team came here a month ago. They brought in their fabric scraps and they wove them on a cricket loom.

JH: You're involved in sustainable and ethical practices with regards to textiles and fashion. How would you define sustainability and/or ethical practices as you understand them, as you believe them to be?

CA: There is the product that's involved. But it's not just the product. It's the people that you employ. Sustainability for me is having a circular economy.

The way I see it, a designer comes to us, and we have our healing arts community that we can employ to cut the fabrics. They can cut it, they can make money from it, and then Weaving Hand can make money also from it. We're doing a circular, sustainable economy that way, by using the fabrics that are most likely going to end up in the landfill or being burned. But we are circling it.

JH: You said in another interview that, as a child, you never threw anything away. There was a lot of mending and repairing instead.

CA: Yeah, in the Philippines you patch things. A friend of mine from the Philippines came here and she said, "I want to fix my umbrella." One of my staff said, "No, you just throw it away. You can get a new one at the CVS on the corner." She's like, "No, no. We don't do that. We're from the Philippines and we repair." We repaired everything. Socks, shoes, I got two pairs of shoes a year.

JH: Same, even though I grew up here. I went to Catholic school and wore a uniform, and my parents got me one pair of loafers or saddle shoes and one pair of tennis shoes.

CA: It's a very modest way of living. I think we are at the height of excess right now. For example, food: you go to the supermarket; I mean, the choices. Sometimes I am so overwhelmed, but then I'm also very thankful. But at the same time, I'm also disgusted.

The Lorax, that's what we are. We think that it's never going to end, it's never going to diminish. It's like an ongoing abundance that's never going to stop, that's the crazy part of it. Water, right? Water. Because we're living here in America, so when I go to different places, it's a different reality.

JH: I have gone to India for the past two years for a few weeks and see how hard it can be for some people to get water. If you're affluent enough, the water comes to your house. You don't think twice about it. But if you're living on the outskirts of a town or in one of the poorer areas, you don't have running water in the house and you have to go to the pump. It's something that we take so for granted. If it were just a little bit harder for us to get water, how much more would we treasure it? The same with garbage, too. In the Philippines, you have to burn your garbage or you see the garbage. You wouldn't throw away an umbrella because it's just one more thing for you to have to dispose of. Whereas here, we just put it in the trash and it's taken away somewhere and we don't know where it goes.

CA: It's such a disconnect. You put it in the trash; someone else takes it and makes it disappear. You don't have to think about it anymore. It's not your responsibility anymore. I think we need to take more responsibility.

JH: It's so hard. I am complicit in this too. I think being a part of a capitalist society is that we're all complicit in our own downfall. Even despite our best intentions, we still play into the system in one way or another. That means that I can't also judge others too harshly, which is not to say that I don't.

CA: I'm totally with you. Because I'm also not innocent. I'm like, "Okay, put it in there. Recyclable."

JH: As a kid, we would go with my dad to the dump if we needed to discard something large. We loved going to the dump. I don't know when I last saw the dump. It's all luxury suburbs in Los Angeles now. I think things get put on a barge and shipped somewhere else now. I have no idea.

CA: I know. That's the thing, you put it on the curb. The truck comes in and then the next day, it's gone. No one has to think about this anymore.

JH: You said in your *Vogue Italia* interview that you were in the Zapotec market in Oaxaca, and that you had this overwhelming sense that you wanted to live a simple life, with no excess and lots of compassion. What does that look like for you?

CA: I see myself living in a place like that; I'm being honest, it's a romanticized view that this is where I want to escape to. But where I am right now in my life, and with my two big children, I can't escape to these places at the moment. But maybe going back to the Philippines could be an option, like in twenty, thirty years.

JH: If it's still there. If it's not under water.

CA: Yeah. If it's still there. I mean, I think this is again coming back to the longing to come home, to the way I remembered it because I was thirteen when I left. It's really a longing to feel grounded again to your ancestral line. My parents bought a big piece of land, and all my cousins are there, and we used to climb trees. It was a very beautiful, free childhood spent in nature. So, when I think about getting old and dying, which I'm not afraid of, that's where I see myself: going back to that life, to a beautiful, peaceful, non-chaotic world.

SOCIAL JUSTICE SEWING ACADEMY

Interview with Sara Trail

JEN HEWETT: I read that you started sewing when you were four.

SARA TRAIL: My grandma taught me. My mom was so overprotective that only my grandma was allowed to babysit me.

JH: I know you grew up religious, right? You were COGIC (Church of God in Christ).

ST: Yes, COGIC. I loved growing up COGIC and was very involved in the church. I was often the assistant to the Bible youth group teacher, which I feel definitely helped refine my teaching skills—from developing patience to engaging youth.

My grandma sewed all the time. I'd get her scraps and all the little pieces that she didn't want. I'd sew them together and make my dog or doll a blanket or a baby outfit. From an early age, I was involved in everything—I dabbled in pottery, I tried beading, I even took welding classes and made stained glass windows from scratch, but sewing was definitely my favorite and the one that stuck throughout the years.

JH: Your parents encouraged you to be creative.

ST: Yes, I was into sewing from ages eight to twelve because my mom owned a residential and commercial building in downtown Antioch. We would always be there after I got out of school. There was nothing for a creative young person to do in downtown Antioch besides go to the local quilt store, Queen B's Quilt Shop, so I asked my mom if I could take quilt classes there. She said, "That's fine. You can walk there from the building. Go and inquire about classes you could take." But the shop staff said, "These classes are for adults, and you're ten." But, I could sew a quarter-inch seam, was proficient with a rotary cutter, and could keep up with the skill level in the classes. My mom talked with the owner. "I know Sara's young, but she actually can sew. I know it's an adult class, but please consider letting her join due to her love for quilting." At the end of the day, the owner believed my mom, so they let me, this twelve-year-old kid, in their $180 weekend class. However, they said, "If people don't like taking a class with a kid, we might ask her to leave."

I definitely was kicked out of a few classes because people didn't want me there. I'd be talking too much, or I'd be sewing too fast. One lady even said, "I did not pay to spend my weekend with kids." So, sometimes the shop would send an email disclaimer to everyone in the class: "We're going to have a younger person in the class, etc." But eventually, my young, determined persistence warmed its way into many of my classmates' hearts and they began to love me—or just tolerate me.

Then I began to take more advanced-level classes and made a double wedding ring quilt. It turned out pretty good. Then I began paper piecing in a book of fifty intricate stars. The Arkansas star, the North Dakota star. I made this paper-pieced quilt that might have taken many people years. Mind you, I'm a kid, so my seams might not have been perfect, but it was complete. Paper piecing is extremely time-consuming. But I had nothing but time in my middle school days.

After having made a few really detailed quilts and feeling fairly confident, I went to a book expo at C & T Publishing. They had a "You want to write a book?" booth, and all these adults were in line because everyone wants to write a book for C & T. I told my mom, "I want to go talk to the people at the booth." My mom said, "Sara, you have to go to college, get a degree, and become someone before you can get a book published. If that's what you want to do, find out the process so you can write one when you're older." I said to C & T, "I want to write a book." Now that I look back at it, I realize the lady was just being polite, but she gave me an overview of the process to write a book with C & T. I took her very seriously. She gave me her card, said I would need to write a proposal, and then I could set up an appointment to submit and show the projects I'd like to be in the book.

I bugged my mom for days to call the lady and make an appointment because I didn't have a cell phone. She finally did, and surprisingly enough, the C & T lady had shared how excited I was with the staff there and said they would love to see the things I had sewn. At that point, I had sewn prom dresses, paper-pieced and double wedding ring quilts, tote bags, aprons, PJs—and more. I brought in a huge trunk show of things and they were extremely impressed. "Wow, you really can sew well for a kid!" and they offered me the opportunity to write a book after that meeting.

JH: How old were you?

ST: Twelve.

I wrote the book *Sew with Sara* and then did a DVD called *Cool Stuff to Sew with Sara* with C & T. Soon after that, I was offered the opportunity to design a fabric line—Folkheart and Biology 101—with Fabri-Quilt. Then, Simplicity contacted me and I flew to NYC. I designed a pattern collection with them. Throughout high school, I was flying around to different JoAnn and local quilt stores, teaching kids how to sew. At first, I was just happy I was teaching kids how to sew. But then after a while, I noticed I was only teaching very affluent kids, none of whom looked like me. I felt I was perpetuating the inequities with regard to access to sewing. My mom explained to me that not many people from marginalized communities have the luxury to spend $75 on a two-hour sewing class with a twelve-year-old. I talked to the locations hiring me to teach sewing to kids to see if I could offer some free classes or even scholarships for low-income young people who couldn't afford the class and materials costs, and they said no. I was even told by a quilt shop owner that, in her experience, kids of color were not interested in sewing. I learned how capitalistic the creative community could be and realized that institutions only wanted me there to teach and to sell the books, patterns, fabric, etc., I had created. I realized the teaching opportunities I was receiving weren't aligned with my intentions. I loved sewing and wanted to share and teach it with any and all young people who wanted to learn—not just to those with parents who could afford it.

So, that's when I opened up a free sewing program at my church. My pastor did a donation call for the congregation. Everybody donated. At that point, I had written a book and he believed in my ability to lead and run this program. He bought ten sewing machines, and after—

JH: Wow, he got some donations. It's that 10 percent tithe.

ST: It really is. My parents donated $100 every Sunday.

The sewing program was so successful. We advertised it in the newspaper and asked for donations and volunteers. We had kids coming to our sewing program who didn't even go to our church. They only came for this class!

JH: Which is great for a mission and ministry.

ST: It was so much fun. We made prom dresses, we made PJs, everyone made a quilt, everyone made a block. It was just a good time by all—and what was so great was the diversity, not just in ethnicity but also in socioeconomic status as well. I was happy that all these youth were enjoying sewing and learning how to make things as much as I did, and I believe the success of this church sewing program debunked any notions that marginalized youth don't have an interest in learning how to sew.

JH: Well, and so many of us are just one or two generations removed from people who sewed. People thinking kids of color don't want to learn how to sew—please . . .

ST: They do. It is just hard to afford classes when they only have one parent paying the household bills. I appreciate all the opportunities and belief that C & T, JoAnn, and Simplicity gave me. They definitely gave me the foundation and confidence to be able to teach young people how to sew. I just had to figure out an additional way to make it accessible to all youth and get rid of the financial barriers barring youth from access.

JH: You did all this stuff in high school and then you went to college. That was always in the books, right? That's why your parents were making you into a well-rounded child?

ST: That's exactly it. I graduated from high school and was immediately off to college.

JH: So, you went to Berkeley. What did you major in?

ST: American studies with a political science and public policy concentration and a double minor in education and African American studies. I double majored and double minored. Obviously, I was confused. I liked education and public policy, but Berkeley didn't have either of those as a major. Honestly, if I could have picked anything, I would have majored in either public policy and education. But, I loved my educational experience at Berkeley because it taught me a perspective of social justice rooted in the historical experience of colonialism, genocide, enforced involuntary servitude, dislocation due to immigration, and forced migration. I thought I was going to go to law school. I started looking at grad schools and my parents said, "Oh, by the way, we're definitely not paying for grad school—you are on your own." I started looking at the tuition for law school.

JH: You would have been $120,000 in debt.

ST: I changed routes and looked at MA degrees in public policy. I thought I'd get my master's in public policy or public administration, but it was still extremely expensive. I then realized if I wanted to make an impact, I could go the policy route for a top-down approach or an educational route for a hands-on impact with young people. I looked at Harvard and found an amazing master's program that was rooted in education, psychology, and public policy, and loved my experience there. An additional bonus is that some of your student loans can be forgiven if you work for a Title I school. I am currently working for a high school serving disadvantaged young people with a majority of them having been in or recently out of jail in the Bay Area.

JH: Is that why you decided to work in a school in the prison system?

ST: I just wanted to be a teacher in a low-income school. If I'm going to be a teacher, I want to be somewhere that I can really make a difference.

JH: Are you a teacher or a principal?

ST: I run a community site, which means I get to teach in-custody (to students in jail), but I also have a whole school site that I run where students who are released from jail come to finish their education. I am able to do enrollments, I get to do the teaching, and I have the agency and autonomy to design the classroom. I love it because it is my site.

JH: Sometime after, or in college, you got a grant for the Social Justice Sewing Academy (SJSA)?

ST: I got the grant the summer before Harvard! I graduated from UC Berkeley in December 2015. I was awarded the Stronach Prize from UC Berkeley in February, then I designed SJSA from February to June. I developed a six-week curriculum, secured a facility to run the program, recruited students, etc. The program was extremely successful and all the kids had a blast. They did youth participatory research projects and designed and created quilts highlighting the inequities faced in their communities. It was initially to be just a one-time summer program. But I really missed working with young people hands-on. So, while I was at Harvard, I developed a workshop model of the SJSA program and I emailed teachers, "Hey, I want to do a workshop at your school. It'll be about A, B, and C. I can make large quilts with every kid contributing a block." The workshop model was successful. The first community quilt that was made featured all these kids' blocks. My friend Robin and I embroidered every block. Every day after class, I'd be up all-night, embroidering these kids' amazing blocks.

I soon realized I needed help. Workshops were amazing and fun, but leading a four-hour workshop with over 60 fifteen-inch blocks would cause me to burn out if I was personally embroidering all the blocks. So, I asked the community to help. I asked the local quilt stores. Then I made an Instagram account and asked for help, to sign up and ask for people to repost their progress. That had a domino effect. One person would embroider a block and I'd say, "Can you please post that you're doing this and ask for other people to sign up?" Nowadays, we'll run a workshop and we'll get 125 blocks from one workshop. With three or four workshops a month, that's over 500 blocks. But today, SJSA is so fortunate to have over one thousand embroidery volunteers. We have an amazing community of volunteers who go above and beyond in embellishing youth students' art. We'd love to get more volunteers. An interesting aspect to note when looking at the intersectionality of our embroidery base—we have very few volunteers of color, very few males, and very few people under twenty-five.

JH: Well, I think that there is a certain amount of privilege to have the time to do something for free.

ST: That is definitely right.

JH: You have to be a certain age and you have to be a certain class.

ST: Absolutely. Because the young people that I know that are sewing or embroidering—most of them are doing it to make a living. They might say, "I love the mission, but I don't have the time," and I totally get it.

JH: To be honest, that's totally fine.

ST: Definitely.

JH: Your embroidery base is filled with women who believe in what you're doing, and they want to do something, too. SJSA may have a bigger aim and bigger work to do, but embroidery is a comfortable thing within their skill level, and I'm not going to knock it at all.
    How do you fundraise?

ST: I have a day job with decent pay. A lot of SJSA's expenses I pay for. Most big grants want you to have five years of proof that you've been doing it, and we don't have that.

JH: Not yet, but you can get seed money.

ST: I've written and we have definitely gotten small grants. The Stronach Prize was the biggest and best grant we've gotten. That allowed me to buy tools and materials. I invested thousands into everyone having a sewing machine, new rotaries, scissors, mats for everything. At the end of that summer program, however, all the materials that I had bought, I gave to the kids who completed the program for them to continue sewing at home.

JH: Tell me about the curriculum for SJSA's workshops.

ST: The kids read critical texts and they learn a lot. We read books from James Baldwin to Michelle Alexander to bell hooks. We read about the criminalization of weed and the war on drugs to white flight and gentrification. Then the youth are assigned research projects—photo voice projects, interviews with community members, do a survey with your peers—and then they make art quilts about it. They become research-informed, activist quilters. I love facilitating their learning and watching their sociopolitical development. It's great to see them become so much more empowered.

As far as workshops go, a student doesn't have to be a good artist, but if they write out their idea to the embroidery volunteer, the volunteer can completely enhance the initial design. I remember one kid wanted to make a block depicting kids in cells, and they kept cutting out all these strips symbolizing bars. And it didn't look good, and so they asked if the cages could be embroidered so they could focus on just designing the kid in the cage. They used water erasable fabric markers to mark the bars, and the embroidery volunteer added all the details of stitched cages—it looked absolutely spectacular.

I feel like the connection between the kid artist and the embroiderer is an intergenerational collaboration. I think seeing the kids feel empowered and excited when their piece is finished, and witnessing them transition from, "My work's going to be ugly. I don't know what to do. Tell me what to make." I always remind them I'm not ever going to tell them what to make. Instead, I say, "Let's just research and let's figure out what you care about. Let's talk about your life."

JH: You have to have a point of view. You can't go through life not having a point of view . . .

ST: It's really about letting them share their narrative. They can talk about their narrative. "Tell me a point where you've ever felt like this." There is an activity that asks, "When did you first realize you were ___?" They can fill in the blank with literally anything they claim as part of their identity—male, gay, short, etc. And kids will just share stories. Sometimes their blocks depict issues from the activity: "I first realized I was low-income. I first realized my parents were using EBT. First realized I was gay." The purpose of the workshop is to provide a space for them to share and create. It's really about owning, and even critically analyzing, their narrative.

A social justice curriculum has to include the lives of all those in our society—both the marginalized and the dominant—and I designed SJSA's curriculum to help equip students to "talk back" to the world. SJSA has activities and workshop models built around different issues. We interrogate power through activities that ask: "Am I hoarding or sharing power? Is my thinking 'either/or' or 'both/and?' Am I pursuing equality or equity?" A workshop I led recently was centered on owning your narrative. We reflected on questions such as: "What story am I telling? Is it truthful and inclusive? Who is telling the story? Who needs to hear the story? Does the messenger affect the efficacy of the message? Are my storytelling methods inclusive or dominant? How else can I tell the story?" Another workshop I led with a group of college students was based on the idea of personal power. We did activities and ended with a reflection on the answers to the questions: "What social privileges do I have? Am I hoarding them or spending them? To whom am I accountable? Am I changing the world by myself or in the community? Am I more concerned with credit or change?"

Additionally, the workshops are often rooted in place-based education where I bring in examples or lessons based on where the workshop physically is. Almost everyone in the Bay Area knows what the San Francisco Pride Festival is, but I've learned very few know about the Stonewall Riots or who Marsha P. Johnson is. In some workshops, we throw out stereotypes or assumptions of the local cities—such as San Francisco smells like pee due to its large homeless population or that the city only houses the rich—and in that workshop, we have conversations about the systemic issues that have pushed families out of San Francisco for the past few decades and the effects of gentrification.

We were at the Houston Quilt Festival and a prominent quilter, who has over 100,000 Instagram followers and a number of books, told me, "You know, Sara. Let me give you some advice, tell you what's wrong with SJSA, and why you don't have any streamlined funding or sponsorships. That's because it's too dark. No one wants to look at quilts about social justice," and explained how funders would love the model of kids sewing, but they would prefer looking at kids making happy things with warmer colors. She berated me for fifteen minutes about how having kids make blocks about social justice issues was wrong, how the model wasn't ever going to be sustainable because it didn't make income. She critiqued the whole model, especially the part of the process involving embroidery volunteers. She didn't get the point of anything. But really, I wanted to let her know SJSA wasn't created for an income model, and I love the intergenerational involvement that embroidery volunteers bring to SJSA. I love witnessing embroidery volunteers take the work to their communities or their quilt group show-and-tell, and watch the conversations that happen when they share their progress on their Instagram accounts. I could have explained to her how it gives everyone a platform to talk about the issues that many young kids are interested in. But instead, I felt immense pressure to bite my tongue because while she was in the SJSA booth, everyone was fangirling her.

JH: It's exhausting being expected to be gracious in the face of entitlement and rudeness.

ST: There's a quote by Arundhati Roy, "There's no such thing as the voiceless. There's only the deliberately silenced or the preferably unheard." Kids all have a voice, but no one's listening to them, unless they come from status or clout— like the Kardashian kids, or they're a young person with a voice that people are currently listening to, like Greta Thunberg. I've been fortunate to have two parents who always made me feel like my voice was heard. Perhaps because of my educational background, I feel like adults have given me the time of day. But the more workshops I've led, the more I realize that kids that look like me weren't ever given the time of day a day in their life. Not only did they not have parents like mine but they also went to an under-resourced or underperforming school, they didn't have mentors, and they didn't have many resources. By the time I was in eighth grade, I'd written a book, designed a fabric and pattern line, and even had Bernina sponsoring me. By the time I graduated from high school, I had been on the Disney Channel. I think all my personal successes and my sewing abilities contributed to my overall confidence, and I wanted to give the access I had to other youth. I realized at an early age how blessed I was, and to me, creating SJSA was an act of sharing resources, creating a network for all youth to feel empowered, and to have access to learning such a fun art form.

CLOSING MEDITATION BY LOI LAING

I believe art-making allows us to deepen connections to our existence and humanity. My practice is a form of meditation and personal metaphor. It is how I process everything that occurs in the present, that which has passed, and what I imagine is yet to come. To combat living with aphantasia (the inability to mentally process visual imagery), I utilize art-making as a way of visualizing the world around me. Rooted in narrative, memory, and emotion, I construct work that is intuitive and has blossomed from discoveries found within the exploration of color and abstraction. I practice the act of surrendering to where the work leads me rather than focusing on my own attachment to a predetermined outcome.

My primary medium of choice is fiber. Using traditional techniques such as hand-stitching, embroidery, and weaving, I examine themes such as domesticity, femininity, and their origins within communities of color. Often practiced by artists in the developing world, these processes have been historically dismissed as craft and not considered within the ambit of art or design. Consequently, research is crucial to my artistic process and yearning to understand non-Western craft production and ways of working, along with their historical context. As a Black woman, my praxis is personal and culturally driven. It is ultimately centered on the goal of reclaiming ancestral knowledge and wisdom handed down throughout civilization, while creating space for others to be self-determined in shaping their own experiences and identities.

CONCLUSION

My crafts have largely been solitary pursuits during the COVID-19 pandemic: the shared print studio I use is closed indefinitely, my in-person printmaking classes have all been canceled, and industry trade shows have been postponed. In many ways, I'm suited to this solitude. I'm an introvert. That declaration may sound strange coming from me, someone who used to teach regularly and who interviewed nineteen people for this book. But, being an introvert just means that I derive energy from solitude and introspection. Introversion is almost a prerequisite for a career as an artist or designer, both of which require the ability to work in solitude for long, focused periods of time. And perhaps, that's where the myth of the lone genius artist, designer, craftsman—yes, man, because the lone genius is almost always coded as male, in addition to being coded as white—comes from. The lone genius works alone, in a vacuum, with no outside influences. The lone genius is a rugged individual, whose success is entirely his doing.

But, the interviews and survey responses for this book, along with my own experience, show over and over again that this myth is false, regardless of whether or not you're a genius (most of us aren't) or a mere maker. Despite my introversion, I miss interacting with my communities in person. I miss the casual back-and-forth in my print studio, where I often learned through watching others work. I miss walking around my classroom, encouraging students and walking them through their technical problems. Yes, I thrive when I'm alone, but the work I do during my quiet time is often informed by the interactions and conversations I have with others.

If there's one thing that writing this book has driven home, it's the fact that we need each other—to learn, to critique, to praise, to guide. Craft and community go hand in hand. We often learn our crafts from our friends or family members, as Rashida Coleman-Hale and Sonya Philip did. Our work, like that of Youngmin Lee and Naiomi Glasses, may draw from our traditions. A life-changing event—such as the death of Dana Williams-Johnson's and Chawne Kimber's fathers, or the birth of Candice English's first child—

358

may provide the catalyst for our journey. Our experiences inform our work, and our communities are central to these experiences.

If craft develops in community, so, too, did this book. I couldn't have written this book without the people featured on its pages. Without their willingness to sit for an hour-long interview or to complete a survey, this book wouldn't exist. Without the beautiful quote from Cecile Lewis that opens this book—one of her survey responses—the title of this book wouldn't be *This Long Thread*. Without the input from my friends, the survey that serves as the backbone of this book would have taken on a very different form. I could go on and on.

Even when we're practicing our crafts solo, we're engaging in connection. Our practices are the culmination of our experiences, our backgrounds, our skills, and our identities. None of these are formed in a vacuum. We draw on and contribute to communities that are far larger than we are. We may each be, as Cecile Lewis writes, just one individual who touches this long thread, but look at what these many hands, this long, long thread can do.

—JEN HEWETT

ACKNOWLEDGMENTS

This book has been a community effort from the very beginning. I'd like to thank Ebony Haight, Sonya Philip, Lisa Solomon, Nichole Ramirez, Adrienne Rodriguez, and Jenna Wolf for helping me devise and vet survey questions. Perhaps, one day, I'll publish all our emails debating the nuances of certain terms, adding questions, and correcting my grammar! Thank you to Lisa Congdon, Stephanie Dodaro, Josie Drury, and Emily Divinagracia for being there, as always. I'm so grateful to George McCalman, who was writing his own book while I was writing mine, for de-escalating more than a few of my freakouts during the writing process. Huge thanks to Katharine Daugherty for providing me with the time and the physical space to start the monumental tasks of reading all the survey responses and organizing my thoughts. Thank you to my editors Jenn Brown, who advocated for this book early on, and Audra Figgins, who saw it through to the end. Thank you to my agent, Kate Woodrow, for championing this book for so long. And, finally, I'm incredibly grateful to everyone who shared and/or completed the survey, took time out of their busy lives to let me interview them, or wrote an essay. This book would not exist without you. Thank you for trusting me with your stories.

CONTRIBUTORS

BIOS

JEN HEWETT

Jen Hewett is a printmaker, surface designer, and textile artist based in the Hudson Valley. Born and raised in California, Jen combines her love of loud prints and saturated colors with the textures and light of California landscapes. Her printed textiles are highly tactile and visually layered. Her first book, *Print, Pattern, Sew: Block Printing Basics and Simple Sewing Projects*, was published by Roost Books in 2018.

AVA GUIHAMA

Ava is a writer from Los Angeles. Currently based in the Bay Area, Ava is a student at the University of California, Berkeley, where they major in American studies with an emphasis on the history and legacy of organized crime. Their writing has been previously published in *The Annex*, *Wilde Magazine*, and *The Secret History*. To learn more about Ava and their work, visit avaguihama.carrd.co.

EBONY HAIGHT

Ebony Haight is a writer living in Oakland, California. She makes clothes, quilts, collages, and some kind of sense. Find her online @ebonyh or heira.studio.

LOI LAING

Born in Alabama and raised in Jamaica, Loi Laing is a multidisciplinary artist working primarily in fiber and paint. Informed by undergraduate studies in sociology and anthropology, her work explores themes of history and the visual language of culture. Loi spent seventeen years as an attorney and educator before dedicating herself to her art practice. She lives in South Florida with her son Kai. You can find her on Instagram @loilaing.

MIA NAKAJI MONNIER

Mia Nakaji Monnier is a writer in Los Angeles, focusing on essays and journalism about art, crafts, and culture. Her work has appeared in *BuzzFeed*, *O, The Oprah*

Magazine, the *Washington Post*, and more. You can find her on both Instagram and Twitter @miagabb and read more of her work at mianakajimonnier.com.

ADRIENNE RODRIGUEZ

Adrienne is the co-owner of A Verb for Keeping Warm, a textile studio in Oakland, California. She is also the coauthor of *Journeys in Natural Dyeing*, published by Abrams in 2020. She enjoys her life as a teacher, researcher, writer, and lecturer on the topics of foraged materials for dyeing with a focus on fungi. You can find her work online at averbforkeepingwarm.com.

JENNA WOLF

Jenna Wolf is a library director at a progressive boarding school, where she guides students to explore and uncover their passions, conduct deep, meaningful research, make things, use cutting edge technology to tell their stories, and inspire them to develop a reading life. As a citizen of Mvskoke Creek Nation (Oklahoma), textile arts, beading, and other kinds of handiwork have always been intrinsic desires and making, a way of life. She cares deeply about the art of Indigenous peoples and how that traditional work informs every aspect of her process and product. She lives in Boston with her partner, Sean.

SHANEL WU

Shanel Wu is a queer Taiwanese American PhD student, currently a settler on Ute, Cheyenne, and Arapaho land (Boulder, Colorado). They are a designer/engineer/tinkerer who researches smart textiles and wearable tech, focusing on incorporating activism, design, sustainability, and anti-colonialism in future tools. They wouldn't have found this position without knitting and handcraft.

PROFILES AND INTERVIEWEES

Tanya Aguiñiga: tanyaaguiniga.com; Instagram: @tanyaaguiniga, @ambosproject
Cynthia Alberto: cynthiaalberto.com; Instagram: @cynthiaalbertoweaver,
 @weavinghand
Stephanie Brown: rebelyarn.com; Instagram: @rebelyarn
Raquel Busa: maquina37.com; Instagram: @maquina37co
Claudia Carpenter: etsy.com/shop/CrochetLuna; youtube.com/c/CrochetLuna/;
 Instagram: @crochetluna

Windy Chien: windychien.com; Instagram: @windychien
Rashida Coleman-Hale: rashidacolemanhale.com; Instagram:
     @ rashida_coleman_hale
Raven Dock: ravendockart.com; Instagram: @ravenkiannad_art
Candice English: thefarmersdaughterfibers.com; Instagram:
     @thefarmersdaughterfibers
Kayla Maressa Fernandez: Instagram: @maressamade
Naiomi Glasses: naiomiglasses.com; Instagram: @naiomiglasses
Brandi Cheyenne Harper: brandicheyenneharper.com; Instagram:
     @brandicheyenneharper
Virginia Johnson: gatherhereonline.com; virginiabjohnson.com; Instagram:
     @gather_here
Shahnaz Khan: maisonshahnaz.com; Instagram: @maisonshahnaz
Chawne Kimber: cauchycomplete.wordpress.com; Instagram: @cauchycomplete
Seema Krish: seemakrish.com; Instagram: @seemakrishtextiles
Stephanie Lee: twinkiechan.com; Instagram: @twinkiechan
Youngmin Lee: youngminlee.com; Instagram: @youngminlee_bojagi
Ellie Lum: klumhouse.com; facebook.com/klumhouse; Instagram: @klumhouse
Kenya Miles: bluelightjunction.com; Instagram: @travelingmilesstudio
Chi L. Nguyen: whatchidid.com; Instagram: @whatchidid; Twitter: @whatchidid
Soukprida Phetmisy: Instagram: @soukprida
Sonya Philip: 100actsofsewing.com; Instagram: @sonyaphilip
Latifah Saafir: latifahsaafirstudios.com; youtube.com/latifahsaafirstudios;
     Instagram: @latifahsaafirstudios
Jessica So Ren Tang: jessicasorentang.com; Instagram: @jessicasorentang
Vanessa Vargas Wilson: craftygemini.com; youtube.com/c/TheCraftyGemini;
     Instagram: @craftygemini
Dana Williams-Johnson: yardsofhappiness.com; Instagram: @callmedwj
Lisa Woolfork: blackwomenstitch.com; Instagram: @blackwomenstitch

SURVEY RESPONDENTS

Laura Albert	Marcela Andaluz	Julie Fei-Fan Balzer
Cynthia Alberto	Yamil Anglada	MJ Barajas
Carmen Ali	Anita Ansari	Mayra Nieves Bekele
Dina Ali	Shubha Bala	Charnita Belcher

Ainur Berkimbayeva

Adriana Blanco

Erica Brant-Warner

Sahara Briscoe

Stephanie Brown

Teryn Bryant

Salina Burns

Raquel Busa

Lucia Calderon-Arrieta

Angela Calero

Claudia Carpenter

Marie Carter

Sandi Carter

Kristine Caswelch

Ava Chan

Sophia A. Chang

Rosie Chapman

Cassandra Chase

Margaret Chess

Katharine Chin

Elaine G. Chu

Emily Clark

Marie Clark

Marlene Clark

Crystal L. Cochren

Margo Coffey Baldwin

Suzanne Coley

S. Haiba Collier

April Corbett

Heidi Corning

Amy Crews

Carol Crosby

Anngillian Cruz

Martine Cumbermack

Tameka Dandrige

Layla DeLeon-Osweiler

Anita DeRuvo

Bhavana Dhaman

Caroline Dick

Raven Dock

Amber Doe

Julie Dunn

Stephanie Echeveste

Coelina Edwards

Grizel Esquivel

Veronique "Nique" Etienne

Kayla Fernandez

Katia Ferris

Vanessa Foo

Kenyatta Forbes

Tanya Forde

Tenille Foreman

Nancy Franklin

Angie Franklin Lord

Loren Gaffin

Sandra Gallardo

Tullika Garg

Izola Gary

Regina C. Gee

Ashley Giddens

Gaye Glasspie

Candy Pilar Godoy

Melissa Gonzalez

Yolanda Gonzalez

Jenn Good

Alicia E. Goodwin

Marilyn Gore

Dennique Graham

Rosalind M. Green-Holmes

Phoenix Gupta

A. H.

Tara Harrison

Amber Heinbockel

Cherri L. Hendricks

Deborah Henry

Lori Henry

Tyshawn Henry

Kaiya Herman Hilker

Adriana Hernandez Bergstrom

Petrina Hicks

Karen Hillman

Noriko Ho

Cheryl Hoist

Shanel Holbrook

Jacqui Holmes Calhoun

Lisa Hsia

Bonnie Hsueh

Ashley Hughes

Tanya Hughes

Lucinda Iglesias

Diane Ivey

Charlene Jackson

Yolanda Jackson

Aliya Jiwani

Michelle Johns

Alicia Johnson

Christi Johnson

Sandra Johnson

Virginia Johnson

Olgalyn Jolly

Alesia Jones

Atiya Jones

Katika Jones

Karen Jordan

Yolonda Jordan

Shirley Karnos
Erin Emiko Kawamata
Jennifer Kee
Timnit Kefela
LaVerne Kemp
Kristina Koo
Heather Kuruvilla
Loi Laing
Lisa Lamson
Simone Lawson
Theresa Lawson
Nicole Lee
Youngmin Lee
Olive Lefferson
DeTiare Leifi
Ciara LeRoy
Cecile Lewis
Madalyn Lind
Grace Lombardo
Ebony Love
Jessie Loveland
Julie Lucero
Ellie Lum
Carole Lyles Shaw
Jessie Maimone
Zairi Malcolm
Whitney Manney
Cynthia Martinez
Margarita Martinez
Roxanne Masters
Georgette Mayo
Lisa McClendon
Lauren McElroy
Bretony McGee
Sienna McMillan
Charlene McNiff

Jeanne Medina
Kim Melikian
Rondica Melvin
Lamar Yvette Mendiola
Gail Mendonza
Lisa Merriweather
Yuko Miki
Sharon Mills-Wisneski
Gina Mittal
Iris Montgomery
Jeania Ree Moore
Christina More
Alicia Morrell
Marilyn Morriss
Veena Mosur
Soumya Mupalla
Debbra Murphy
Jocelyn Murray
Cecilia Nelson-Hurt
Denise Nembhard
Carolyn Norman
Angela Obeso
Maria Parker
Valerie Dionne Parker
Elisabeth Perez
Samira Petaawii
Gail Pettiford Willett
Soukprida Phetmisy
Lisa Pinedo
Annemarie Quevedo
Wendy Raigosa
Rachel Rangel
Roberta Rennie
Ana Reyes
La-Shonda "Lala" Rice
Lisa Rice

Tracey Ricks Foster
Tracey Rivers
Julie Robinson
Yetunde Rodriguez
Cecelia Romero Likes
Lia Rose
Rhonda Ross
Merimar Rossi
Charon Rothmiller-Cash
Joya Roy
Doris Rushing
A. S.
Latifah Saafir
Jamie Sandoval
Joy Sanga
Lisa Santoni Cromar
Wei Jing Saw
Amanda Scott
Veronica Sew
Cherrelle Shelton
Lisa Shepard
Lily Shih
Christina C. Shuy
Kass Silas
Belinda Silver
Amanda Smith
Murl Smith
Rochelle Smith
Karen Sorey
Charla Soriano Jaffee
Luz Sotomayor
Natasha Stewart
Danielle L. Stringe
Sharon Sutton
Tracey Tabata
Christine Tawatao

Maybelle Taylor Bennett   Kandra Wilbur   Afifa
Alyssa Thaxton   Jacqueline Denise Wilder   Andrea
Elaine Tom   Aniqua Wilkerson   Angel
Christina Torres-Rouff   Lisa Williams   Belen
Helen Trejo   Shannita Williams   Catherine
Andrea Tsang Jackson   Stephanie Williams   Jane
Tina Tse   Jenevieve Womack   Jennifer
Erin Tsurumoto Grassi   Karen Wong   Karen
Sarah Vanphravong   Tiffany Wong   Mercedita
AJ Velasquez   Bri Woods   Nkese
Ashwini Venkatesan   Lisa Woolfork   Paetrice
Maria Villar   Shanel Wu   Roxanne
Kay Washington   Carrie Young   Teri
Tracy Weyhenmeyer   Erica Yuen   Thaise
Diana Wheatley   Kristl Yuen   Zhanna